# A HISTORY
## *of*
## MADISON COUNTY VIRGINIA

*Claude Lindsay Yowell*, B.S., M.S.

HERITAGE BOOKS
2012

# HERITAGE BOOKS
### AN IMPRINT OF HERITAGE BOOKS, INC.

Books, CDs, and more—Worldwide

For our listing of thousands of titles see our website
at
www.HeritageBooks.com

A Facsimile Reprint
Published 2012 by
HERITAGE BOOKS, INC.
Publishing Division
100 Railroad Ave. #104
Westminster, Maryland 21157

Originally published 1926 by Shenandoah Publishing House

— Publisher's Notice —
In reprints such as this, it is often not possible to remove blemishes from the original. We feel the contents of this book warrant its reissue despite these blemishes and hope you will agree and read it with pleasure.

International Standard Book Numbers
Paperbound: 978-1-58549-385-2
Clothbound: 978-0-7884-9322-5

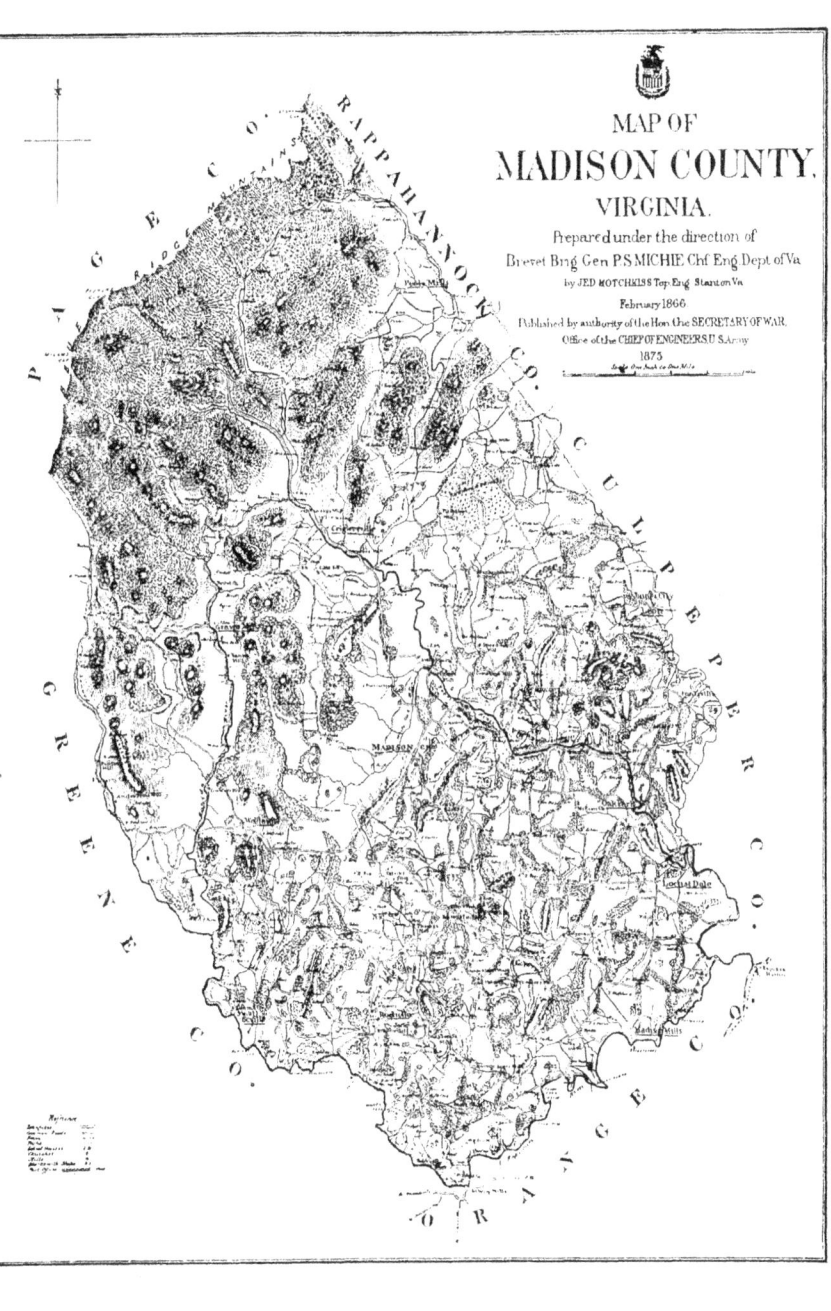

The real history of the human race is the history of tendencies which are perceived by the mind, and not of events which are discovered by the senses. *Buckle.*

Historical facts should not be a burden to the memory but an illumination of the soul. *Lord Acton.*

To love truth for truth's sake, is the principle part of human perfection in this world and the seed plot of all virtues. *Locke.*

The greatest teacher of man is man, and history is the record of men and their achievement. *Winterburn.*

History is a school of truth, reason and virtue. *Guizot.*

# Table of Contents

| Chapter | | Page |
|---|---|---|
| | Preface | 11 |
| | Introduction | 13 |
| I. | The Genealogy of Madison County | 19 |
| II. | Geography of Madison County | 26 |
| III. | Exploration and Early Settlement by the Whites | 32 |
| IV. | Madison As a Part of Orange and Culpeper | 46 |
| V. | Madison County Organized as a Separate County | 53 |
| VI. | Madison County in Our Wars | 62 |
| VII. | The Church History of Madison | 85 |
| VIII. | The School System of Madison County | 105 |
| IX. | Economic History | 112 |
| X. | Social Customs of Yesterday | 123 |
| XI. | The Present | 131 |
| XII. | Miscellaneous Data | 138 |
| XIII. | Interesting Incidents | 150 |
| XIV. | Manufacturing | 161 |
| XV. | The Colored People of Madison County | 165 |
| XVI. | Conclusion | 172 |
| | Appendix | 179 |
| | Bibliography | 193 |
| | Index | 195 |

# PREFACE

From childhood I have been interested in history. To me it is a living subject filled with facts which deal with the life of human beings. I like to study the way people act, for to me they are the most interesting things in the world.

There has been, however, one group of people in which I have been especially interested. These have been my home people—the people of Madison county, Virginia. I love Madison county and I love its people. This love that I hold has created within me a desire to see their history recorded.

I have hoped for some years to see some citizens of the county record the events that have occurred. Many other counties in Virginia have written histories and are seeking to preserve their records. In fact, for the last few years there has been an increased effort to preserve historical records over the entire United States. I see no reason why Madison should not be represented in this move of reviving the glorious events of yesterday.

I have waited, but no one has undertaken the task I desired to see done. I have waited until I have realized that the time is ripe for some one to undertake this task.. There are many sources through which we may secure knowledge of our county's history, which if they are not preserved now, will in a few years be lost forever. Realizing that the time is ripe to preserve these records, having a burning desire to record the achievement of our forefathers, and possessing a love for Madison county and its people have been the causes which led me to attempt to write this book.

I dare say that no one who reads the pages of this book will see as many errors and weak points as I see myself. I can assure you, nevertheless, that I have tried to the best of my ability to present to you true facts in a simple way. I am not presenting this book to you in a finished form, for I could not hope to do that; neither could you expect me to do it. I am presenting this book only as a beginning in the collection and recording of our county's history. My purpose has been to arouse an interest among the people, so that sometime in the future the county would produce an historian who would do justice to the work before him.

I am aware of the fact that criticism of this book will arise: in fact, I want it to arise. I want the people to become interested in their history; I want them to think about their history. I want them to be dissatisfied with present conditions and seek to achieve perfection, for if they do not become interested enough to want better kept historical records they cannot hope to make progress.

How I would like to see Madison county have an historical society composed of citizens of the county who would each year record the facts of that year!

My problems and handicaps have been many in writing this book. In the first place there has not been any work of this nature in the county. I have not had a model to follow, nor a work on which to build. In the second place, all the facts I have given had to be gathered here and there and many of them were hard to find and get straight. Then, in the third place, some records are so vague, brief and complicated, it is almost impossible to get the material desired. There are also many other problems which I will not take time to mention, for I am sure the reader will see them.

My problems and handicaps, however, have been alleviated to a great extent by many loyal citizens of the county, and I desire in the beginning of this book to express my gratefulness to them. First of all I want to mention Mr. W. E. Bohannon to whom most of the credit of this book is due. He not only gave encouragement and help in every way, but also much valuable material. I take not the honor of being the first to gather facts and conceive the idea of recording them in this manner, for this honor belongs to Mr. Bohannon. Then there are others who have helped in various parts of the book. Mr. J. N. Miller helped in the history of the school system; Mr. J. W. Sprinkle on the church history; and Finks Gordon on the history of the colored people. I also talked with many older people; received answers to questionnaires from others; was given help by county officials, librarians, etc., and from many, many people received help of every kind all of which I wish to acknowledge and to whom I wish to express my most grateful thanks.

The English historian, Bryce, states in his *History of the Holy Roman Empire,* "For until they can look forward, men must look backward." It is my desire that the people of my county may look back to the noble deeds of their ancestors and then look forward to greater and nobler achievements. I love the people of Madison county, therefore I dedicate this book to them.

# INTRODUCTION

### Events As An Outward Expression of An Inward Feeling

Events occur, but ideas continue; for this reason history is important. Events of themselves may be unimportant; their importance lies in the fact that they are always an outward expression of an inward feeling; they show us how people think; and we know that as they think, they will act. This has been recognized by great philosophers during all ages. Many years ago, the great French philosopher, Descartes, had as his motto "Je pense donc je suis" (I think; therefore, I am). Even before that, the Bible stated, "As a man thinketh, so he is." Events may occur quickly, but ideas are usually slow in developing. Ideas pass from one generation to another; they are more important than events; but, if it were not for the outward event, we would never know the inward idea.

The events that occurred in Madison county have not been important in the nation's history, nor in the history of Virginia; yet, to us who are citizens of Madison, they are important, for they show us the ideas under the influence of which our lives have been molded. They show how our ancestors thought, and how, after thinking, they acted. Some of their acts may have been mistakes; if so, let us not make the same mistake again. If their deeds were right and were crowned with success, let us follow their example and achieve greater success. It would be foolish for succeeding generations not to profit by the experience of former ones.

A knowledge of history should arouse within us pride for the noble deeds of our ancestors and that pride should create a desire never to place a blot upon the fair record left by our forefathers. There are many facts connected with the history of Madison county and its people of which any who possess such a heritage, may be proud. Oh, what a burden it is upon the present generation to continue the noble actions of the past! What a responsibility it is to keep our characters clean and to add something to the civilization of former ages!

So many of us are prone to think only in terms of the present and forget or neglect the past and the future. I like to think of this world's civilization as a great monument of stone upon which each generation places one more block. The past has built it up to the present; the present is now making its contribution; while the future will, generation by generation, add to this structure carrying it nearer to perfection and closer to the throne of God. It is, then, the duty of each generation to lay a firm stone on which others may build. Many times in the history of the world faulty stones have been placed in the structure of a country's civilization. For a while this faulty stone lay unnoticed; then, after a few years, the structure began to totter and at last came to earth with a mighty crash. Egypt flourished in its day; but at last, fell because of the life of its citizens; the same was true of Babylon, of Chaldea, of Assyria, of Greece, of Rome, and of many other nations. The same will be true of us if we do not build our civilization with stones of noble deeds. It is sad to find events in the history of our county which may be considered as faulty stones, and to find people who have placed a blot on the fair record of their family. I am glad, however, to say there are very few examples of either of these in the history of our beloved county.

The events which have taken place in Madison which were due to the toil and achievement of our ancestors should inspire us to greater patriotism, and should create within us a greater love for those who have lived and died. This love and heritage of common traditions should bind us closer together, and form for us a common heritage. Similar traditions and a community inheritance are the greatest elements in the patriotism of any group of people. We have only to look to the World War for an example of this. It was common traditions, similar language, race, and blood which caused the little nations of Poland, Czecho-Slovakia and Jugo-Slavia to retain a nationality for years suppressed. Patriotism should not be applied to the defense of one's country in time of war only; it should also be active in times of peace. It is just as patriotic to obey the laws of the land, to perform the various duties of a citizen, and to seek to make one's country better as it is to march to war. The Stars and Stripes are over us always, and always we need loyal citizens to uphold them.

History points out to us universal facts. There are facts which happen over and over again, or, in other words, are universal. These facts are universal because man is man, and does things which distinguish him from other animals. The God-idea is a universal fact; there has never been any nation or tribe of people who did not believe in some God and who do not today worship some deity. A tendency to produce the beautiful is another universal fact: there has never been a group of people on earth who has not attempted to produce some form of beauty. It may have been beauty of sound, which is music; it may have been beauty of language which is literature; or it may have been beauty which appealed to the eye, as painting, architecture, or sculpture. These and other facts are universal to mankind; there are other facts universal to communities only.

Some of these facts universal to Madison county are as follows: the people of the county have not been rich in material wealth; they have possessed a greater wealth; they have always possessed noble characters and have lived noble lives; they have always been industrious, honest, kind and hospitable; they have not caused their neighbors to fall; they have suppressed no one; nor have they blasted homes for the sins of the people. On the other hand they have lifted the fallen, have cared for those in need and have given a helping hand and sympathetic heart to those who needed and deserved them. It is a universal fact that the people of Madison have lived and still live simple, yet noble lives.

To know the past often enables us to lay aside prejudices and become citizens of mankind and of the world. It broadens our views and enlarges our sympathies. The world has not made progress through any certain group of individuals, but has progressed through the labors of all mankind; hence no study can be compared with history in the broadening of the mind. Every race and every nation has made its distinctive contribution to the advancement of mankind. Palestine has given us our religion; Greece our art; and Rome our laws. We may differ from the views held by some, yet we should respect their viewpoint and see their good rather than their evil. If the people of this world expect to approach a lasting peace they must all become citizens of the world. To become a citizen of the world one must lay aside prejudice, envy, selfishness, and intolerance and must have love, understanding, tolerance, and cooperation.

There is no better place to begin this world citizenship than at home; in Madison county.

The historical events which have occurred in the county and the achievements that have been made, have not been made by one little community, but by the county at large. From this we see the necessity for expanded patriotism, greater tolerance and more perfect cooperation. When we have extended our patriotism to the limits of the county then we are ready for a greater expansion and not until then. Events are built one upon another, and do not occur without some relationship to other events. Automobiles could not be made before gas engines; nor could gas engines be made before iron could be worked; nor could iron be worked before fire could be made. So it is with patriotism; it must begin in the community and extend first to the county; then, to the state; later on, to the nation and, at last, embrace the world.

History does not teach partisanship but citizenship. It took both patricians and plebeians to build Rome; likewise it took only a clash between the nobility, bourguoise and peasants to cause the bloody French Revolution. Political parties and social classes are necessary and beneficial; but, history testifies that, when they take the place of citizenship, there is danger of destruction. Rome had its parties and made progress until those parties cared more for themselves than they did for the welfare of Rome; then, Rome crumbled into dust. France had its parties, until those parties became so exclusive and self-centered that the Revolution arose and with it, came a change. These and other examples from different parts of the world teach us the folly of placing one group of people over another group, or, of placing one's party above the state. It is the welfare of all the people, and not of a few which should interest us most.

We should be able to see that the progress of Madison county has not been achieved by Republicans nor by Democrats, but by the combined efforts of both. The achievements of the county have been due to its citizens, not to its political parties. Political parties are essential and beneficial in their place, but destructive and blighting out of their place.

We hear so much today about aristocracy; what is aristocracy? There are only two classes of aristocrats recognized by history as deserving the name of "aristocracy". They are the aristocrats of achievement, and the aristocrats of character. David, St. Paul, Washington, Lincoln, Lee, and men of that type, were aristocrats of character. Pericles, Newton, Jefferson, Galileo, and such men, were aristocrats of achievement. You will notice that these men were not aristocrats because of what their forefathers did, but because of what they themselves did. So far as history is concerned, our aristocracy is determined by the individual. We Madisonians should not feel that we have any claim to aristocracy because of what our forefathers did. Their deeds belong to them; if we would be true aristocrats, we must show ourselves worthy of the title. We may, and we should, be proud of what our forefathers did; but to us is left the task of doing something worth while ourselves.

No one can make a study of history and not see that beyond man there is some great power; a hand that guides the destiny of mankind. Events do not occur by chance, neither does man seek higher things without a cause. Man does not understand himself nor many things in this world, but he does understand that his power is limited and that there are things beyond his power. Mankind has been nursed from the infancy of barbarism to the present state of civilization, as a child is nursed from infancy to mature age. Who nursed mankind? Has it not been God? One may open the pages of history anywhere and find many great men who are famous for their deeds. Do we not find that their good deeds have lived while their evil deeds have perished? This proves that there is a God who rules. We find many achievements of citizens of Madison which are far from the power of man; therefore, they must have been wrought by God.

History teaches us that selfishness does not pay. The question for us to answer is: What would the world be like if all the people were like us? Are we doing our part for the advancement of the world? Are we leaving behind us great deeds?

"Lives of great men all remind us
We can make our lives sublime,
And departing leave behind us
Footprints on the sands of time."

The purpose of this introduction is to mention briefly a few of the laws of history and start the reader to thinking of the meaning of events. It is to be hoped that he will see the connection between past, present and future. The keynote of the future is:

"Build thee more stately mansions, O my soul,
As the swift seasons roll!
Leave thy low-vaulted past!
Let each new temple, nobler than the last,
Shut thee from heaven with a dome more vast,
Till thou at length art free,
Leaving thine outgrown shell by life's unresting sea!"

# A History of Madison County, Virginia

## CHAPTER I

### THE GENEALOGY OF MADISON COUNTY

Events occur, not alone, but as links in a chain of events which have transpired in the past, happenings which make it possible for others to follow them in the future. Of this the formation of Madison county is an example. It was possible for Madison to be established as a county in the way in which it was, only after certain other events had occurred. It was necessary that Madison should be formed after the formation of other counties. This produced a family tree, so to speak, a genealogy of Madison county. To some it may seem that to trace the genealogy, or to seek the genesis of Madison county is of relative unimportance, for as history it appears to be insignificant. Taken separately it may be insignificant, but in its similarity to a greater event, namely, the development of the United States, it is of the greatest significance. It is important because it is a very complete miniature example of the formation of the states of the United States.

The history of America may be divided into four distinct, yet overlapping epochs.

The first is the epoch of discovery. In the latter part of the thirteenth century, Europe began to emerge from its slumber of the Dark Ages. Then it was that literature, art and science began to be revived; then it was that ships began to venture out into the seas, which before this time had been believed to be inhabited by demons. Many adventurers became bold, casting aside their old beliefs and traditions which had so long filled their hearts with terror and hindered the expansion of civilized nations. Of these there was one adventurer who forged ahead of his time, one who had a vision of a new land beyond the seas. This man was Christopher Columbus, a native of sunny Italy.

On October 13, 1492, three small ships of Portugal, sailing under the command of Columbus, sighted land in the west. Little did the men on board realize that this event would revolutionize the world. It did not change the world at once, for no event does that; but as we look back over the vista of years and see the links in the chain of happenings following the discovery of America, we realize that it was one of the most important events in history. The change took place slowly, and although America was discovered in 1492, the first permanent settlement was not made until one hundred and fifteen years later.

The second epoch in American history was that of colonization. For various reasons, Europe entered into an era of colonization in the seventeenth century. This era of colonization followed as a natural sequence the era of discovery, which had taken place in the fifteenth and sixteenth centuries. We are very prone to think that America as a nation began with colonization, but this is untrue. The American nation, as we use the term, did not begin until much later; not until the environment of a new land had transformed European people into a new nation. The first colonies established in America were only frontier settlements of European countries. The early colonists were not Americans as we think of them today. They were European in thought and action, and were at first dependent upon the mother countries. This condition remained for many years; in fact, as long as the colonies were confined to settlements along the eastern coast, and a change did not take place until the colonial frontiers began to expand westward. However, as this expansion began to take place, it marked the end of the second age of American history, or more broadly speaking, the end of direct European influence.

The third epoch in American history may be called the age of Americanization, for it was during this age that America became independent of European influence. The age of Americanization began with the expansion of the seacoast colonies, and ended with the disappearance of the frontier in 1890. During this period the frontier life developed American traits, the effect of environment began to be seen, the colonists removed from the direct influence of European life began to develop a new mode of thought adapted to their surroundings. This change marked the real beginning of America, the birth of American institutions and the development of a new nationality of people known as Americans.

The fourth epoch marks the development which has occurred since 1890, after the disappearance of the western frontier. The fourth age is one of Industrialism, one of internal development, one of expansion within.

The genealogy of Madison county is interesting because it is an example of the change that took place during the second and third epochs of American history. It shows the westward expansion of the seaboard colonies and the change that this expansion produced.

In order to show the westward expansion of the seaboard colonies we will begin the genealogy of Madison county with the first settlement of Virginia. The first permanent settlement made in Virginia was made on the island of Jamestown in 1607. The settlement consisted of one hundred and five colonists and was the first permanent settlement made by the English in North America.

Twenty-seven years passed; years of hardships, of suffering and troubles. Many of the first colonists died during these trying years, but as new ones continually came from England, the little colony grew in population, and by 1634 they numbered 5,119.[1] At this time the colonists were no longer all living on the island of Jamestown, but had become scattered over the plantations that bordered along the rivers in the tidewater section of Virginia.[2]

As long as the colonists lived at Jamestown the original government satisfied their needs but when expansion began to take place it was necessary to make a change. This change occurred in 1634. People who lived on the outlaying plantations were too far distant to attend court and other legal functions at the original colony, so the country was divided into eight shires, or what would now be called counties.[3] The colonists still were Englishmen and knew no other system except the English, consequently, they provided that each of the shires should be governed as English shires. As a result lieutenants were appointed the same as in England but with the special duty of supervising wars against the Indians. Sheriffs were elected as in the mother countries and exercised the same powers. Sergeants and bailiffs were also appointed when necessity required them.[4]

In tracing the genealogy of Madison county we are concerned with only two of the original shires, namely, Northumberland and York. Theoretically the land now known as Madison county was a part of these two original shires.

York was originally called Charles River, taking its name from the river Charles, which in turn had been named for Charles I, King of England. This shire included all the plantations lying on both sides of the river Charles and contained in 1634 a population of five thousand and ten.[5]

In 1645 the name Northumberland was given to the Indian district, Chicacoan. This shire was situated at the mouth of the Rappahannock river and like York included all the plantations bordering on that river.[6]

It is not definitely known when the shires became known as counties. However, it is known in 1642-43 the name of the shire Charles River had changed to the County of York, and the river below the confluence of the Mattaponi was called York river.[7] Northum-

---

[1] Robinson, M. P., Virginia Counties: Those Resulting From Virginia Legislation, Page 36.
[2] Ibid. Page 36.
[3] Ibid. Page 36.
[4] Henning, William Waller. Statutes at Large of Virginia. Volume 1, Page 224.
[5] Robinson, M. P. Virginia Counties: Those resulting from Virginia Legislation, Page 66. Henning, William Waller—Statutes at Large of Virginia, Page 249, Volume 1.
[6] Robinson, M. P. Virginia Counties: Those resulting from Virginia Legislation, Page 36. Henning, William Waller—Statutes at Large of Virginia, Vol. 1, Pages 294-352.
[7] Scott, W. W., History of Orange County, Page 17.

berland was created a county by the governor and council of Virginia in 1645, but this action was not confirmed by the General Assembly until 1648.[1]

The land now known as Madison county was unexplored when the counties of York and Northumberland were formed, yet these two counties were the first theoretically to own this land, as their western boundaries were indefinite. It is interesting nevertheless, to trace the genealogy of Madison county from this early settlement, for it shows the gradual westward expansion of the frontier.

The frontier began with the original shires but as it gradually moved westward, new counties were formed, similar to the development of the states. New counties were formed as a necessity created by the distance of the backwoodsmen from the former county courts. Like the mother county the newly formed ones were not given any western limit.

The frontier did not reach what is now Madison county until the early part of the eighteenth century. Before this time there were no white people living within the limits of the county, consequently, the counties formed prior to this time only theoretically owned this territory. It was not until after the formation of Spotsylvania county that the white man began to settle the present Madison county. Thus the genealogy of Madison before the formation of Spotsylvania is very vague.

Lancaster, the first county to be formed on the western side of York and Northumberland, was formed in 1651 from the scattered settlements along the Rappahannock river which was then owned by these two original shires.[2]

Old Rappahannock was the next to be created. It was formed on the western side of Lancaster in 1656.[3] This was the third county made upon the Rappahannock river, but did not exist very long, as it was divided in 1692 into the two counties of Essex and Richmond.[4]

Essex was formed from the northern part of Old Rappahannock and later gave part of her territory to Spotsylvania,[5] but as Spotsylvania also received a part of her lands from King William and King and Queen we will now turn back and trace the history of these two counties.

King William was formed from King and Queen in 1742.[6] King and Queen was formed from New Kent in 1691.[7] New Kent

---

[1] Robinson, M. P., Virginia Counties: Those Resulting From Virginia Legislation, Page 86.
[2] Robinson, M. P., Virginia Counties: Those Resulting From Virginia Legislation, Page 86.
[3] Robinson, M. P., Virginia Counties: Page 66.
[4] Robinson, M. P., Virginia Counties: Page 56.
[5] Robinson, M. P., Virginia Counties: Page 86.
[6] Robinson, M. P., Virginia Counties: Page 56.
[7] Robinson, M. P., Virginia Counties, Page 56. Henning, William Waller—Statutes at Large of Virginia, Volume 3, Page 94.

THE GENEALOGY OF MADISON COUNTY      23

was formed from York and James City in 1654.① This completes the genealogy until the formation of Spotsylvania.

After the formation of Spotsylvania the genealogy of Madison is much more easily traced because each new county was formed directly from one other county.

In 1720 the General Assembly passed an act for erecting the county of Spotsylvania. The act was as follows:

"Preamble, That the frontiers towards the high mountains are exposed to danger from the Indians, and the late settlement of the French to the westward of the said mountains."

"Enacted, Spotsylvania county bounds upon Snow Creek up to the mill, thence by a southwest line to the river North Anna, thence up the said river as far as convenient, and thence by a line to be run over the high mountains to the river on the northwest side thereof, so as to include the northern passage through the said mountains, thence down the said river until it comes against the head of the Rappahannock, thence by a line to the head of the Rappahannock, and down that river to the mouth of Snow Creek, which tract of land from the first of May 1721 shall become a county, by the name of Spotsylvania county."②

The county was named for Lieutenant-Governor Spotswood, then acting governor for the colony.③

Without the help of boundaries subsequently established and maintained to this time, it would be difficult to define the lines laid down in this statute. Interpreted by these it would be safely affirmed that on the east and south the county would be bounded as now: "Snow Creek," the line with Caroline county, empties into the Rappahannock ten or fifteen miles below Fredericksburg. The North Anna is the southern boundary of the Orange line: "up the North Anna as far as convenient" is obscure but unimportant, and may be interpreted as meaning all the way to its source. The ultimate source of this river is near the top of the Southwest Mountains, and but a few feet from the turnpike leading from Gordonsville to Harrisonburg. Taking this spring, which is not far from the Albemarle line, as the starting point for the "line over the high mountains to the river on the northwest side thereof so as to include the northern passage through said mountains," we have approximately the present lines of Orange and Green Counties with Albemarle to the top of the Blue Ridge. This about forces the conclusion that the "northern passage" means Swift Run Gap, through which this same pike crosses the Blue Ridge. At the time the county was formed the only passage across the mountains had been made by Governor Spotswood in 1716, known as the "Expedition of the Knights of the Golden Horseshoe." The "river on the northwest side" of the mountain is our Shenandoah,

---

① Robinson, M. P., Virginia Counties, Page 62. Henning, W. W.,—Statutes at Large of Virginia, Volume 1, Pages 387-88.
② Statutes at Large of Virginia, Volume 4, Page 77—Henning, William Waller.
③ Slaughter, Philip—A History of St. Mark's Parish, Page 1.

then called "Sherrando" and "Shenando," and by Spotswood "the Euphrates;" down the river until it comes "against the head of the Rappahannock:" this would bring us about Front Royal, the county seat of Warren; thence by a line to the head of the Rappahannock River, say about the corner of Fauquier, Warren and Rappahannock, and then down to the beginning, following the line of the sources of the Rappahannock, and the Rappahannock itself to Snow Creek. These boundaries can easily be traced on any modern map of Virginia.[1]

Orange county was formed from Spotsylvania in 1734. The act for the formation of Orange was somewhat as follows:

"Whereas divers inconveniences attended the upper inhabitants of Spotsylvania County, by reason of their great distance from the Courthouse and other places usually appointed for public meetings: Be it therefore enacted, by the Lieutenant-Governor, Council and Burgesses, and this present General Assembly, and it is hereby enacted by authority of the same; that from and immediately after the first day of January now next ensuing the said county of Spotsylvania be divided by the dividing line between the parish of St. George and the parish of St. Mark: and that part of the said county which is now the parish of St. George remain and be called and known by the name of Spotsylvania county: and all that territory adjoining to and above the said line, bounded southerly by the line of Hanover county, northerly by the grant of Lord Fairfax, and westerly by the utmost limits of Virginia, be henceforth erected into one distinct county, to be called and known by the name of the county of Orange."[2]

The terms of the statute need explanation in this, "southerly by the line of Hanover." Louisa was then part of Hanover. "The grant of Lord Fairfax on the north." As then understood, Lord Fairfax's southern limit was the Rappahannock river, as it is shown today.[3]

In order to understand the dividing line between Spotsylvania and Orange as stated in the act above, it is necessary to give part of the act defining St. Mark's parish, which was as follows:

"Enacted, Whereas many inconveniences attended the parishioners of St. George's parish, in the county of Spotsylvania, by reason of the great length thereof, that from January 1st, 1730, the said parish be divided into two distinct parishes: From the mouth of the Rapidan to the mouth of Wilderness Run: thence up the said Run to the bridge; and thence south to the Pamunkey River: the part below the said bounds to be known as St. George's Parish, and all the other part which lies above the said bounds to be known as St. Mark."[4]

On March, 1748 an act was passed for the formation of Culpeper, a part of the act reads as follows:

---
[1] Scott, W. W.—History of Orange County, Virginia, Page 19.
[2] Henning, William Waller—Statutes of Virginia, Volume 4, Page 450.
[3] Scott, W. W.—History of Orange County, Virginia, Pages 19-20-21.
[4] Scott, W. W.—History of Orange County, Virginia, Page 22.

"For the greater ease and convenience of the inhabitants of the county of Orange in attending courts and other public meetings be it enacted by the Lieutenant-Governor, council and Burgesses of this present General Assembly and it is hereby enacted by the Authority of the same that from and immediately after the seventeenth day of May next ensuing the said county of Orange shall be divided into two counties that is to say all that part of the county lying on the south side of the Rappahannock river to the head of the Conway river shall be one distinct county and retain the name of Orange county and all the other part thereof on the north side of the said Rappahannock and Conway river commonly called the Fork of the Rappahannock shall be one other distinct county and called and known by the name of Culpeper county."①

In the above the wording of the boundary is somewhat confused. The Conway River is a tributary of the Rapidan which is in turn a tributary of the Rappahannock. Thus the boundary line between Orange and Culpeper was the Conway and Rapidan. "The Fork of the Rappahannock" was the fork of the present Rappahannock and Rapidan.

In 1792 Madison was formed from Culpeper as a separate county. Thus its genealogy is completed. The act for the formation of Madison will be given later.

Chart showing the genealogy of Madison county.

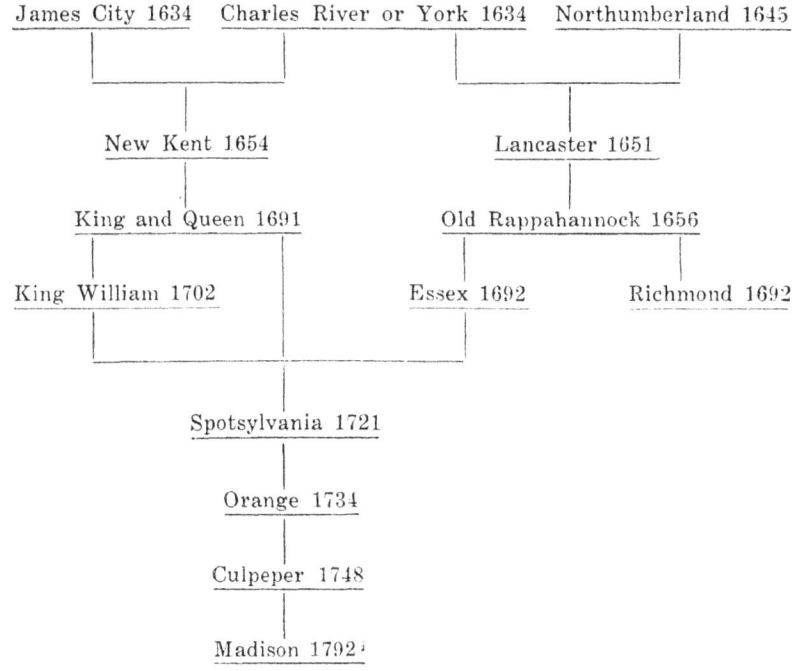

① Robinson, M. P., Virginia Counties: Those Resulting From Virginia Legislature, Page 204.
② Robinson, M. P., Virginia Counties: Those Resulting From Virginia Legislature, Pages 163-171.

## CHAPTER II

### GEOGRAPHY OF MADISON COUNTY

Madison county, Virginia, lies on the eastern slope of the Blue Ridge Mountains, in the Piedmont section of the State. It extends from the Blue Ridge Mountains on the north, to the Rapidan river on the south, and from the Conway or Middle river on the west, to Hughes river on the east.[1] Its longest dimension measured northeast and southwest is about thirty miles. Its total area is 336 square miles; being surpassed in size by sixty-two other counties in the State.[2] However, the assessor's books in the county show an average taxable acreage of 205,000, which makes a little more than 336 square miles.[3]

Madison is bounded by the following counties: on the northeast by Rappahannock, on the east by Culpeper, on the southeast by Orange, on the southwest by the Conway and Rapidan rivers which separate it from Greene and on the northwest by the Blue Ridge Mountains which separate it from Page. Except for a straight line on the northeast, which divides Madison from Rappahannock and a part of Culpeper, the county is elliptical in form, the longest dimension being northeast and southwest. It lies totally between the 78th and 79th degrees of longitude, and between the 38th, and 39th degrees of latitude.[4]

A line drawn in a northeast direction from the center of the county, and measured in that direction seventy-five miles would end in the center of Washington, D. C., the national capital. Likewise, a line drawn southeast from Madison C. H. and measured in that direction sixty miles, would end in the city of Richmond, the capital of the State.[5]

Madison county has remained as originally established by an act of the Assembly which was passed in 1792. The boundary as given in this act is as follows:

"Beginning at the mouth of the Robinson River, thence up the same to the mouth of Crooked Run, thence up said Run to the mountain road, where Tennants church formerly stood, thence a straight course to the head of Hughes River in the Blue Ridge, thence the same course continued to the top of the ridge and to the line of Shenandoah county, thence westwardly on the top of the ridge with the lines of the counties of Shenandoah and Rockingham to the lines of Orange, thence with the lines of Orange county to the beginning."[6]

---

[1] Michie, P. S., Map of Madison County.
[2] Whitehead, Thomas, Virginia: A Handbook, Page 279.
[3] Assessor's Books of Madison County. Volume 1920.
[4] Michie, P. S., Map of Madison County.
[5] Michie, P. S., Map of Madison County.
[6] Henning, William Waller, Statutes at Large of Virginia, Volume 13, Page 558.

It must be borne in mind that changes have taken place in the counties which adjoin Madison, since Madison was formed. Greene was formed from Orange in 1838[1]; so that the western boundary from the top of the Blue Ridge to Wilhoit's Ford on the Rapidan River now separates Madison from Greene. Likewise, Rappahannock was formed from Culpeper, in 1833.[2] Thus the line from near Slate Mills to the top of the Blue Ridge is no longer between Madison and Culpeper, but between Madison and Rappahannock. Page was formed from Rockingham and Shenandoah in 1831.[3] Thus the line on top of the Blue Ridge is now between Madison and Page. The change in the counties that surround Madison has in no way affected Madison; it is at present the same as originally formed.

The topography of the county is similar to that of a basin; its edge, except where streams have cut through, is much higher than the center. The exact center is near the Hebron Lutheran church. Here the altitude is only five hundred feet above sea level, while on the northwest side, which has the highest edge, the altitude is thirty-five hundred feet.[4]

The topography of the entire county has been formed by erosion, consequently, its surface is composed of hills and valleys. That the topography of Madison has been formed by erosion is plain to everyone. For it will be noticed that the mountains and hills, except the Blue Ridge, run parallel to the streams. The hills and mountains which are now near the streams have been protected against erosion by quarries of stone, but where the hills contained little stone the streams have cut wide valleys. The widest valley is that of the Robinson River which is near the center of the county, and is several hundred feet lower than any valley near it. If a canal were cut from Hughes river on the east, or the Rapidan river on the west, their waters would flow into the Robinson River Valley.[5]

Madison is watered by four principal rivers, all of which have their source within the bounds of the county, and empty into the Rappahannock, or into streams which lead to this river. Hughes River, which takes its name from an early settler who patented land there, has its source on the line between Madison and Rappahannock in what is commonly called Nicholson's Hollow. This river forms part of the boundary line between the two counties and flows into the Hazel River, which is a tributary of the Rappahannock. The Robinson River, named for one of the first patentees of land in the vicinity of its source, is purely a Madison stream, for its entire length lies within the bounds of the county. It rises in the Blue Ridge near

---
[1] Robinson, M. P., Virginia Counties: Those Resulting From Virginia Legislation. Page 53.
[2] Robinson, M. P., Virginia Counties: Those Resulting From Virginia Legislation. Page 66.
[3] Robinson, M. P., Virginia Counties: Those Resulting From Virginia Legislation. Page 64.
[4] Michie, P. S., Map of Madison County.
[5] Michie, P. S., Map of Madison County.

the two peaks Haywood and Double Top, and flows into the Rapidan River near Locust Dale. The Rapidan, whose present name is a contraction of Rapid Anne, was named for Queen Anne of England. This river rises near the peak called Fork Mountain, and after flowing in Madison for some distance becomes the southern boundary of that county as well as of Culpeper. It flows into the Rappahannock a few miles above Fredericksburg. The Conway was also named for an early patentee. Its source is near the line between Madison and Greene, and forms the boundary between these two counties until it flows into the Rapidan near Seville. There are many smaller streams in the county known as runs, which form tributaries of these rivers. Some of the latter are: Elk Run, Maple Run, Great Run, White Oak Run, Deep Run, Muddy Run, Fleshman's Run, Popham's Run, Quaker Run and Mulato Run. All of these streams are rapid, so there is a possibility of a vast development of water power.[1]

The Blue Ridge Mountains with their many peaks and lower parellel ranges form the backbone of the county, and are perhaps the most conspicuous and most wonderful feature in the physical geography of Madison. Some of the peaks in the Blue Ridge rise to the height of 3,500 feet above sea level. In the northeastern corner of the county, the Old Rag is the most prominent. It takes its name from the fact that it is almost one solid mass of huge rugged stones. This peak rises to the height of 3,000 feet above sea level and falls almost abruptly into the slightly rolling lands called Champlain. Near the center of the northern rim of the county is a peak called the Double Top, so called because of a notch in its summit. This peak rises to the height of 2,500 feet. In the Blue Ridge proper there are four well known peaks lying in Madison, all of which are about 3,500 feet high; the Haywood situated a little to the right and behind the Double Top; Skyland, almost directly behind the Old Rag; Folk Mountain, a little southeast of the Double Top; and the Hawk's Bill, just south of Folk Mountain. In addition there are many lesser peaks or mountains distributed over the entire area of the county, the names of some of these are: Meadow, Allen, Banks, Neal, Simpson, Tom, Lost, Medley, Thourafare, Mitchell, Garr, Sheep, German, Rouse, Carpenter, Aylor, Deal, Blakey, Sag, Ball and Beamer's Head. Most of these small mountains are named for early settlers who owned them.[2]

The following minerals have been discovered in the county, but none have been fully developed: graphite, ochre, steatite, iron (magnetic and hematite), and copper. There have been two attempts made to mine copper in Madison, one in what is called Dark Hollow, and the other near Stony Man. The Dark Hollow mine is situated about one mile to the southwest of Milum (Fisher's) Gap. The

---

[1] Study made by Mr. W. E. Bohannon.
[2] Michie, P. S., Map of Madison County.

exposures of copper ore found in this vicinity are reported to have been worked before the Civil War, but after that were abandoned for many years. The working of the Dark Hollow mine known as the Old Shaft is located at an elevation of about 250 feet above the confluence of the two headwater branches of the Robinson River. This shaft and the small opening to the southwest was made some years ago. The New Shaft is an incline forty two feet in length located one hundred feet below the mouth of the Old Shaft.[1] Several other shafts were made but have all been abandoned. The ore found in these openings comprises native copper, blue and green carbonates, a little cuprite and some chalcuprite. These workings are located quite close to the contact of basalt and syenite. A copper mine was begun much later to the northeast of Milum Gap near Stony Man Peak but after going down sixty feet this was also abandoned. The ore from this mine was about the same as that from the Dark Hollow mine.[2] Madison has a large variety of ores but their quantity does not justify mining. The deposits are only folds in the mountains. This condition is usually true in all the mines on the eastern side of the Blue Ridge.

The nature of soils is largely controlled by geological formations. This fact is well illustrated in Madison county. An arm of the large secondary formation of the Triassic period which extends from the Rapidan River through Culpeper county and other counties to the Potomac River, extends across the southeastern part of Madison, crossing the Robinson River above its mouth, and having a width of one or two miles. Where the formation is a red or chocolate colored shade, the super-imposed soil is of excellent quality. Where gray sandstone predominates, the soil is of medium fertility, but easily improved.[3]

Between the secondary deposit and the Rapidan River the underlying rocks for twelve or more miles are mostly epidote and greenstone, similar to those of the adjacent southwest mountain range of Orange county, the decomposition of which furnishes potash and lime. The Madison lands adjacent to Orange county appear to be of better quality, owing to some admixture of sand from the adjacent sandstone belt, and furnish in many places soils remarkably well adapted to the culture of grapes, and particularly the valuable Catawba grape, which it is difficult to raise in many sections.[4]

The portion of the county lying between the secondary deposits and the region adjacent to the foothills of the Blue Ridge Mountain is underlaid with gneissoid sandstone, decomposing granites and metamorphic strata, all of which are azoic, and furnish upon disintegration but little lime and potash or other ingredients of value.

---

[1] Watson, T. L., Mineral Resources of Virginia. Page 509.
[2] Watson, T. L., Mineral Resources of Virginia. Page 509.
[3] Whitehead, Thomas, Virginia: A Handbook. Page 280.
[4] Ibid. Page 280.

The soil in this belt, except upon the streams, is of medium quality, either gray or red, but readily improved. Adjacent to the foot-hills of the Blue Ridge, the stones show marks of the metamorphic or igneous action accompanying the elevation of the Blue Ridge, and produce fertile soils.[1]

The Blue Ridge extends along the entire northwest border of the county, throwing out long spurs, some of which nearly attain the height of the parent Ridge. Its top and more elevated slopes furnish excellent grazing when cleared. There cattle thrive well, owing to lower temperature and freedom from annoyance by insects. The lower parts of the mountains and the numerous and beautiful valleys and glens of Madison are eminently adapted to the growth of grapes, apples and other fruits. Fruit abounds very plentifully in Madison where the elevation of the land is between eight and fifteen hundred feet above sea level. In this range of elevation late frost rarely ever injures fruit. No section of Virginia is better adapted to the growth of pippins and other valuable apples.[2]

Upon the rivers and creeks of the county are numerous bodies of very rich lands. One of the largest of these is on the Robinson River near Madison Court House, where there are about fourteen hundred acres in one bottom. This was evidently once the bottom of a lake.[3]

As Madison is a rural county, its chief occupation is farming. There is a wide variation of agricultural products, the chief ones being grain, hay, cattle, hogs, sheep, poultry, dairy products, fruits and lumber. The valleys furnish the farm lands, and the hills and mountains are covered with valuable lumber including an enormous amount of oak, pine, walnut, hickory, ash, locust and poplar. It was estimated a few years ago by an experienced lumber and timber inspector that there was sufficient locust timber standing in Madison county to furnish locust pins to string every mile of telegraph and telephone wire in the United States.[4]

Madison is divided into three magisterial districts, namely, Robinson, Rapidan and Locust Dale. The first takes its name from the river of that name as the district is located on that river; the second is also named because of its location on the Rapidan River; and the third is named for a village of the same name which was one of the first post offices established in the county. Of these districts the Robinson is the largest, the Locust Dale next in size and the Rapidan the smallest.[5]

The people of Madison are chiefly of English, Irish, Scotch-Irish and German descent, with the English and German the most numerous, and the first settlers. Nationality can easily be traced by the

---

[1] Whitehead, Thomas, Virginia: A Handbook, Page 280.
[2] Ibid. 281.
[3] Ibid. 281.
[4] Evan's Almanac for 1907.
[5] Court Order Books of Madison County.

family names now in the county. The community near the Hebron Lutheran Church has the largest percentage of German population.①

There are eight voting precincts in the county, namely, Criglersville, Brightwood, Graves Mill, Madison Court House, Nethers, Oak Park, Rochelle and Wolftown.②

---

① Answer to Questionnaires.
② Registration Books of Madison County.

## CHAPTER III

### Exploration and Early Settlement By The Whites

The best information that can be obtained, shows that the hills and valleys now known as Madison county first met the gaze of a white man in 1669. These hills and valleys were then covered with dense forest and knew only the tread of the Red Man and of wild beasts. Many changes have taken place within the two hundred and fifty years that have since passed. It is only when we find some relic, such as an arrowhead, that our thoughts turn back to those days when the whoop of the Indian, and the howl of the wolf was heard over the hills and vales of Madison.

All of us are familiar with the Powhatan Indians who lived in the tidewater region of Virginia. History has given us an account of their customs, religion, and dealings with the early white settlers, but has preserved little concerning the Indians in the Piedmont section of our state. These latter were more warlike, more hostile to the white man, and less civilized than the Powhatans. These tribes were not related by blood nor united by alliance; they were mortal enemies. Had the Indian tribes of Virginia preserved written records they would be filled with accounts of conflicts waged between the Indians of the high and those of the low country, or in other words, between the Powhatans and Mannahoacks.

It is said that in 1608 Captain John Smith visited the falls of the Rappahannock River; instead of the generous welcome which a stranger now receives from the hospitable dwellers upon this beautiful stream, he was greeted with a war-whoop, by the fierce Mannahoacks who then roamed in proud independence upon its wooded banks.[1]

The Indians who lived in the Piedmont Section, were called Mannahoacks. This general tribe was composed of eight smaller tribes, or clans, all of whom were subject to the Mannahoack chieftain. These eight small tribes lived on the head-water branches of the Rappahannock River, and caused the colonies endless troubles. Many of the defensive measures necessary after the first struggles of the white man with Indians near Jamestown, were directed towards stopping the insurrections of this tribe.[2]

Strachey, one of the first writers of Virginia, gives us an account of the Mannahoacks, in which he states that the Mannahoacks differ little from the Powhatans in nature, habit, or condition; they are, however, more daring against the white man and are more warlike than other Indian tribes.

---

[1] Slaughter, Philip, History of Saint George's Parish, Page 5.
[2] Sams, C. W., The Conquest of Virginia and the Forest Primeval, Page 369.

The eight tribes of the Mannahoacks were as follows: the Mannahoacks proper, who inhabited Spotsylvania and Stafford counties; the Snackakonies, who inhabited Spotsylvania; the Whonkenties and the Tauxitanians, who inhabited Fauquier county; the Tegninaties and the Hasinungaes, in Culpeper; the Ontponies and the Stegarkies who inhabited Orange county.①

Among the peculiar customs of the Indians were their methods of burying the dead. Usually they put all into one large mound which was generally oblong shape, and extended east and west. Some have thought that they covered the bones of those who fell in battle on the spot where they fought; others ascribe the mounds found to the custom said to prevail among the Indians, of collecting at certain periods of time the bones of all their dead where-so-ever deposited at the time of their death, and burying them at one central place; while still others suppose them to be the general sepulchres of towns. Some of these mounds have been found and excavated in Orange, Greene, Page and Albemarle counties.

There are several traditions of Indian graves handed down by the older people of the various communities in Madison. Some of these mounds or graves appear to be unusual, but none of them have been investigated and proven. For example, there is one situated near Banco. This mound is in the woods near the summit of a hill on the Chapman farm where there is no possibility of the land having been cleared. It is now about four feet above the level of the ground, twenty-five feet long, and about fifteen feet wide. Mr. W. H. Weaver, one of the oldest men in the county says that he was told, when a small boy, that this was an Indian grave, and that this tradition had been passed down from colonial days.

No record can be found showing that there was ever any serious troubles with the Indians in Madison; however, as late as 1754 there were some minor troubles in the county. We do not know when the Indians entirely disappeared, but many conclude that they were still in the county until after the Revolutionary War.

Slowly the Indians were driven westward by the waves of white settlers. This was true of the Mannahoacks, for they were finally driven beyond the Ohio River where they mingled with other tribes, losing their tribal name and adopting that of the tribe of which they became a part.

There are many legends about the Indians in Madison county which are interesting and some of which are doubtless true.

There is a small valley near Syria known as Shotwell's Hollow, which has been owned by the Shotwell family since 1740. Tradition states that when this family bought the land the Indians had a trail against the Blue Ridge above the valley. This trail followed the Blue Ridge and was used by the Indians in going from southwest

---

① Sams, C. W., The Conquest of Virginia and the Forest Primeval. Page 370.

Virginia into the northern part of the State. It is reported that the Indians would pass along this trail and molest the patches of corn growing near it. Mr. W. E. Bohannon, a citizen residing near this community says that he found traces of this trail.

It is also related that in the neighborhood near Syria an old woman lived in colonial days, who had been scalped by the Indians but strange to say, had survived this ghastly ordeal.

Tradition has preserved an account that in the early history of the Hebron Lutheran Church two sentinels were placed at the door of the church building during preaching to guard against Indian attacks. It has also been stated that the congregation of this church could see Indian camp fires burning on the Haywood Mountain beyond Criglersville. These German settlers are said to have lived on friendly terms with the Indians. In their excursions the Indians sometimes camped near the Hebron community, visited the settlers, and even allowed themselves to be coaxed into their homes where they were received with kindness.[1]

There are several legends of the Indians connected with the Blue Ridge. One of these legends is that the Indians had great reverence for this mountain. They would prostrate themselves before it in reverence to the Mountain Spirit whom they supposed dwelt there. Another is, that the Indians used copper which they claimed to have mined in the Blue Ridge near the present copper mine in Dark Hollow. Still another is that the peak known as "Old Rag," a peak in the Blue Ridge near Etlan, contained enough gold to put shoes on every horse in the surrounding neighborhood. Near Locust Dale is a farm known as "Indian Trace," it takes its name from the tradition that an Indian trail crossed this farm and that the usual camping place was near the present residence of Mr. L. W. Hill.

There is a record in Orange county dated 1742, while Madison was a part of that county, which reads as follows: "Sundry Indians among them Manincassa, Captain Tom, Blind Tom, Foolish Zach and Little Zach were before the court for terrifying one Lawrence Strother, who testified that one of them shot at him, that they tried to surround him; that he turned his horse and rid off but they gained on him till he crossed the Run. Ordered that the Indians be taken into custody by the sheriff until they give peace bonds with security, that their guns be taken from them until they were ready to depart out of this colony, they having declared their intentions to depart within a week and gave bond."[2]

After Madison was formed in 1792 there is no record in the county writings concerning Indians. The only visible proof that we have today that the Indians roamed over Madison at some former period of time is the arrow heads that are found very frequently over

---

[1] Huddle, W. P., Hebron Church, 1717-1907, Page 50.
[2] Scott, W. W., History of Orange County Virginia, Page 56.

## Exploration and Early Settlement

the entire area of the county. Sometimes when we see these small relics we cannot help feeling a touch of pathos for that vanquished race. Although the Indian was a terror to the early settler, yet this was his home and he was the original American.

John Lederer, a German physician, hired by Governor Berkley, is said to have been the first white man to stand upon the soil now known as Madison county. Lederer's Journal, giving an account of his exploration, was printed in an English translation at London in 1672, and again at Rochester, New York, in 1902. If this report be translated so as to conform to modern geography, the account of his expedition would be somewhat as follows:

Lederer started on this expedition, March 9, 1669, from the Chichahomminy Indian village at the falls of the Pamunkey River accompanied only by three Indian guides. He pursued his way up the river and passed its head-spring on the thirteenth. On the next day he gained from a hilltop his first distant view of the Blue Ridge, lying like a cloud on the horizon, before which the Indian guides, in reverence to the mountain spirits, prostrated themselves howling out in a barbarous manner, "Okee paeze," that is, "God is nigh." The day following he crossed the Rapidan River and was then traversing the western edge of the Piedmont, a land of sunshine and clear rushing streams, nestled securely under the southeast band of the blue mountain wall.

On the seventeenth of March, after nine days of travel, the little party was under the face of the mountain, in Madison county. Lederer found the slope and approaches densely set with hardwood timber, which offered as great an obstacle to the traveler as did the height and steepness of the range.

A full day was required to ascend the mountain. The horses were left at the foot, but even to man, the dense underbrush offered almost insuperable obstacles. At last the summit was reached, which was probably here as elsewhere about a mile wide, and so windswept by winter blasts as to be only partially timbered. The eyes of the traveler naturally sought first of all the west, but here met great disappointment for the view was cut off by higher ridges, a sight that afterwards was to prove discouraging to Virginia explorers who were made to feel there was no end to the mountains.[1]

This expedition has been doubted by some historians chiefly because of its errors in geography. Perhaps it was a forgery, that will never be known; its truth or its falsity can never be proven by anyone, but it is true that such an account existed in England in 1672.

Another exploration party the account of which no one doubts came in 1716. This party was composed of Governor Alexander Spotswood and his famous "Knights of the Golden Horse-Shoe."

---

[1] Alvord, C. W., and Bidgood, Lee. The First Exploration of the Trans-Alleghany Region by the Virginians, Page 64.

This expedition started from Germanna, and was composed of about fifty merrymen, if accounts be true, who were supplied with an extraordinary amount and variety of liquors. The route followed by this merry party lay completely within the bound of what was then Spotsylvania county. It is certain that in this expedition the explorers traversed a part of Madison. They crossed from what is now Orange into Madison at the old German Ford, thus crossing the Rapidan River about one-half mile above its junction with the Robinson. The expedition evidently passed near what is now Woodbury Forest from which place Swift Run Gap may be seen, and from here the party made their way to this gap.[1] The explorers had thus blazed the trail into a new land which in a few years was to feel the settler's tread, and under-go transformation from a dense forest to a prosperous community.

These early explorers leave us a very vivid picture of the territory, that later became Madison county. This picture is very different from the one we see today. Then all the land was densely wooded with large timber, and in most places very dense with vine and underbush. Game was very plentiful; there were deer, bears, wolves, foxes, and other smaller game. Large herds of deer could be seen grazing on the small patches of land cleared by the Indians, or where a few blades of grass sprang up in the less dense forest. Wolves roamed in packs and at night their howls broke the stillness of the surrounding hills. It is interesting to know that there were wolves in Madison as late as 1812, for in this year there are records which show that bounties were still given for their scalps. Foxes, which today furnish so much sport for Madisonians, were much more plentiful then and could be seen by a traveler at all times of the day. Bears roamed over the forest seeking food wherever they could find it. All early records show that bears were so plentiful that several could be killed in one day by a traveler who was not hunting them. Otters and beavers paddled up and down the small streams seeking food and building dams. What a change has taken place in a few years! All of this larger game is gone; the smaller game, much less plentiful; the Red Men, almost forgotten; and the hills and vales, once covered with dense forest, now wave with beautiful grain.

The white man has produced this change. After the settlement of Jamestown, the frontier rolled westward like the waves of the sea. The sturdy frontiersmen hurled back before them the forest, the larger game, and the Indians. Each generation pushed the frontier one step farther. Each new family ventured out into the virgin forest just a little more; to clear a small patch of ground on which to raise corn and tobacco, build a small cabin and live in contentment. Their children followed the example of their parents, and in turn pushed still farther westward to the edge of the frontier and there built their

---

[1] Slaughter, Philip. History of St. Mark's Parish.

homes. This process continued until the Blue Ridge was reached. This mountain furnished a barrier which checked the tide for a few years, and before it could be overcome the valley of Virginia was settled by colonists from the North. Thus the tide from eastern Virginia did not cross the Blue Ridge but turned southwestward and passed through the Cumberland Gap into the Blue Grass region of Kentucky.

It was over one hundred years after the settlement of Jamestown before the frontier reached Madison, for we know it is very doubtful that any white people lived in Madison before Spotsylvania County was formed in 1721.

The King of England was supposed to own all the land that England had laid claim to in America; from time to time he would make grants of this land to his favorites in England, or to prominent colonists in America. The grants were made beyond the frontier before the territory was settled; thus the early settlers would secure legal rights to their homes not from the crown but from these great land owners or proprietors. This was true of what is now Madison county. The entire tract of land, within the head-waters of the rivers Tappahannock, alias Rappahannock and Quiriough, or Potomac, the courses of those rivers, and other parts in Northern Virginia were granted at different times by King Charles, the First and Charles, the Second to Lord Hopton and others, and subsequently by King James to Lord Culpeper, who had purchased the rights of the other parties. However, when Lord Culpeper died he was survived by only one daughter who married Lord Fairfax, and thus, Lord Fairfax became proprietor of this large domain, commonly known as the Northern Neck of Virginia.

From the wording of the original grant to Lord Culpeper it would seem that the boundaries of his lands were very indefinite. The people of England knew little about the geography of Virginia; thus conflicts followed. In 1705 Governor Nott of Virginia in the name of the King granted 1920 acres of land to Henry Beverley in the forks of the north and south branches of the Rappahannock River. Lord Fairfax objected to this grant on the grounds that it was within the limits of his grant. The question then arose as to whether the south (Rapidan) branch or the north branch of the Rappahannock was the chief stream. The contention became so heated that the Governor and the Council of Virginia appointed commissioners to meet with those of Lord Fairfax to survey these rivers. This commission met and reported in 1706 that the rivers were of equal magnitude, and the matter was dropped.①

Later Governor Alexander Spotswood patented land in what is now Madison county to German settlers, believing this land to be his by a grant given him by Queen Anne. The contention was renewed

---

① and ② Slaughter, Philip. History of St. Mark's Parish. Pages 23-26.

Hebron Community

between Governor Spotswood and Lord Fairfax in regard to whom owned the land between the Rappahannock and the Rapidan Rivers. This contention not only involved the original owners of the land, but also the settlers who were there. The English, who had patented land under Lord Fairfax, realized that if the land belonged to Governor Spotswood they would lose the legal right to their homes; while the Germans, who had patented under Governor Spotswood, also realized that if the land belonged to Lord Fairfax, they would lose their homes. The contention became very bitter and in 1733 Lord Fairfax made a complaint to the King that patents had been granted in the name of the crown in this disputed territory. The King in council ordered the Governor of Virginia to appoint another commission; on the part of the Crown, he appointed William Byrd, John Robinson and John Grimes. Lord Fairfax also appointed a commission to represent his interest. The commissioners of Fairfax were Charles Carter, William Berkley and William Fairfax. On August 3, 1736 the King's commission met at Williamsburg and made their report. Lord Fairfax was not pleased with the decision; he took the report of this commission to England and had the matter referred to the Lords of Trade. The question was assigned and the decision was made in favor of Lord Fairfax[1] His grant then extended to the Rapidan River instead of the Rappahannock. In rendering their decision, the Lords of Trade made provision for those settlers who had patented land under Governor Spotswood. This was that the German settlers should not be molested, as they were innocent of the mistake, and that the decision made by the Lords of Trade should be to them a legal basis to their homes. This decision has served to this day as the legal foundation for the land patented by the German settlers in the Hebron Church community.

Now let us turn to these settlers themselves, these hardy, robust founders of Madison county. It is interesting to note that we would be able to judge the nationality of the early settlers to a surprising degree, should we have no other information than the parts of the county in which they settled. The German or Dutch settlers came from the lowlands of Europe and we find them making their homes near the rivers in the swamps which others avoided. They sought land which corresponded nearest to the land of their childhood. One distinct settlement of these Germans came into Madison county very early; these settlers and their descendants have played a very prominent part in the county's history; even today their names are very prominent.

It was in the year 1717 that a little band of Germans left Germany attempting to make their way to Pennsylvania. The vessel that was to bring them to America stopped at London and there the captain of the vessel was imprisoned for several weeks because of debt.

---

[1] Slaughter, Philip, History of St. Mark's Parish, Pages 23-26.

By this delay part of the ship's provisions was consumed while in port so that many of the passengers died of hunger while crossing the Atlantic. The remainder never reached Pennsylvania, for a storm arose and they were driven south, landing on the shores of Virginia. Here they were sold by the captain of the ship in order to pay their transportation charges. They were bought by Governor Spotswood and became his indentured servants. He settled them on the South side of the Rapidan River near Germanna, in what is now Orange county, where he three years before had established a German reform colony consisting of twelve families from Naussau-Siegen.[1]

Of the colony of 1717 eight of the colonists are known: they were Christopher Zimmerman, Matthew (Michael) Smith, Michael Cook, Andrew Kerker, Henry Snider, Christopher Paulur or Parlur, (later known as Beller, Barler and Barlow), Hans Herren Burger (Harnsburger), and John Motz. The other twelve of this colony are, probably, Conrad Amburger, Balthaser Blankenbaker, Nicholas Blankenbaker, Matthias Blankenbaker, Michael Clore, George Sheible, George Mayer, Michael Kaifer, Michael Holt, George Utz, Zacharias Fleshman and Andrew Bullenger. The last twelve named and Nicholas Yager, John Broyles, Philip Paulitz, Henry Snider, Michael Smith and Michael Cook were sued in the courts of Spotsylvania in 1724 for their passage money.[2] From all accounts the number of families in this German colony must have been at least twenty-four. The particular locality from which they came is not known, but from the naturalization papers of Nicholas Yager and his son Adam, we are informed that the former was a native of Hesse and that the latter was born near Dusseldorfin in the Dukedom of Newburg, Germany.[3] In the Moravian diaries it is said they came from Wertemburg. The Reverend Casper Stoever, one of the pastors of this congregation of German Lutherans, states that they were from Alsace, the Palatinate.

The chief cause of the immigration of this colony to America was persecution. In a few words the condition of Germany at this time was as follows: The wars of Louis XIV and that of the Spanish Succession had almost exhausted Germany, and especially those people along the border. In addition to the wars the extravagance of the rulers and the contention that existed between the different religious sects caused the colonists to sail to the New World; among those who emigrated we find the colony of 1717.

Governor Spotswood employed these Germans in his iron mines near Germanna and also at odd times they did a little farming; this proved of great assistance to them in the future. Their lot was a sad and bitter one at Germanna, and at last they decided to seek land of their own. They pushed out into the wilderness and found the land

---
[1] Huddle, W. P., Hebron Church, 1717-1907, Page 2.
[2] Huddle, W. P., Hebron Church, 1717-1907, Page 4.
[3] Huddle, W. P., Hebron Church, 1717-1907, Page 5.

which they desired, on the banks of the Robinson River and White Oak Run in Madison (then Spotsylvania County). In moving from Germanna to their future home they moved up the Rapidan River, crossing this stream, according to tradition, at the old German Ford just below Madison Mills. They pushed on towards the mountains in the distance until they passed the place where Madison Court House now stands; here they came to a halt and settled on both sides of the Robinson River and White Oak Run within a circle with a radius of about eight miles.

The place of their new settlement is described in old records as being at "Smith's Island," for White Oak Run was first called "Island Run," because there was an island near its mouth. All of the deeds of this period are described by their position on Island Run.

All the colonists did not move at the same time. Tradition has preserved thirteen surnames which are said to be of the first settlers. They are: Aylor, Blankenbaker, Carpenter, Zimmerman, Crigler, Finks, Hoffman, Clore, Yager, Utz, Wayland, Souther, Crisler and Weaver. However, new settlers continued to arrive, and within eight years this colony numbered about three hundred.[1]

The time of the removal of the first German settlers to what is now Madison cannot be fixed definitely; however, it was not earlier than 1724 and not later than 1726. From the information, that may be procured, we may conclude that the migration began to take place in 1724. One of the sources to which we may refer in this matter is an order taken from the court order books of Spotsylvania county giving some Germans the privilege of making roads; the one, to clear a road from the ferry at Germanna to Smith's Island up to the Rapidan; the other, to lay out and make the most convenient road for the so-called German Mountain Road. From this order we would base the settlement at about 1725.[2]

The names of the Germans who first patented land on the Robinson River and White Oak Run are: Zacarias Fleshman, Henry Snider, John and Michael Tower or Tomer (doubtless Tanner or Turner), Matthias Blankenbeker, Nicholas Blankenbeker, Belthaser Blankenbeker, John Prial (Broyles), George Utz, George Sheible, Nicholas Yager, Christopher Zimmerman, Michael Smith, Jacob Crigler, Michael Clore, Michael Cook, George Mayer, George Woodroof, Matthias Beller, Michael Kaifer, William Cimberman (Carpenter) and Michael Holt. Two days later John Motz and John Harnsburger bought land, these patents were dated June 24, 1726.[3]

Then on September 28, 1728 the following persons patented land: Michael Holt, William Carpenter, John Rouse, John Thomas, Christopher Thomas, Christopher Zimmerman, Jacob Broyles,

---

[1] Huddle, W. P., Hebron Church, 1717-1907, Page 11.
[2] Huddle, W. P., Hebron Church, 1717-1907, Page 14.
[3] Huddle, W. P., Hebron Church, 1717-1907, Page 15.

Thomas Wayland, George Woods, Michael Clawse, John Clawse, Cyracus Fleshman, Peter Fleshman, Frederick Cobler, Robert Tanner, Michael Costler (Crisler) and Thomas Wright.①

The following settlers patented land later; Jacob Holzolaw, Sept. 27, 1728; John Hoffman, Sept. 28, 1729; Edward Ballenger, (South side of Deep Run) 1733; George Long, Sept. 17, 1731; Pattas Blankenbeker, March 2, 1732; John Michael Stolts, April 11, 1732; Conrad Amburger, John Carpenter and Joseph Bloodsworth, June 20, 1734; Jacob Manspoil and Andrew Garr, October 3, 1734. The deeds of these settlers show that four hundred acres was the customary size of a patent.②

The first work of these settlers after arriving at their new home was to build a fort and stockade on the north side of the Robinson River, on what is now known as the Thornton Utz farm. This fort was used for protection against the Indians and also as a church. Although the forest was dense and the land hard to clear for cultivation, the colony grew and prospered and soon became a progressive community. It was in this community and by these people that a school was begun, for the teaching of religion, reading, writing and arithmetic. This achievement cannot be praised too highly for this school was the first authentical public school for white children in the Old Dominion.③ This and many other things were performed by the early German settlers, for which their memory will be cherished by Madisonians.

Now let us turn to the English settlers. There has been a great deal of contention between Madisonians concerning who were the first to come into the county. Some claim that the Germans in the Hebron Church community were the first in what is now Madison county; while others contradict this and claim that the English settlers were already in the county when the German congregation came.

Although historical data on this is very meager, we are able to gather some information about the English settlers from the few records which have been preserved. Mr. Scott in his History of Orange county states that the colony settled by Governor Spotswood at Germanna in 1714 was the first settlement in Orange county.④ Thus, it is certain that in 1714 there were no settlers in what is now Madison, as Orange was nearer the original settlement of Virginia and was thus settled before Madison. Then two years later, in 1716, Governor Spotswood made his memorial passage across the Blue Ridge. An account of this passage has been preserved, which shows that Germanna was the frontier settlement at that time, and that the lands beyond this were still in virgin forest. Thus, we are certain

---

① Huddle, W. P., Hebron Church, 1717-1907, Page 16.
② Deed Books A and B, Culpeper County.
③ Virginia Magazine of History of Biography, Volume XIII.
④ Scott, W. W., History of Orange County, Virginia, Page 79.

that no settlements were made in Madison prior to 1716; which brings us within nine years of the time when the German settlers settled on the Robinson River.

Before Spotsylvania was formed in 1721 several large grants were made beyond the frontier in the territory that later became known as Spotsylvania county; consequently, these grants could have been in what is now Spotsylvania, Orange, Culpeper, Greene or Madison counties. These grants, however, were not made to settlers because they were exceedingly large grants. They were speculative and in most cases the grantees never lived on the lands, but as the tide of settlers reached these grants they were divided into homesteads and sold. Thus the land dealers in the tidewater counties would speculate on the frontier lands. When Spotsylvania was formed these grants were recorded in the county records. The grants made before 1721 within the limits of what later became Spotsylvania were as follows: 1712, to Larkin Chew and Augustine Smith; 1717, to John Madison and John Rogers; 1718, to Francis Thornton, Anthony Thornton and William Strother; 1719, to Thomas Jones, Robert Beverley and James Bridgeforth; 1720, to William Skrine and Ruben Welch; 1722, Robert Coleman, William Hansford and John Quarles.[1]

The largest of these grants were those of Robert Beverley and Thomas Jones who patented 15,000 acres; of James Taylor, who patented about 10,000 acres; and of Larkin Chew who patented over 20,000 acres. Chew's grant is very interesting because it shows how fast the settlers came after the frontier reached his grant; by 1740 his grant had been divided into thirty homes.[2]

It is certain that the earliest settlements in Madison were made while Madison was a part of Spotsylvania, and that the first deeds made to land now in Madison were recorded in Spotsylvania. Although there have been many changes in the names of streams and other physical features of this territory, we are able to get some idea of the location of the land described in these old deeds made two hundred years ago.

One very common phrase in these deeds is that the land described lies "in the folks of the Rappahannock." This gives us a more definite idea as to its location for we know that it means this land was either in what is now Madison or Culpeper counties. It could however mean only Madison, for in that day the Rapidan River was often spoken of as the Rappahannock. This being true, it would mean that the land thus described would be "in the folks" of the Rapidan and Robinson Rivers. Patents thus described in the Spotsylvania records prior to 1734 when Orange was formed are as follows: Oct. 7, 1724, Joseph Waugh to Alexander Spotswood; Aug. 8, 1726, John

---
[1] Crozier. W. A., Deeds of Spotsylvania County.
[2] Crozier. W. A., Deeds of Spotsylvania County.

Shelton to Augustine Smith; Nov. 1, 1726, Augustine Smith to Mary Slaughter; Aug. 6, 1728, William Smith to Francis Thornton; Nov. 5, 1728, Augustine Smith to Robert Slaughter; Feb. 4, 1728, Augustine Smith to Thomas Slaughter; Jan. 18, 1728, Thomas Guy to Robert Eastham; Dec. 17, 1728, Alexander Spotswood to Thomas Burn; June 3, 1729, John Hadocks to Francis Thornton; Sept. 2, 1729, Henry Willis to Philemon Cavenaugh; Mar. 3, 1729, Thomas Guy to John Bond to George Wheatley; Dec. 4, 1733, William Carpenter to Michael Cook and Michael Smith, trustees of the German Church; May 17, 1734, Benjamin Rush to Anthony Strother; Aug. 6, 1734, John Mercer to Charles Carter.[1]

The deed of William Carpenter to Michael Cook and Michael Smith, trustees of the German Church, which was without a doubt in Madison proves that "In the folks of the Rappahannock" could certainly mean in what is now Madison county.

There are other instances where the deeds are described as being, "In the great folk of the Rappahannock" which like those "In the folks of the Rappahannock" could have been either in Madison or Culpeper. The deeds thus described are as follows: June 4, 1728, Samuel Wright to John Finalson; October 3, 1727, Joseph Copper to John Kirk; June 3, 1729, John Kilgore to Joseph Haddock; April 7, 1730, Isaac Norman to John Read; July 7, 1730, John Roberts to Roger Oxford; Oct. 6, 1730, John Ashley to William Smith; Nov. 30, 1730, James Pollard to Samuel Ball; Jan. 23, 1730, John Kilgore to John Haddox; Mar. 2, 1730, John Asher to Robert Boarman; July 6, 1730, John Duett to William Smith; Aug. 3, 1731, George Wood to John Hoffman; Aug. 3, 1731, Philemon Cavenaugh to Davis Yancey.

Likewise, there are two deeds for land described as being "In the little folks of the Rappahannock" which certainly meant in the forks of the Rapidan and Robinson Rivers. One of these deeds was made Dec. 2, 1729, when Isaac Bledsoe transferred one thousand acres of land to Robert Jones. The other was made April 2, 1733, when a deed was granted by Charles Morgan to William Smith. It will be noticed that both these deeds are later than those of which we have been speaking.

There is only one deed recorded in Spotsylvania which describes the land as being, "In the folks of the Robinson;" this was made by Theophelus Eddins to Alexander Waugh Nov. 8, 1733. The earliest patent that we are sure was made by an Englishman in Madison was in 1726, when Colonel Joshua Fry patented 1,000 acres of land in the forks of the Robinson River.[2] In 1724 Anthony Strother

---

[1] Crozier, W. A., Deeds of Spotsylvania County.
[2] Slaughter, Philip, History of St. Mark's Parish, Page 134.

patented land, "under Double Top."[1] In 1736 Edmund Broadus patented land in Madison; he was an ancestor of John A. Broadus.[2]

The conclusion that we may draw from all these deeds is that, German and English settlers came about the same time. The Irish and Scotch-Irish came at a later period and will not be discussed here, but it may be said that they did not come in a group as did the Germans and the English.

The English settlers in contrast to the Germans sought the high lands. We may account for this in several ways. In the first place their mother country was not lowland like the German's; they sought land that resembled the mother country. Then again, the high lands were more easily cleared of the forest, and tobacco grew there better than on the low lands. As tobacco was used as currency at that time we would expect them to seek ground that was best adapted to its culture.

On most of the mountains of Madison may be seen today the remains of old colonial cabins, and signs of clearings that have now grown up into forests. The descendants of these early settlers have now forsaken their old homes and have moved into the more fertile valleys and among the smaller hills. These early forefathers of our have been forgotten; only a few piles of stone mark where their cabins once stood; even their graves are unmarked; yet, they performed their task in the great chain of events and made it possible that we may live a better life. Their achievements live on and their blood still flows in the veins of the Madisonians. We may say with one accord that their lives were not lived in vain.

---

[1] Slaughter, Philip, History of St. Mark's Parish, Page 169.
[2] Slaughter, Philip, History of St. Mark's Parish, Page 134.

## CHAPTER IV

### MADISON AS A PART OF ORANGE AND CULPEPER

*(As a Part of Orange County)*

Madison was a part of Orange county from 1734 to 1748, a period of fourteen years. In 1734, almost fifty years before Madison was formed into a separate county, Orange was separated from Spotsylvania. Thus what is now Madison became a part of this new county of Orange.

The first court in Orange was held in January 1734. At this court twenty-three justices were named for the county and took the oath of office. They were: Augustine Smith, Goodrich Lightfoot, John Taliaferro, Thomas Chew, Robert Slaughter, Abraham Field, Robert Green, James Barbour, John Finlason, Richard Mauldin, Samuel Ball, Francis Slaughter, Zachary Taylor, John Lightfoot, James Pollard, Robert Eastham, Benjamin Cave, Charles Curtis, Joist Hite, Morgan Morgan, Benjamin Borden, John Smith and George Hobson. Some of these evidently lived in what is now Madison. However, it was evidently some of these eight; Abraham Field, John Finlason, Richard Mauldin, Samuel Ball, James Pollard, Charles Curtis, John Smith, and George Hobson.[1]

Colonel Henry Willis, an ancestor of Mrs. Ambrose Madison of Woodbury Forest, became the first county clerk. Benjamin Cave, an ancestor of the Madison Cave family, qualified as sheriff with Thomas Chew and James Barbour as sureties, and William Henderson as under-sheriff. Early deed books in Madison show that James Barbour owned land there. James Wood obtained a commission from the President and masters of William and Mary College, dated November 1734 to be surveyor for the county. Zachary Lewis and Robert Turner were sworn as attorneys to practice law in the new county. The court unanimously recommended John Mercer to prosecute the King's causes in court. James Cowherd and John Snow were named as overseers of the highway.[2]

At the next term of court many constables and surveyors of the highway were appointed. Some of these men were Madisonians and some of the highways were in what is now Madison county. Christopher Zimmerman, a member of the Hebron Lutheran Church, was appointed to survey the highway "from the German Road to Potatoe Run;" John Howard, "from the Chapple Road to the

---

[1] Scott, W. W., History of Orange County, Virginia, Page 27.
[2] Scott, W. W., History of Orange County, Virginia, Page 28.

Rapidan Cave Ford;" John Garth, "from the Mountain Road along Mr. James Taylor's 'rolling' road and thence to the Rapidan River." It was from the latter that we perhaps get the name of Barnett's Ford today.①

The first jury ever empanelled in the county was at the following August term of court for the purpose of trying an assault and battery between James Porteus and Jonathan Fennell, alias Fenney. The jury was composed of the following: Benjamin Porter, foreman, Francis Browning, Francis Williams, James Stodgill, Leonard Phillips, William Richardson, George Head, John Conner, John Bomer, William Bohannon, William Crosthwait and Isaac Bletsoe. The verdict was fifteen shillings damage.② Of those on this jury the last three were perhaps Madison county men.

The first grand jury met in November with Robert Cave as foreman. This jury was composed of Abraham Bletsoe, Francis Browning, William Bryant, William Pannill, Edward Franklin, Philip Bush, Anthony Head, William Kelly, Henry Downs, John Bransford, David Phillips, John Howard, George Anderson, Mark Finks, William Carpenter, and George Woods.③ Of this grand jury the following perhaps lived in what is now Madison; Mark Finks, William Carpenter, George Woods and George Anderson.

As there was no court house, Mr. William Robertson's house, on Black Walnut Run, was designated as the place where court should be held until a place could be agreed upon for building a court house. It was at this place that the first court was held in 1734.

At the same term of court Thomas Chew, was ordered to build a prison on his plantation, "a log house, seven and one half feet pitch, sixteen long and ten wide, of logs six by eight at least, close laid at top and bottom, with a sufficient plank door, strong hinges and a good lock." It was further ordered that two hundred pounds of tobacco and a cask be paid for the building of said house.④

A debate was held to decide upon the best place to build a court house. The custom in those times was to build the court house in the center of the county, or as near the center as possible. In this instance, however, the court was divided; one part was in favor of the center; others favored Raccoon Ford, which was at that time some distance higher up the river than now. Eight favored the former and six the latter situation. The size of the county may be seen from that fact that it could not be ascertained whether the mouth of the Robinson, which is in the corner of Madison, or Raccoon Ford was nearer the center. Justices Smith, Chew, Barbour and Taylor favored a point just below the mouth of the Robinson on the south side of the Rapidan. Mr. Lightfoot agreed that this was nearer the

---
① Scott, W. W., History of Orange County, Virginia, Page 29.
② Scott, W. W., History of Orange County, Virginia, Page 30.
③ Scott, W. W., History of Orange County, Virginia, Page 30.
④ Scott, W. W., History of Orange County, Virginia, Page 31.

center but insisted on the north side of the Rapidan. Messrs. Field, Green, Finlason, Ball, Pollard, and Francis Slaughter declined to answer the question as to the center, but insisted on Raccoon Ford, or thereabouts and the north side of the river.[1]

At the June term, 1735, Charles Carter and William Beverley reported as to the agreement they had been ordered to make with Colonel Spotswood for land on which to build the court house; their agreement, however, was ignored, for in October 1736 another proposal was made and the Court, after debate, agreed that the house be built at the place appointed by the commissioners "near the Governor's Ford on the south side of the Rapidan."[2]

In November, the Court made an agreement with John Branham, whereby he leased twenty acres of land upon which to build the courthouse, this plot to include the spring most convenient to Cedar Island Ford. Branham was to receive one hundred and twenty pounds per annum. Thomas Chew and William Russell were appointed to lay off the land and designate the location of the court house.[3]

In July 1738 a notice was given that at the next term the Court would make an agreement with workmen to finish the courthouse, and at the February term of court following, Peter Russell was employed to keep the building clean and "provide candles and small beer for the justices." Thus it appears that it took nearly two years to build this courthouse. It seems certain, also, that the first real courthouse owned by the county was located near the present Somerville's Ford. Henry Willis was paid thirteen thousand and one hundred pounds of tobacco for building the prison and three thousand three hundred and fifty pounds for finishing the courthouse.[4]

In November 1739, Willis took out a license to keep an ordinary near the court house.[5] These ordinaries, where entertainments for man and beast was provided, were usually owned by the gentry, and at that time the court set the prices asked. Thus in 1735, this order is entered in the Orange County records, "The court does thus set and rate liquors; rum the gallon, eight shillings; Virginia brandy, six shillings, a hot dyet (diet), one shilling; a cold dyet, six pense; a lodging with clean sheets, six pense."[6]

From these court records of Orange county between 1734 and 1748 we are able to get a very interesting account of laws and courts of that time. The laws, although very much like those of England at the same time, were what we today would consider cruel and harsh; they were also very diligently enforced by the justices. The justices felt as important in their office in the county in America as their

---

[1] Scott, W. W. History of Orange County, Virginia. Page 32.
[2] Ibid. Page 32.
[3] Ibid. Pages 33-36.
[4] Ibid. Pages 33-36.
[5] Ibid. Pages 33-36.
[6] Ibid. Page 122.

## As A Part of Orange and Culpeper

models, the squires, did in England, the mother country. To a certain extent, they were very important; for they had much more power and many more duties than these officials have now. As already stated there were twenty-three squires in the vast area then included in Orange county. These squires were the leaders in their community in both legal and religious activities. In their legal capacity they watched over their immediate community, keeping order and giving legal advice. This, however, was not their greatest responsibility; as it was presiding over the county court and thus serving in the capacity of what is now a circuit court judge. In their religious capacity they served as wardens and leaders in the parish churches. It was not strange for them to serve in the two capacities for at that time the government and the Episcopal Church were inseparable.

The harshness of the laws in those days is shown by examples of actual cases tried in the courts. The death penalty was inflicted for a very small offense. In the early days of this county, hog stealing became a very common practice; a law was passed placing the death penalty on the second conviction of a theft of this kind. Negro slaves were punished very severely as examples for other slaves. There is a record of a case in which a slave was hanged for killing his master, his head was then severed from his body and placed on a pole in the court yard, as a warning to other slaves who were meditating the same crime. Another record shows that a negro was hanged for stealing $10.00 worth of merchandise from a store. The most awful case was that of a negro woman, named Eve, who was tied to a stake and burned to death because she poisoned her master.[1]

The law extended over a much wider field than it does today, in that it looked after the morals of the people. If a father did not educate or train his children in Christian principles, they were taken away from him by the court and bound out to someone else. An example of this occurred in 1742 when the court ordered that a man, named Dodson, should have his children bound out by the church wardens.

Presentments for swearing, oaths and non-attendance at church were common occurrences. Everyone was compelled to attend Church and the Church must be the parish Episcopal.

In 1743 Pat Leonard was ordered to the stocks for calling the sheriff a liar. Jacob Saunders was ordered to receive twenty-five lashes at a common whipping post for being a vagabond and for cheating at cards.[2]

No outstanding event occurred while Madison was a part of Orange. This period of time was not an era of events but one of prosperity. The settlers lived in peace and made progress in clearing

---

[1] Scott, W. W., History of Orange County, Virginia. Pages 133-136.
[2] Scott, W. W., History of Orange County, Virginia, Page 124.

and cultivating their lands. As the Indians were fast disappearing and were no longer a menace to the settlers, they could now devote all of their time to the pursuits of peace. This they did and the result was that great progress was made. We may judge the prosperity of the settlers of Orange by the fact that only fourteen years were required to increase the population enough to justify the creation of another county. This new county was Culpeper and with the formation of this county, what is now Madison no longer remained with Orange, but became a part of Culpeper.

## Madison As Part of Culpeper

The original county of Culpeper was formed from Orange in 1748. It included what is now Culpeper, Madison and Rappahannock. Culpeper took its name from Lord Culpeper, who was the original proprietor of the land known as the "Northern Neck of Virginia." This grant included all of Culpeper county as it was when formed.

The act which made Culpeper a separate county was passed in 1748. This act for dividing Orange and forming Culpeper has been given elsewhere in this book. Although the act for the formation of the county was passed in 1748, the first court was not convened until 1749. As in other newly formed counties, there was no courthouse in which court could be held; until a courthouse could be built, court was held in the home of Robert Coleman. From the records that have been left it is evident that Mr. Coleman's home was near the present courthouse.

The town of Fairfax became the county seat, but was not established as a town until ten years later in 1759. Pursuant to an act of the General Assembly, passed at a session held in Williamsburg, February 22, 1759, the town of Fairfax was laid off on twenty-seven acres of land originally owned by Robert Coleman. The courthouse was located on lot No. 24, which is now on the corner of Davis and Main Streets. The town was laid off by William Green, Philip Slaughter, Nathaniel Pendleton, and William Williams. The plan of the town was submitted to the county court on Tuesday, June 21, 1759, and ordered to be recorded. Many years later the name of Fairfax was changed to Culpeper.

Roger Dixon qualified as the first clerk and served in this capacity from 1749 to 1772.[1] He was followed by John Jameson who served from 1772 to 1810.[2] Robert Slaughter was appointed as the first sheriff of the county.[3]

---

[1] Court Order Books of Culpeper County. County Clerk's Office. Volume "A", Page 4.

[2] Court Order Books of Culpeper County. County Clerk's Office. Volume "A", Page 75.

[3] Same Volume "A", Page 3.

The first surveyor of Culpeper was a man who afterwards became very famous. George Washington, became county surveyor of Culpeper in 1749, and served in this capacity for three years. The marriage of his brother Lawrence with Miss Fairfax made him known to the proprietor of Northern Neck, and it was this acquaintance that led to his becoming county surveyor. Washington was then in his seventeenth year, and there was nothing unusual about his daily life. In the county court of Culpeper we find the following records July 20, 1749, "George Washington, gentleman, produced a commission from the President of William and Mary College, appointed him Surveyor of this county, which was received; and thereupon took the usual oath of his Majesty's person and government; and took and subscribed the adjuration oath and test, and then took the oath of Surveyor, according to law."[1]

The first general enumeration made in the county was not an enumeration of the people but of tobacco plants. Thus, as early as 1728, several groups of men were appointed to count the tobacco plants; of this number, two were from what is now Madison. George Woots (Woods) and Michael Cook were appointed to count the plants from the mouth of the Robinson River up to the Great Mountain, which was the Blue Ridge.[2] The next enumeration of which we have any record is that of the population of the county taken by the Federal Government in 1790. This was two years before Madison had separated from Culpeper; hence, the figures for Culpeper include Madison also. The census returns for Culpeper county show the following figures: 3,372 white free males over sixteen years of age; 3,750 white free males under sixteen years of age; 6,682 white free females; 70 unclassified free persons; and 8,226 slaves. This makes the total population of the county 22,105.

Many of the earliest patents made to land in Madison can be traced through the records at Culpeper. We find in these records that Lord Fairfax still made patents after Culpeper county was formed. One rather interesting patent recorded at Culpeper is made by Thomas Smith to a large tract of land lying on Island Run (now White Oak Run); he sold this patent to James Barbour, Sr., while he in turn divided it and sold it to settlers. The names of those to whom this land was sold and the dates of their deeds are as follows: Thomas Barbour, 1757; George Utz, 1764; Adam Garr, 1765; Ambrose Barbour; 1765; John Graves, 1770; John Willson, 1770; John Wayland, 1771; Antony Berry, 1772; John Sampson, 1773; Adam Broile, 1772; Michael Swindle, 1773; Michael Telp, 1773; John Sales, 1773; William Campe, 1775; John Porter, 1786; and John Archer, 1789. This division shows us how quickly the county was being developed, and gives also the names connected with this development.

---

[1] Slaughter, Philip, History of St. Mark's Parish, Page 28.
[2] Slaughter, Philip, History of St. Mark's Parish, Page 115.

Two notable events occurred in the history of our county while Madison was a part of Culpeper. These events were the French and Indian War and the Revolutionary War. The Revolutionary War will be discussed in another chapter; consequently, only the French and Indian War will be discussed here.

During the course of the French and Indian War, the legislature of Virginia passed numerous acts for the defense of the frontier, for paying the troops, and for supplying the army with provisions. In the seventh volume of Henning's Statutes is found a schedule appended to an act passed in September 1758, giving the names of soldiers to whom pay was due, together with the names of other persons who held accounts against the colony for work done for the army, for provisions furnished, etc. The names of those who seem most likely to have been in Madison are as follows:

| | |
|---|---|
| William Brown | David Devoid |
| George Watherall | Corelius Mitchell |
| John McDaniel | John Wilhite |
| John Thomas | John Bowman |
| William Wall | Jacob Wall |
| Nicholas Yager | Daniel Delaney |
| William Twiman | John Care |
| Adam Baland | Andrew Carpenter |
| Matthias Weaver | Lewis Fisher |
| John Plunketpeter | John Glove (Clure) |
| (Blankenbeker) | Mattias Rouce (Rouse) |
| William Yager | Alexander Waugh, Jr. |
| Edward Jones | William Jones |
| Abraham Bledser | Daniel Wright |

Aside from the wars that occurred during the forty-four years that Madison was a part of Culpeper, there is very little known concerning the events that took place. It is very difficult to place material definitely on only a part of the county that far in the past.

## CHAPTER V

### Madison Organized As A Separate County

Exactly three hundred years after Columbus discovered America, an act was passed by the Virginia Assembly for the formation of Madison county. This act provided for the division of Culpeper into two parts, each of which was to be a separate county.

Culpeper, at the time of its formation, was a very large territory, including what is now Culpeper, Rappahannock, and Madison counties. The vast extent of this one county later gave rise to a great inconvenience which had not existed when it was formed. When Culpeper was formed into a county in 1748 only a part of it was thickly settled; this was the southeastern corner; consequently, the court house was not placed in the center of the county, but in the southeastern corner. The court house, at the time it was built, was placed in the center of the population, but later the center of population changed; other parts of the county became thickly populated, especially the northwestern corner, or what is now Madison county. This growth of population and the inconvenience placed upon those living in the remote parts of the county to attend the county court caused agitation for a division.

Like all human endeavors, the movement for the formation of a new county had its opponents. Some ridiculed the idea, calling the new division the "little cow pasture;" like all ridicule it, perhaps, had a serious effect at the time it was uttered, but later it developed into humor. Regardless of ridicule and objections the county was formed and became a large "cow pasture," for farming today is the chief occupation.

The act for the division of Culpeper and the formation of Madison was passed, December 4, 1792, but did not take effect until May 1, 1793. This act, besides specifying the bounds of the county, provided for the beginning of its government as follows:

Section Two: "A court for the said county of Madison shall be held by the justices thereof on the fourth Thursday in every month after the same shall take place, in like manner as provided by law for other counties, and shall be by their commissions directed.

Section Three: "The justices to be named in the commission of the peace for the said county of Madison, shall meet at the house of John Yager, Jr., in the said county upon the first court day after the said county shall take place, and having taken the oath prescribed by law, and administered the oath of office to and taken bond of the sheriff according to law proceed to appoint and qualify a clerk, and fix upon a place for holding courts in the said county, at or as near the center thereof as the situation and convenience will admit, and thenceforth the said court shall proceed to erect the necessary public buildings at such a place, and until such building be completed to appoint any place for holding court as they shall think proper. Provided always that the appointment of the place for holding court, and of a clerk, shall not be made unless a majority of the justices of the said county be present; where such a majority shall have been prevented from attending by weather or of their being at the time out of the county, in such case the appointment shall be postponed until some court day when a majority shall be present.

Section Four: "It shall be lawful for the sheriff of Culpeper to collect and make distress for any public dues and officers fees which shall remain unpaid by the inhabitants of the said county of Madison, at the time the said county shall take place, and shall be accountable for the same in like manner as if this act had never been made.

Section Five: The governor with the advice of the council shall appoint a person to be first sheriff of the said county of Madison who shall continue in office during the term and upon the same conditions as are by law appointed by other sheriffs.

Section Six: The court of the said county of Culpeper shall have jurisdiction of all actions and suits depending before them at the time the said county of Madison takes place and shall try to determine the same, and award execution thereof.

Section Seven: The said county of Madison shall remain in the same district with Culpeper, for which district courts are holden in Fredericksburg, to all intents and purposes as if this act had never been made. In all future elections of a senator, the said county of Madison shall be of the same district as the said county of Culpeper."[1]

In pursuance of the above act the first court convened in Madison, was held on the fourth Thursday and Friday, May 23 and 24, 1793. This court was held at the home of John Yager, Jr., a few miles north of the present court house on the farm now owned by Mr. W. L. Payne.[2]

There were no cases of interest tried at this term of court for the entire time was consumed in administering the oath of office to the new officials. It was customary at this time for the first sheriff of a new formed county to be appointed by the governor of the state. This rule was obeyed when Madison became a county, for Henry Hill was appointed by the governor to act as sheriff with Robert Hill, Daniel Brown and William Wallis as his under-sheriffs, or what would now be called deputy sheriffs. Robert Hill and Daniel Brown gave security for Henry Hill. The first clerk of the county was not appointed by the governor, nor elected by the people, but was appointed by the court. John Walker, Jr., received this appointment and gave as his securities John Walker and James Walker, Jr. The court next proceeded to appoint an attorney for the commonwealth; this appointment was given to John Walker, Sr. It is interesting to

---

[1] Henning, W. W., Statutes at Large of Virginia. Volume XIII, Pages 558-9.
[2] Court Order Books of Madison County, No. 1, Pages 1, 2, 3.

note that two of the most important positions in the county were given to members of one family.[1]

Until recent years the office of county surveyor was considered very important. The first court did not have power to appoint a county surveyor; it could only recommend one, subject to his ability to receive a commission. George Hume received this recommendation by the court, and later secured his commission, but resigned in July of the same year. After the resignation of George Hume, the vacant office was filled by Henry Wayland, who remained county surveyor for many years. James Barbour and Andrew Finks were the securities for Henry Wayland. It was usually customary for the county surveyor to survey all new roads made in the county, but the first county surveyor of Madison was relieved of this duty. Only a short time before Madison was formed, Culpeper had appointed road surveyors for the part of the county that became Madison; the first court held in Madison decided to let these men remain in office until their term expired.[2]

Before any lawyers were allowed to practice in the county, they were required to take the oath of allegiance. Robert Peacock, Robert Voss, Robert Taylor, James Bell, Richard Henry Yancey and John Shackleford took this oath at the first court and were given permission to plead cases. William Wirt, who later became famous as an attorney-general, was given permission to practice law in the county at the next term of court, which met in June, 1793.[3] This concluded the work of the first term of court, with the exception of granting George Eve license to perform marriages, and appointing John Gibbs an assessor of taxable property.

The new county was named Madison in honor of James Madison, who was at this time a leader of the Democratic Party in Congress. The most important achievement performed by Madison prior to the formation of Madison county and while he was a leader in Congress, was the introduction of seventeen amendments to the Constitution, twelve of which were passed by Congress and ten ratified by the necessary number of states. These amendments went into effect November 3, 1791, and are the first ten amendments to the Constitution of the United States. James Madison was not born in Madison county, nor did he ever live there. His home was at Montpelier, just across the line in Orange county. Some of his family, however, did live in Madison, and he owned property there. It has always been a law in Madison county that anyone desiring to build a mill on any stream must first secure permission from the court. The first permission of this kind was granted in 1793 to James Madison, Jr., James Madison, Sr., Francis Madison and William Madison to build the mill now known as Madison Mills.[4]

---

[1] Court Order Books of Madison County, No. 1, Page 2.
[2] Ibid. Page 2.
[3] Court Order Books of Madison County, Volume No. 1, Pages 1-10.
[4] Court Order Books of Madison County, Volume No. 1, Page 25.

At the next term of court which met June 27, 1793, a place was considered for building a court house. The members of the court were unanimously in favor of selecting a place that was in the center of the county, or as near it as possible. After some deliberation it was decided that the land belonging to William Carpenter, known as Finnell's old field, would be the most suitable, as this was for all practical purposes in the center of the county and was an ideal site for a town. This field was situated on a large hill or ridge, which commanded a beautiful view of the surrounding hills and valleys; above all, the Blue Ridge was visible for miles of its length lying like a sleeping giant beyond the hills and valleys clothed in the pale blue tint which gives it its name. This tract of land selected was part of a patent originally granted to the German settlers by Alexander Spotswood.

The court house lot was surveyed by Henry Wayland August 28, 1793, and the deed was dated September 26 of the same year.[1] At this time two acres were bought for the court house lot at a cost of five shillings, which in present currency would be about eighty-five cents. This lot was deeded to the first justices appointed by the governor for the county, who had taken the oath of office at the May term of court. They were: James Barbour, William Walker, Robert Alcocke, William Chapman, Reubin Fry, Merry Walker, Ambrose Barbour, Robert Beale, Ambrose Medley, John Henshaw, Jeremiah Kirtley, Thomas Graves and John Wetherall.

Court continued to be held at the home of John Yager until the December term 1793; then, it was moved to the home of John Graves. It seems that only one term of court was held at the home of John Graves; this was the December term 1793, for at this time the court ordered that the next meeting should be held in Finnell's old field. However, it did not meet in this field, but in the home of Thomas Brooks, since at the February court it was ordered that Thomas Brooks be paid for court being held at his residence. Records do not show why so many changes were made, nor do they tell us where court was held until the court house was built.[2]

It was suggested by the court in July 1793 that a court house and other necessary buildings be built on the land bought for this purpose. This suggestion was ignored at this term of court and did not materialize until September. In September the suggestion was again made, and this time met the approval of the court, for James Barbour, William Walker and Ambrose Medley were appointed as a commission to make plans for the new court house. This committee then met and drew up plans which were submitted at the next term of court. Their plans met with the approval of all that were concerned, and the court house was later built to conform to these plans.[3]

---

[1] Deed Books of Madison County, Volume No. 1, Page 25.
[2] Court Order Books of Madison County, Volume "A", Page 130.
[3] Court Order Books of Madison County, No. 1, Page 8.

This building was made of logs. It was forty-two feet long, twenty-four feet wide, with a pitch of twelve feet to the roof. The interior was divided into three rooms and equipped with fire-places in two rooms. The total cost of the building was one hundred and eighty-one pounds, English money.[1] The building served as the court house for thirty-four years, until it was replaced by the brick building which is in use at the present time. When the old building was built its architectural design was not considered; service was the only consideration. This was not true of the brick building, for, by this time, the citizens had begun to consider both service and beauty. An architect named Phillips was employed to design and build the new court house. Today Madisonians are proud of a tradition which gives a greater architect's opinion of their court house. This tradition is that when Stanford White, the architect of Madison Square Garden, New York City, was building Cabell Hall at the University of Virginia, he made a visit to Madison and while there inspected the present court house and pronounced it an excellent piece of architecture.[2] There is another tradition, which adds to the solemnity of this house of justice; this is that it is built in a graveyard. It has been said by older people in the county that when the foundation of the present court house was dug many skeletons were unearthed. These could not have been placed there by the settlers, for the old court house stood on this same plot of land; our only conclusion is that it was an Indian grave.[3]

At the June term of court, 1793, the court ordered that a county jail be built. A committee was appointed to supervise this work, and the same committee was appointed which had served in this capacity when the first court house was built. They were James Barbour, William Walker and Ambrose Medley. The first jail, like the first court house, was a log building, sixteen feet long, twelve feet wide, with a ten foot pitch to the roof. The walls, floor and ceiling were made of logs, leveled to a square edge of a thickness of nine inches. In order to make the walls thicker and the possibility of criminals escaping less, the entire interior of the building was lined with oak boards two inches thick and securely nailed with spikes five inches long. Pine heart shingles were used for roofing; these shingles were three-fourth of an inch thick and twenty inches long, being placed on the roof so as to show six inches. Only one window was made and this was made secure with iron bars one inch square, the opening between each bar being not more than two inches wide. The door was five feet long and two and one-half feet wide with flat bars two inches wide and three-fourth of an inch thick; also a double door was made of inch plank. Another jail was built in 1795, and it is

---

[1] Ibid. Page 122.
[2] Statement of oldest people.
[3] Statement of oldest people in the county.

The Court House

probable that both these jails were used at the same time. A few years later a third jail was built; this also was made of logs a part of which is now in the building used as an office by Dr. Clore. The present jail is the fourth one built by the county. All the jail buildings have stood practically on the same spot of ground. At the February term of court 1794, it was ordered by the court that a pair of stocks be built in the jail in which to place the worst criminals. This was done by Henry Wayland at the cost of six pounds and six shillings.[1]

When Madison was formed into a county the state required that each county be divided into districts and that each district furnish a company for the county militia. This was a custom and requirement handed down from colonial days, being then necessary against Indian attacks. All men from twenty-one to sixty were required to serve in this militia or general muster. Madison was divided into twelve districts, each of which had its captain, lieutenants, and other necessary officers. Then there were other officers for the entire county, of which the lieutenant-colonel was the chief. Reubin Beale was appointed as the first lieutenant-colonel of the Madison Militia; Jasper Haynes was made major of the first battalion; and Jeremiah Kirtley was made major of the second battalion. This system of county militia continued until the Civil War, but was never used after that time.[2]

The first division of the county which corresponds to the present magisterial districts, was made in March 1794. The county was then divided into three districts known as numbers one, two and three. The first district was composed of all the land lying on the northeast side of the Robinson River. The second district was situated on the south side of the Robinson River above the road leading from Russell's Ford to Crawford's Ford. The third district was also on the south side of the Robinson River and was below the road which leads from Russell's Ford to Crawford's Ford. These divisions were created because of the necessity arising from the supervision of election and the care of the poor. Henry Hill became the first supervisor of district Number 1; Merry Walker, of district Number 2; and Ambrose Medley, of district Number 3. Some years later these districts were slightly changed and became known by the names which they bear today, namely: Robinson, Rapidan and Locust Dale.[3]

When the county was formed it was customary to have county courts instead of circuit courts as today. The first form of court held in Madison was a county court that met once each month. This was not presided over by a judge, but by five justices of the county. These justices were recommended by the court and appointed by the governor. The senior member of the board of justices served as the

---
[1] Court Order Books of Madison County, Volume No. 1, Pages 6, 37.
[2] Ibid. Volume No. 1, Page 24.
[3] Court Order Books of Madison County, Volume No. 1, Page 48.

chief judge in the court room. This chief justice also served as sheriff; if he did not desire to serve, he could farm out the office to someone else; thus, the sheriff was not elected by the people as he is today, but each year the senior justice automatically became sheriff.[1]

The county courts were the only ones held until 1809, when a so-called Superior Court was established. This court met twice each year in May and October. It had jurisdiction over the larger cases and also served as a court of appeals from the county court. In 1831 this court was changed to the Superior Court of Law and Chancery, but retained somewhat its same jurisdiction and form, and met at the same time as the old superior court. After the Civil War the justice county court was abolished and a judge took the place of the justices. However, court continued to meet each month, the same judge serving, perhaps, in several counties. In 1904 the court ceased to meet each month but instead met once every two months. This is the form now in use.[2]

When the Superior Court was established in 1809 the first grand jury was as follows: Andrew Gassell, William Bradford, Robert Hill, Joseph Towles, Churchill Gibbs, Paschal Earley, James Wood, Simeon Lewis, William Twyman, William Crow, Edmund Gaines, John Walker, Leonard Barnes, William Jones, Robert Beale, William Booton, John Booker, Martin Barnes, Michael Yager, George H. Allen, James Barnett and Joseph Brock. The first case to be tried was that of Samuel Morris, who was indicted for the murder of Abraham Ramsbottom. The first jury, and the one to try the above case, was composed of Edward Simms, Jonas Blankenbeker, Lewis Crigler, William Chapman, Henry Price, Thomas Chapman, Zachriah Shirly, Adam Wayland, Joseph Carpenter, John Rucker, John Smith, and Michael Clore. This jury found Morris guilty of murder in the second degree and fixed his penalty at twelve years in the penitentiary. Hugh Holmes was the first judge of the court in Madison. Madison has produced one very famous judge, Daniel R. Fields. Judge Fields was born on the Garr place at Garr's Run. He was the judge of the circuit court for thirty-six years. William Wirt, who later became United States Attorney-General, lived near Locust Dale and pleaded his first cases in Madison county. Benjamin Cave was the first clerk of the Superior Court.

When Madison was formed in 1793 there were no post offices in the county. The first to be established was Madison Court House, January 1, 1801. It was named for the county and was situated at the county seat. This was made an incorporated town March 20, 1875.

Leon, formerly called James City, taking its first name from the James family, of which Jesse and Frank James were members,

---

[1] Statement of oldest people in the county.
[2] Court Order Books of Madison County, Volume No. 7, Page 1.

was established on October 1, 1810. The name of this office was changed to Leon on November 25, 1840. This was the second post office to be established in the county.

The third was Locust Dale, first established as Locust Grove, March 8, 1823. The name was changed to Locust Dale May 28, 1825. This office was discontinued October 21, 1830, but re-established November 13, 1830.

The fourth post office established in the county was Wolftown formerly called Rapidan, established January 7, 1828. The name of the office was changed to Wolftown on October 28, 1857.

Criglersville was established January 2, 1833. It takes its name from the Crigler family, who were among the first settlers in the community.

The other offices in the county were established as follows: Achsah, April 7, 1905; Aroda, June 15, 1922; Aylor, September 28, 1904; Banco, October 10, 1901; Brightwood, formerly known as Fleishman's Shop, later Dulinsville, March 6, 1855; Duet, 1901; Elly, October 5, 1905; Etlan, October 18, 1899; Grave's Hill, February 9. 1841; Haywood, August 4, 1880; Madison Mills, January 20, 1848; Nethers, 1875; Novum, 1895; Oak Park, April 25, 1854; Oldrag, July 1, 1919; Peola Mills, August 10, 1848; Pratts, November 13, 1883; Radiant, March 18, 1885; Rochelle, March 25, 1854; Ruth, December 3, 1900; Shelby, 1892; Syria, December 19, 1898; Twyman's Mill, 1868; Uno, 1891; Hood, 1881; Woodbury Forest, 1910; Zeus, March 22, 1902.[1]

---

[1] All information concerning post offices came from the Post Office Department at Washington, D. C.

## CHAPTER VI

### Madison County In Our Wars

#### The Revolutionary War

It must be borne in mind that Madison was a part of Culpeper during the Revolution, as it was not formed into a separate county until 1792; therefore, it is hard to find records for this period and to separate them into purely Madison history. Unfortunately the records dealing with the Revolution were all destroyed; could they be found, it would be a difficult task to separate the history of the two divisions of the county. Hence, in discussing the Revolution we are forced to use a great deal of the general history of Culpeper; we remember in so doing that we are also discussing the history of Madison.

We are familiar with the causes that led to this war; especially how the cry was against "Taxation without Representation." The colonies of the new world claimed that England placed unfair taxes on them and gave them no direct representation in her legislative bodies. They did not complain so much of the burden of the taxes that England placed upon them, but they detested the principle. They claimed that England did not have a moral nor a legal right to deal with her colonies as she did.

The real cause of this war was neither taxation nor representation; it was the natural phenomenon which takes place when two nations are united under one government. The interests of the American colonists had become separated from those of the mother country; consequently, they desired to have their own government. The colonists who fought in this war proved loyal to their Anglo-Saxon blood, which made them lovers of liberty. They desired freedom and independence in order to follow their own desires and mold their own fate. In the course of the war the colonists proved that they were willing to pay the price of freedom. They also proved their valor, courage and endurance as sons of a new land and of a new nation; they established a precedent which has been handed down through the years which have followed until it has become a characteristic principle of our nation. This principle is that the citizens of this great nation are willing to fight for abstract principles and to lay down their lives that right may prevail. We may well be proud that our county did its part in this war, and we should honor our forefathers because of the price they paid for what we now enjoy. Culpeper was exceedingly prominent in the cause of liberty prior to the war, as well as during the war. When the question of the Stamp

Act was being discussed and agitated, Culpeper was one of the first counties in the state to protest to the governor against this act of oppression. This protest expressed the views of the people concerning the Stamp Act and the unfairness of its provisions. The protest was written and signed on Monday, October 21, 1765, by sixteen justices of the peace of Culpeper county. The protest was made to Governor Fauquier, the governor of Virginia, and in order to make it more emphatic the justices at the same time resigned their commissions. The address was as follows:

"To the Honorable Francis Fauquier, Esquire, His Majesty's Lieutenant.

Governor and Commander-in-Chief of the Colony and Dominion of Virginia. The humble address of the Justices of the Peace of the county of Culpeper.

"Sir: At a time when his majesty's subjects in America are so universally alarmed on account of the late proceedings of the British Parliament, and the enemies of America employed and representing its colonies in an odious light to our most gracious Sovereign and his ministers, by the most ungenerous interpretation of our behavior, we beg leave to take this method to assure your Honor of our inviolable attachment to and affection for, the sacred person of his Majesty, and the whole Royal family.

"And from your Honor's well known candor, and benevolent disposition we are persuaded that we at the same time be permitted to lay before your Honor those reasons which have determined us to resign the Commission of the Peace under which we have sworn to act as magistrates in this county.

"It seems to be the unanimous opinion of the people of America (and a few in England), that the late acts of Parliament by which a stamp duty is imposed upon Americans, and a court of vice-admiralty appointed ultimately to determine all controversies, which may arise, concerning the execution of the said act, is unconstitutional, and a high infringement of our most valuable privileges as British subjects, who, we humbly apprehend, cannot constitutionally be taxed without the consent of our representatives, or our lives and properties be affected in any suit, or criminal causes, whatsoever, without first being tried by our peers.

"And, as the execution of the said act does, in some measure, depend on the county courts, we cannot, if consistent with the duty which we owe our country, be, in the smallest degree, instrumental in enforcing a law which conceives as in itself, shaking at the very foundations of our liberties, and if carried into execution, must render our prosperity unhappy and ourselves contemptible. In the opinion of all men who are the least acquainted with the British constitution, we shall, in that case, no longer be free, but merely the property of those whom we formerly looked upon as our fellow subjects.

"Permit us Sir, to add that we shall hope his Majesty and Parliament will change their measures and suffer us to enjoy our ancient privileges, and if we should incur the displeasures of our Sovereign by thus endeavoring to assert our rights, we should look upon it as one of the greatest misfortunes which could befall us.

"We do heartily and sincerely wish his Majesty a long and happy reign over us, and that there never may be wanting a Prince, of the illustrious House of Hanover, to succeed him in his dominions, that your Honor may continue to enjoy the favor of our Sovereign, long govern the people of this ancient and loyal colony, and that the people may again be happy under your mild and gentle administration as they have formerly been, is what we most devoutly pray for."

(Signed)

| | | |
|---|---|---|
| N. Pendleton | John Strother | Benjamin Roberts |
| Robert Green | Henry Pendleton | Daniel Brown |
| John Slaughter | George Wetherall | Henry Field, Jr. |
| W. Eastham | William Brown | Joseph Wood [1] |
| Ambrose Powell | William Green | |
| William Williams | Thomas Scott | |

As the clouds of war grew thicker and conflict became inevitable, it was suggested that each county in Virginia should organize a Committee of Public Safety. Culpeper organized such a committee in 1775, with James Barbour as county lieutenant and commander-in-chief of the Culpeper Militia. The committee itself was composed of the following men: John Jameson, Henry Pendleton, James Slaughter and John Slaughter. There were others on this committee who are not definitely known. However, they were probably from the list of justices of the county at that time; these were Henry Field, William Ball, William Green, Ben Roberts, Joseph Woods, John Strother, Sam Clayton and James Pendleton.[2]

The Virginia Convention met in St. John's Church on March 20, 1775. At this convention Patrick Henry moved that Virginia be put in a state of defense and in support of this resolution he delivered his immortal speech, ending with words, "Give me liberty or give me death." The meeting of this convention so alarmed Lord Dunmore, then governor of Virginia, that he caused the powder to be removed from the old magazine at Williamsburg. This arbitrary act of Lord Dunmore so aroused the superstition of Patrick Henry, who had recently been made commander of the State Militia, that he issued the call for volunteers and marched toward Williamsburg. Upon his summons one hundred and fifty men from Culpeper, one hundred from Orange, and one hundred from Fauquier answered the

---

[1] Green, Notes on Culpeper County and St. Mark's Parish.
[2] Ibid.

call. These men came together and pitched their first camp in a field about one-half mile west of the town, then known as Fairfax, now, Culpeper. These were the first minute men raised in Virginia, of whom John Randolph of Roanoke later said in the United States Senate, "We were raised in a minute, armed in a minute, marched in a minute, fought in a minute, and vanquished in a minute.⁽¹⁾

This group of patriots formed themselves into a regiment and chose Lawrence Taliaferro, colonel; Edward Stevens, lieutenant; and Thomas Marshall, father of Chief-Justice John Marshall, major. The flag used by this group of men, better known as the Culpeper Minute Men, bore in its center the figure of a rattlesnake coiled in the act of striking; above this was the inscription "The Culpeper Minute Men." On each side were the words "Liberty or Death," and beneath, "Don't tread on me." The corps was dressed in green hunting shirts with the words "Liberty or Death" on their breasts. They wore in their hats buck-tails; and in their belts, tomahawks and scalping knives. This uniform gave them a very weird, savage, and warlike appearance. It is said that their appearance terrified the inhabitants of the country through which they marched and that during their stay in Williamsburg they were called by the inhabitants of that town, "Men from the Indian Country."⁽²⁾

After they were mustered at Fairfax, Patrick Henry called them to Williamsburg. Shortly after their arrival at this place about one hundred and fifty of them, who were armed with rifles fit for service, marched into Norfolk county and were engaged in the battle of Great Bridge. This was the first battle of the Revolutionary War fought on Virginia soil. The battle took place on December 9, 1775, and was a victory for the Americans. After the battle of Great Bridge, Lord Dunmore retreated to Norfolk and was followed closely by the Americans. The British were unable to hold Norfolk, and on January 1, 1776, they set fire to the city. Only a part of the Culpeper Minute Men were at the burning of Norfolk; the others had not yet been able to secure proper equipment and were still encamped near Williamsburg.⁽³⁾

By an ordinance of the convention of 1775 the colony was divided into eighteen districts, one of which was composed of the counties of Orange, Culpeper and Fauquier. Each of these districts were required to enlist a battalion of five hundred men in ten companies of fifty men each with requisite officers; a colonel, lieutenant-colonel, and major, ten captains and lieutenants, a chaplain, surgeon, etc.⁽⁴⁾

During the war Culpeper organized eight companies of eighty-four men each, making a total of six hundred and seventy-two men, not including officers. These eight companies were organized by the

---
[1] Howe, Henry, Historical Collection of Virginia, Page 237.
[2] Ibid. Page 238.
[3] Ibid. Page 239.
[4] Ibid. Page 239.

following captains: John Green, John Thornton, George Slaughter, Gabriel Long, Gabriel Jones, John Gilleson, Abraham Buford, and McClanahan, a Baptist preacher. No one has been able to estimate how many of these men lived in what is now Madison, but there are several things which would lead us to believe that Madison furnished her quota. One reason for believing this is, that there were a good many Baptists and German Lutherans in the part of Culpeper that later became Madison, and history tells us that these two denominations were very loyal to the cause of liberty. The second reason is that the pensioners reported in 1835 were about equally divided between Madison and Culpeper.[1]

It is impossible to follow the Culpeper Minute Men all through the war; at various times they were divided, some taking part in battles of one section, while others were assigned to other leaders and took part in other battles. We do know, however, that a large part of them were with Washington in his campaign in New Jersey and Pennsylvania and took part in the battles of Brandywine and Germantown. It is, then, evident that they were with Washington when he made his memorable crossing of the Delaware and were also at the battles of Trenton and Princeton. They were with Washington during the terrible winter he spent at Valley Forge; and there, from the stories told, we judge they endured many privations.

There were, also, Culpeper Minute Men in the Southern Campaign conducted against Lord Cornwallis; a company, commanded by Abraham Buford, was defeated by General Tarleton near Waxham, North Carolina, and others were engaged in the battle of Mammoth Court House and in the storming of Stony Point. John Jameson, who was the clerk of Culpeper at the beginning of the war, organized a company and it was he who was in command of the men who captured Andre.[2]

We are fortunate in securing the names of a few veterans in this war who are known to have lived within the present bounds of Madison. They are as follows: Ambrose Madison, a relative of President Madison, who lived at Woodberry Forest and held several official positions during the war; Captain Ambrose Bohannon, who served as paymaster during the war, and had his home near where Mr. Hiram Berry now lives; Colonel Fry, who lived near Madison Court House, and at the beginning of the war ranked above Washington.[3]

Lieutenant Churchill Gibbs was a very brave soldier, both in the Continental Line and State Militia. At the close of the war he was offered a grant of land and a pension. He accepted the land but

---

[1] Slaughter, Philip, History of St. Mark's Parish, Page 43.
[2] Green, Notes on Culpeper County and St. Mark's Parish.
[3] Slaughter, Philip, History of St. Mark's, Pages 132-133.

refused the pension; after his death, his family accepted the pension and drew $10,000 in unpaid dues.[1]

Rev. William Carpenter, Sr. and Rev. William Carpenter, Jr., were both at Yorktown when Cornwallis surrendered.[2]

Others who served but whose careers are not known are: Jimmie Shotwell, Rev. Samuel Carpenter, Ephraim Utz, Adam Fisher, Captain Welch, Ambrose Richards, Leroy Kennedy, James Clatterbuck, Hy Fowles, John Harrison, Tavener Jones, Humphrey Major, John Spauldin, William Twyman, Abraham Tanner, William Taylor, Hy Towles, Larner Watson, William Yowell, John Breedlove, Jacob Rouse, Samuel Delph, Jacob Tanner, Lewis Rouse, Benjamin Rush, John Henderson, William Roebuck, Benjamin Smith, James Debord, John Birk, John Graves, General Zachary, William Smith, Nicholas Yager, Matthias Weaver, John Blankenbeker, and Matthias Rouse.[3]

*The War of 1812*

On June 1, 1812, President Madison sent a message to Congress in which he enumerated the various grievances of the United States against England. These grievances were practically all concerned with commerce and the Indians in the Northwest. The message sent to Congress spoke of the insolent conduct of the British cruisers in searching American vessels on American coasts; of the impressment of American seamen; of the seizure of American ships and of the British intrigues with the Indians of the Northwest.

The South and West were in favor of the war, which Congress declared on June 18th. The United States government depended on volunteers to prosecute this war. Most of the fighting was done on water and in an attempt to invade Canada. The fighting on water was much more successful than the attempt to invade Canada. Many privateers did some excellent fighting and their names have gone down in history as immortal heroes.

Unfortunately muster rolls have been preserved only for the men in the county who were drafted, consequently, we have no records at all of the men who volunteered for service; thus, there are no records that tell anything about the part Madison played in the War of 1812. There is a tradition that William Madison organized a regiment of men from Madison county and marched as far as Fredericksburg; on arriving there, he found that peace had been made, and disbanded his

---

[1] Statement of Mr. W. E. Bohannon.
[2] Garr, J. W., Genealogy of the Descendants of John Garr, Page 89.
[3] Crozier, W. A., Virginia Colonial Militia.
  Garr, J. W., Genealogy of the Descendents of John Garr.
  United States Pension Reports.
  Court Order Books of Madison County.
  Family Questionnaires.

regiment and returned home. How true this is cannot be proven, for as yet no records have been found to confirm the report.

As the people of Madison were very loyal during the Revolution, naturally we should expect them to be the same in the second war against England. During this war James Madison, who was well known and much admired in Madison county, was president; consequently, we would expect the people of Madison county to take more interest in the war because of him.

Through various sources the names of a few Madisonians who served in this war have been preserved. They were: Absalom Crisler, Solomon Garr, David Wilhoit, Adam Miller, Jacob Crigler, Abraham Clem, Fielding Smith, Sr., Major Finks, Benjamin Garr, Roland Berry and Lynn Banks.[1]

## The Mexican War

In the Florida Treaty of 1819 the United States surrendered claim to Texas, and a few years later she became a state of Mexico. It was not long after this that settlers from the United States began to pour into Texas, and President Adams, foreseeing trouble with Mexico, authorized the American minister to propose the purchase of Texas; this proposal Mexico refused. Americans continued to move into Texas, and by 1835 there were 30,000 Americans living there. They decided to drive out the Mexicans and establish an independent state; after some fighting they succeeded in carrying out this plan and the new state asked to be annexed to the United States. Texas would have been annexed to the United States in 1837 but for the anti-slavery people, for Texas was to become a slave state. It was not annexed until 1845.

The annexation of Texas produced a rupture between the governments of the United States and Mexico; war began and Congress authorized the enlistment of 50,000 men and the appropriating of $10,000,000 to carry on the war.

Again we are without records showing what Madison county did in this war. We know, nevertheless, that some men enlisted from the county and that some of these men received training which was to be of benefit to them in the Civil War. Those who are known to have enlisted are: Knelus Blankenbaker, Latham Yager, Captain Strother (captain of the Madison Cavalry in the Civil War), and General Kemper, who distinguished himself in the Civil War.

## The Civil War

Volumes have been written on the causes, campaigns and results of the Civil War; hence, it is not necessary to say more concerning

---

[1] Garr, J. W., Genealogy of the Descendents of John Garr.
Family Questionnaires.

that in this book. There is, however, one point in regard to its causes to be made clear and remembered. There have been arguments on state rights and causes of this nature, but most historians have forgotten that they were only immediate causes. They were, so to speak, only sparks of a greater fire. All events have immediate causes, which begin action; but, behind these causes, are other causes which are greater, more far reaching and more important.

The Civil War was caused primarily by a separation of the interests of two groups of people. The South and the North had been growing apart for many years; just as the American colonies had grown away from England before the Revolutionary War. To begin with the North and South had become separated along economic lines. In the South cotton was king, while the interests of the North were centered in commerce and industry. The South spent its capital, energy and all its other resources in the culture and production of cotton, while the North did the same for factories and channels of commerce. This dissimilarity of economic interests tended to draw the two sections apart and to create them into two unworkable halves.

The people of the North lived either on small farms or in towns, while in the South there were few towns and many large plantations. This difference in the mode of life had a tendency to separate the two sections socially; thus, the social customs of the two sections became different.

Again labor conditions were different; in the South, the negro slave produced more profit than in the North; consequently, the slaves became concentrated in the Southern States; not because of moral reasons but because of economic reasons. Labor in the North was supplied by immigrants from Europe and the condition of these foreigners in the Northern factories was little better than that of the slave in the cotton field. There was not enough difference in the labor system of the North and South to justify a moral war, nor did it create one; it helped to create war, in that there was great antagonism between the two orders of labor.

Many other differences could be enumerated, but these are sufficient to show that the two sections grew apart, each forming into a solid unit of its own. National unity was destroyed. In fact there came to be two nations living under one government, and this could not endure very long without some great event taking place, which would divide them into two governments or restore them to their former unity. This event came and we call that event the Civil War.

The above is sufficient to show that the causes to which we so often attribute the Civil War are after all not real causes, but rather results. Modern historians are beginning to lay aside slavery and state rights as causes of strife between the states and are placing more emphasis upon the economic causes and the conditions resulting from the formation of a union of the two sections.

Although the remote causes of the Civil War were not state rights nor slavery, we must not forget that these two causes played a great part. How did Madison stand on these two questions? This county was in favor of state rights, as was shown just after the formation of the new county. In 1798 Congress passed the Alien and Sedition Acts, which were opposed by Thomas Jefferson; he wrote a set of resolutions in which he defined the constitution as a compact between sovereign states and that the powers of Congress were delegated and limited. The resolution declared, "That whensoever the general government assumes undelegated powers, its acts are unauthoritative, void and of no force.[1] These resolutions passed the Virginia Legislature in 1798, the representatives from Madison voting in favor of them. In 1830 was passed the tariff bill to which South Carolina so seriously objected and which she finally nullified. The question was placed before the voters of Madison and they decided that South Carolina had a right to nullify this act. From the above examples and through other sources of information, it is evident that the people of Madison county from the beginning have been believers in the rights of separate states.

The Piedmont sections of the South were not adapted to the growth of cotton; consequently, slavery was not found as popular in those sections as in other parts of the South. Madison was not an exception; the county was not adapted to the culture of cotton and slavery was not favored to a very marked extent. In 1831 and 1832 the South discussed the abolition of negro slavery. The question was discussed and voted upon in Madison; the fact that the resulting vote was about even shows that slavery was in no great favor in the county. There are other things also in the history of the colored people which show that Madison was not a very strong slave holding county.[2]

The tax bill receipts of Madison in 1851 show that out of eight thousand and eighty-six, only two thousand, two hundred and sixty-one slaves were taxed. This would make an average of a little over two slaves to each family paying taxes. This also proves that Madison was not in the Civil War because of slavery, for the people of the county would hardly have gone to war because of two slaves.[3]

When the contentions of the North and South at last developed into actual war, Madison threw herself into the conflict with her usual determination and courage. The greatest gift that could be given was the blood of her sons, and this she gave freely. In the course of the war Madison men bore their part in the fortunes of the Army of Northern Virginia, sharing alike joy and sorrow with their

---

[1] Latine, J. H., A History of the United States, Page 210.
[2] Election Returns.
[3] Tax Book of Madison County for 1851.

great commander whom they came to adore and reverence, as we today adore him, Robert E. Lee; and we, also, admire the men who fought under his banner.

During the war Madison was represented in the following companies of the Army of Northern Virginia: Company "C," 4th Virginia Cavalry; Company "A," 7th Virginia Infantry (Richardson's Guards); Brook's Battery Artillery, Booton's Reserves, Carter's Battery Artillery, Letcher's Battery, Booton's Heavy Artillery, Company "K," 7th Virginia Infantry; Company "L," 10th Virginia Infantry; Company "G," 12th Virginia Cavalry; Charlottesville Artillery, Rockbridge Battery, Rice's Battery, Company "I," 1st Virginia Cavalry.[1]

Of these companies, Company "C," 4th Virginia Cavalry, Company "A," 7th Virginia Infantry, Company "K," 7th Virginia Infantry, Company "L," 10th Virginia Infantry, and Booton's Heavy Artillery were composed chiefly of Madison men; in the other companies mentioned there was not quite so large a per cent of them.[2]

The first soldiers to be taken from the county belonged to the Richardson's Guards. The history of this company was somewhat as follows: "The company was organized in 1858. After John Brown's raid it was ordered to Charleston, now in West Virginia, for guard duty and witnessed the execution of Cooke, Copprice, Green and Copeland, the associates of John Brown in his raid on Harper's Ferry. In April 1861, it became Company "A," 7th Virginia Infantry, commanded by Colonel James L. Kemper. At the reorganization of the army at Yorktown, Virginia, in 1862, all the old officers were restored, except N. W. Crisler, who had been promoted to captain and quartermaster of the regiment. W. O. Fry was made captain; Thomas V. Fry, first lieutenant; W. F. Harrison, 2nd lieutenant; and George N. Thrift, 3d lieutenant. The company took part in nearly all the battles fought by the Army of Northern Virginia from Bull Run to Appomattox. It was in the campaign with General Hoke in North Carolina and participated in the capture of Plymouth, North Carolina. Its history is linked with that of the Army of Northern Virginia, sharing its fortunes alike in victory and defeat. On May 21, 1864, three regiments of the brigade, the first, seventh, and eleventh were unloaded at Melford Station, Caroline County, Virginia. In a short time the enemy appeared. Major George Norton assumed the command, ordered out skirmishers from the seventh and eleventh regiments, held the ground for several hours, and checked Grant's advance. The seventh lost heavily in killed, wounded and captured. The brave stand made by Major Norton with only a handful of men delayed Grant for nearly a day, thus enabling General Lee to reach the neighborhood of Hanover Junction

---

[1] Muster Roll Book of Madison County.
[2] Ibid.

in advance of General Grant. Had Major Norton retreated instead of showing fight Grant would doubtless have cut off General Lee from his base of supplies at Richmond."[1]

The condition of the South became critical during the trying winter of 1863-1864. Not only did the resources of food and equipment become low but the army dwindled away. Regardless of this condition the spirit of the South was yet unconquered, and as a last great effort she called her old men and boys to arms in her defense. The men and boys of Madison heard this call and organized Booton's Reserves in June 1864. The company came together at Madison Court House and from there marched to Richmond to help defend their capital city. Their march was not a direct one to Richmond, but was by way of Charlottesville, Lynchburg, and Farmville. On arriving at their destination, the company was taken to Belle Island and there used to guard prisoners. The company remained on this island until late in September, when it was ordered to Chaffin's Farm; there it was put into line, and saw actual service until the close of the war.

Booton's Heavy Artillery was organized by Captain Booton at the beginning of the war. This artillery was placed at Yorktown, Virginia, but after Captain Booton became too old for service, he retired and his company was disbanded.

The Madison Cavalry or Company "C," 4th Virginia Cavalry was organized at Madison Court House in the beginning of the war, and was with Lee in all the important battles from Manassas to Appomattox. This company has been considered by Madisonians as the most outstanding company of men in which Madison was represented in the Civil War. It may well be so regarded, because it was the company that contained the largest per cent of Madisonians, and it did credit to the county by bravery and conduct.

Madison did her part in furnishing men, and those men fought nobly and bravely. We cannot honor and praise them too highly; their deeds will ever live in our memory. The causes of the war may be forgotten, but never can we forget the valor and bravery of our soldiers. They fought for what they believed to be right and never did soldiers fight with more courage, valor and endurance.

During the Civil War there was only one battle of any consequence fought in Madison County; this was a cavalry engagement. However, that does not mean that no actual warfare occurred in the county. Although very few battles were fought, the county was used extensively as campaigning grounds. Milum's Gap was one of gaps in the Blue Ridge used by Confederates to connect the Shenandoah Valley with Richmond; consequently, Madison was traversed many times. The campaign in which the battle of Cedar Mountain occurred is an example of this.

---

[1] Muster Roll Book of Madison County.

Before the campaign Jackson was encamped near Richmond. He was stationed there in order to be of assistance to Lee who feared the advance of McClellan on Richmond by way of the James River. General Pope thought that Jackson would soon break camp and march by way of Gordonsville across the Blue Ridge into his famous campaigning ground in the Shenandoah Valley. For this reason Pope directed his forces in such a way to intercept his passage. Lee soon learned that McClellan's plan was to leave the James River; he sent A. P. Hill to reinforce Jackson in order that they together might attack Pope. After being reinforced, Jackson advanced with twenty-eight thousand men and encamped near Gordonsville. This was in July, 1862. On July 16, a body of Pope's cavalry crossed the Rapidan and advanced through Orange Court House towards Gordonsville.⁽¹⁾

By this time Ewell's Division had advanced and encamped near Liberty Mills on the road to Madison Court House, remaining there until August 7th. In the meantime there had been many small cavalry skirmishes in Madison, but so small that they are not recorded. Pope was then near Culpeper; on August 7th, Jackson decided to attack him, and breaking camp at Gordonsville, marched in the direction of Culpeper. On the morning of the 8th, Jackson, who had then crossed the river into Madison encountered the federal cavalry and drove them back towards Culpeper. Brigadier-General Robertson was the commander of the Confederates in this skirmish. On the 8th, a part of the Confederates marched in the direction of Madison Court House.

A part of the federal cavalry retreated towards Culpeper making a feeble resistance. The other part fell back towards Madison Court House and were pursued by the Confederates. At several points they attempted to rally but each time were unable to do so; finally, after covering a distance of about five miles, they broke and ran leaving about twenty prisoners in the hands of the Confederates.

The battle of Cedar Run was fought on the 9th. In this battle Robertson's cavalry was stationed on Jackson's left; Colonel Jones, who had been sent to Madison Court House, returned towards evening, and after dark was passed to Jackson's right and front.⁽²⁾

In the darkness the Confederates charged the federal cavalry and forced them to take shelter under the infantry. A prisoner in this charge gave the first information of Seigel's arrival with reinforcements for Banks. The following day all the cavalry with Jackson was put under the command of General J. E. B. Stuart. In the battle of Cedar Run the Federals lost 2400 and the Confederates 1300.⁽³⁾

---

⁽¹⁾ McDonald, W. N., A History of the Laurel Brigade, Pages 78-80.
⁽²⁾ McDonald, W. N., A History of the Laurel Brigade, Pages 80-81.
⁽³⁾ Dodge, A. B., Bird's Eye View of the Civil War, Pages 70-71.

CONFEDERATE MONUMENT

Just before the battle of Fredericksburg, Jackson was ordered to move across the Blue Ridge. He began this movement November 20, 1862 by moving up the Valley to New Market, across the Massanutten and Blue Ridge into Madison. The army camped the first night on the east side of the Blue Ridge near Syria; from this place they moved on towards Madison Court House, camping there several days. The weather was cool and the march long; it has been said that many of the soldiers were without shoes, and that their feet were bleeding. From Madison the army moved past Orange to the vicinity of Fredericksburg arriving there December the 1st. While the army was in the vicinity of Madison Court House General Jackson wore for the first time a new regulation coat with the wreath and hat. His appearance in this uniform caused a great deal of amusement among his men; for, his dress before this had been a rusty grey coat, intended for a colonel, and a little dingy cloth cap which lay flat on his head, or rather forehead.[1]

The only battle of any consequence fought on Madison soil occurred at Jack's Shop (now Rochelle) September 22, 1863. Here Stuart had an engagement with the federal cavalry which threatened at one time to end in a serious situation for the Confederates. McDonald in his "History of the Laurel Brigade" gives us an account of this engagement, in which he states the following: "Of this affair no reports can be found from Confederate sources, while the Federal commander, General John Buford, contents himself with speaking of it as a great Federal success."[2]

"It appears that General Buford with one division of federal cavalry started for Madison Court House, September 22, on a reconnaissance down the Gordonsville turnpike, expecting to connect with another division under General Kilpatrick in the vicinity of Jack's Shop.

Stuart hearing of Buford's coming went out from Liberty Mills with a portion of Hampton's division and encountered him near Jack's Shop. He hurled regiment after regiment upon the strong columns of the enemy without making much impression. In the midst of this struggle, Kilpatrick's division, with Davis's Brigade in front, struck the turnpike just in the rear of Stuart's column.

There was a rush of riders in hot haste informing Stuart of his danger, and the sound of small arms in the rear soon made the Confederates understand the gravity of the situation. Between the two Federal divisions Stuart was now hemmed in and naught but a cool head and steady valor could extricate him.

Colonel Davis had come upon Stuart unexpectedly, and the surprise was mutual. It looked to the Confederates, who were aware

---

[1] Early, Jubal, Autobiographical Sketch and Narrative of the War Between the States. Pages 165-166.

[2] McDonald, H. B., History of the Laurel Brigade. Pages 174-178.

of Buford's hostile presence in their front, as if a trap had been cunningly laid for bagging Stuart and his whole army.

Stuart, however, was equal to the occasion. Placing the guns of Chew's Battery in an open field, at a point from which a range and a view to both front and rear could be had, the battery opened in both directions at the same time. The bullets from the sharpshooters of Buford and Kilpatrick now interlapped among the Confederate ranks. The perilous situation of the Confederates was understood by every soldier, but inspired by the coolness and gallant bearing of Stuart, as he quickly made disposition, every man resolved to do his best.

The task of breaking through Kilpatrick's line and re-opening the way to Liberty Mills was chiefly assigned to Jones' Brigade, then under the command of Colonel Funsten. A part of this command dismounted and advanced into the woods, while the mounted men charged where the opening would permit. On the left was the 7th under Lieut-Colonel Marshall, and on the right, the 11th, under Major Ball.

The 12th under Colonel Massie, occupying the center advanced upon the woods, close to the edge of which was a rail fence separating it from the open field. Openings in the fence were quickly made in the face of a heavy fire from the enemy's mounted and dismounted men in the woods. The nature of the ground was such that organization could not be preserved, and soon men and officers of different regiments were mingled almost en masse and were rallied around the person of General Stuart, who urged and led them into action.

It was fortunate that Stuart met the rear attack of Kilpatrick with such promptness and vigor; for, had there been delay sufficient for Kilpatrick to throw his whole force across Stuart's line of retreat, with Buford's strong division pressing his front line, it would have been hardly possible for Stuart to have escaped the net set for him without the loss of his artillery and a good part of his command.

The fighting in this engagement was close and fierce with both sabre and pistols; there were some notable instances of personal adventure and heroism, rewarded afterwards by General Stuart with official mention and recommendation for promotion.

Having swept Kilpatrick from his path and put him to flight, Stuart withdrew from the engagement with Buford; but was followed by him, however, almost to Liberty Mills. Here, Stuart crossed the Rapidan and was reinforced by Wilcox's division of Confederate Infantry. The losses in this fight, while considerable on both sides, considering the short time they were engaged, are not mentioned in either the Confederate or Federal reports, except that Colonel Davis reports that Major McIrvin of Kilpatrick's staff, Captain Hasty of the Second New York and sixty-nine prisoners fell into the hands of the Confederates. Major McIrvin was captured by private B. C. Washington of Company "B," 12th Virginia Cavalry, in a hand to hand fight, in which Washington disarmed McIrvin by a cut across his sabre hand. Washington was promoted to a second lieutenancy for his services.

The severest loss to the Confederates in this engagement was in the death of that splendid soldier, Captain John H. Magruder of Company "B," 7th Regiment, who fell in the assault on Kilpatrick's column.

Thaddeus Baney of Company "B," 12th Virginia and Lieutenant John Green of the brigade staff, were also among the killed.

After the affair at Jack's Shop there was comparatively little fighting along the cavalry front for two weeks. Many of the men were given furloughs to go home and procure fresh horses, while others gave themselves up to making the most of their freedom from active service.

On the 10th of October all were again in the saddle near Madison Court House with Colonel Funsten of the Eleventh commanding the brigade.

General Lee had begun his flank movement on Meade's army, and was engaged in what is known as the Bristoe Campaign.

As the success of the movement depended upon its secrecy, the cavalry were expected to screen the march of Lee's infantry. Funsten's command was in front of the column that moved toward Woodville on the Sperryville turnpike. It moved for the most part over blind roads through fields, twisting and turning in under the shelter of the woods and hillocks to avoid observation from the Federal signal posts on the peaks of the neighboring mountains.

On the morning of the 11th the command had reached Sperryville and was marching along the road that leads to Culpeper."[1]

In 1924 Mr. W. E. Bohannon wrote a very fine article on this battle. The general outline of his article corresponded with this account, but he made an important contribution by adding some interesting incidents and by giving local color to the narrative. As this article has recently appeared before the people and is of the same general outline of the above, it will not be repeated here.

A part of the Confederate army again traversed Madison just after the Gettysburg campaign in 1863. Early arrived at Madison Court House, June 28th, and was here joined by other divisions which came through Thornton's Gap. After remaining near Madison Court House until June 31st, the Confederates moved to the vicinity of the Robinson River near the road from Liberty Mills. They crossed the river into Culpeper the next day and came to a halt at Pisgah Church. This was the end of the campaign in Federal territory.[2]

---

[1] McDonald, History of the Laurel Brigade.
[2] Early, Jubal, Autobiography. Pages 284-285.

Early's army was again in Madison in October 1863. Meade's army was now in Culpeper and Lee determined to move around Meade's right to attack him. This movement began October 8th. Early moved by Madison Court House on October 10th, crossing the Robinson River and camping three or four miles from it. That evening there was a sharp fight with the cavalry. On the 11th the Confederates moved into Culpeper and the Federals retreated across the Rappahannock.①

In 1864 Rosser's brigade encamped near Wolftown. This brigade broke camp May 4, 1864 and again joined Lee's army. It passed the infantry in breastworks at Mine Run and encamped on Lee's right.②

The examples above will suffice to show that the Civil War, unlike most of the wars in which our country has been engaged, was not far away from our country but was witnessed by our ancestors in their homes, where we now live. There are perhaps many other examples which could have been placed here but those campaigns were rather insignificant as historical data.

Much could be told in regard to the period that followed the Civil War; however, it is sufficient to say that the people of the county went to work immediately to overcome the losses incurred by war. They toiled without murmur and deserve to be honored. Reconstruction days were not as hard in Madison as in many sections of the South where the colored population was greater. The county was never under the "carpet-bag-rule," nor did it suffer much from "scalawags." The people managed their own affairs, and the losses of the war soon began to be repaired.

### The Spanish-American War

This war with Spain was due to the Spanish policy in the West Indies and some of her other possessions. Her policy became so cruel and inhumane that the United States went to the aid of those people who were receiving such harsh treatment from the Spaniards.

The war from the beginning was a very unequal contest, for the Spaniards were not in any way the equal of the Americans. The United States did not draft any men for this war but depended upon volunteers.

Madison, as always, had some sons in this war. Only two are known to the author, Messrs. Jack Lillard and John Finks; there were perhaps others. Nevertheless, we see that Madison was represented.

---

① Early, Jubal, Autobiography.
② Ibid. Pages 343-345.

## World War

It is useless to review the causes of the World War. In Europe they were deep rooted and even now cannot fully be explained. It requires the master touch of time to put the finishing touches on all events. It takes a number of years to bring to light all the elements that enter into such a tremendous event as the World War.

The reasons for the United States entering into this conflict are known more or less definitely to all of us. It was chiefly for the protection of humanity and the finer institutions of man. It was, so to speak, a crusade for humanity like the crusades of old for the birthplace of Christ. Of course it would be foolish to say that was the only motive and that everyone had that motive in view. There were evils, and evil motives in this war as there are in all wars.

We should be proud that our county so well expressed itself in the right motive and worked with the greater and nobler goal in view.

When the flames of war began to burn in 1914 our county was largely pro-German, and remained so until 1917. The reason for this was two-fold. Governor Spotswood in his administration of Virginia, imported thirteen German families and settled them on the Rapidan River at Germanna Ford; Spotsylvania county, starting the first iron industry in this county. It proved a failure. These people moved and settled on the Robinson River over two hundred and seventy years ago; therefore, a large portion of the population of Madison is of German blood. They have made good, honest, hard-working, thrifty, law-abiding, church people. This was the only class of immigrants our people had come in contact with and they had made good; hence, it was natural that those who knew them should sympathize with Germany.[1]

Things continued in this way until the sinking of the Lusitania, and until Germany had begun her murderous attacks by submarines on every craft that undertook to sail the briny deep. Then it was that the feeling of the people slowly began to change; German brutality opened their eyes. When Congress declared war, the people of Madison almost without exception got behind the government, and stood firmly until the end, using men, money and their best energies to aid the government in every way possible. It would be wrong to leave the impression that there were no slackers. There were a few, as is always the case; however, the number was small and as they kept quiet, they did the government little or no harm.[2]

The churches as a body were extremely patriotic. Special services were held to bless all the acts of our government, to strengthen the minds and hearts of our people, and to give them fortitude to meet successfully and carry through that which they had undertaken; in

---

[1] Report of the Madison County War History Commission.
[2] Ibid.

the belief that by so doing we were serving our Lord and Savior. The church members made flags and took part in all the drives for money; they worked untiringly in the Red Cross activities which among our people carried on to the fullest extent. Larger crops were raised, as well as more cattle, hogs, and sheep; everyone worked; men, women and children—each one in his own sphere; an idle person was looked upon with scorn. There was little or no suffering, yet all economized in every possible way.

The county, not being near the main line of travel, did not come actually in contact with the hurry and bustle of war. There were no hospitals or camps near, yet the people felt their duty and heeded its call. Our women went to work knitting sweaters, socks, and rolling bandages. Prior to our entrance into the war a drive was made in behalf of the Belgians for old clothing and provisions; many wagon loads were collected and shipped.

The only active organization in the county was the Red Cross. Its membership was over 1200, and many others worked for and with it. Our free schools were organized and worked in all drives; through their activities a great many war savings stamps were sold. Beside the public schools there is one preparatory school in the county, Woodberry Forest. This school has an enrollment of about 140 boys. They were unanimously patriotic during the war; both faculty and students took an active part in every movement. Soon after the United States declared war, this school added a military department, and trained its students in military practice. This course was followed throughout the full period of hostilities, and quite a number of boys entered the army.

Madison county furnished 252 men for the service in the World War, of which 172 were whites, and the other 80, negroes. Of the white men in service, 27 volunteered and 145 were drafted. There were six white men killed in battle, and eight died in camp; also, six negroes died in camp. In money, Madison raised the following:

| Purpose | Quota | Subscribed |
|---|---|---|
| Young Men's Christian Association | $ 1,050.00 | $1,615.00 |
| United War Work | 4,900.00 | 5,200.00 |
| Young Women's Christian Association | | 124.70 |
| Armenian and Syrian (First Drive) | 500.00 | 1,300.00 |
| Armenian and Syrian (Second) | 500.00 | 650.00 |
| First Liberty Loan | 12,000.00 | 9,000.00 |
| Second Liberty Loan | 28,800.00 | 19,550.00 |
| Third Liberty Loan | 50,000.00 | 56,000.00 |
| Fourth Liberty Loan | 75,000.00 | 112,000.00 |
| Victory Loan | 75,000.00 | 100,000.00 |
| War Saving Stamps (matured) | 150,050.00 | 127,415.25 |
| Red Cross | | 7,852.76 |
| Total | | $439,707.20 |

(1) Report of the Madison County War History Commission.

This was a per capita of $43.97 per head of population.

The boys from Madison county who went to the battlefields during this war belonged to the Blue Ridge or 80th Division, the 159th Brigade, and the 318th Regiment. There were of course some boys from the county who belonged to other divisions, regiments and brigades but the majority were in this classification.①

W. H. Waldron has written a history of the 80th Division in which he briefly summarizes its activities. Condensing this and picking out the subject matter which deals with the 159th Brigade and the 318th regiment, we are able to get a glimpse of the activities through which the men of Madison passed.

One of the original twelve divisions of the National Army, the 80th or Blue Ridge Division, was organized August 27, 1917, at Camp Lee. It derived its name from the fact that the enlisted personnel of the division was drawn from Virginia, West Virginia and the western part of Pennsylvania, the Blue Ridge Mountains being common to these states.

There were many associations of the past that drew these men together. Their forefathers had borne the brunt of the Revolutionary War, and the War of 1812; they had gained respect for each other in the Civil War. There were immense values attached to these common traditions.

Within the division, the territorial character of the personnel was wisely emphasized by the localization of the units in component elements of the command. The 159th Infantry and the 314th Machine Gun Battalion were formed exclusively of men from Virginia. The Tidewater or Eastern section made up the 318th Regiment, and it was to this regiment that most of the Madison men were assigned.

The division was most fortunate with respect to the men who were called upon to organize it. Brigadier General C. S. Farnsworth had charge of the 159th Infantry Brigade with Colonel Bryant H. Wells commanding the 318th Infantry.

Various changes in the command of the units occurred before the division sailed for France. General Farnsworth was promoted and was succeeded by General Jamerson; Colonel Bryant H. Wells was relieved from the command of the 318th Infantry and was succeeded by Colonel U. G. Worrilow.

May 17, the division began the movement to France. The 318th Infantry embarked at Hoboken for Brest on the great ship Leviathan. This ship was unsuccessfully attacked May 30, at the very entrance to the harbor of Brest by a flotilla of German submarines, the strength of which was estimated at from seven to two crafts.

---

① Muster Rolls of Madison County.

An agreement had been reached with the British whereby ten American divisions were to be assigned to the British training areas in France and to receive training and equipment at the hands of the British army. The 80th Division was fortunately selected for this training service, which was to give to it practical experience of war in the British trenches before being engaged on a large scale in the American Sector.

From the port of debarkation, the division was transported to Calais where the troops exchanged American for British arms. Before the middle of June, the division was assembled in the Samer training area, several miles east of Boulogne under the tutelage of, first the 16th Irish, and then the 24th British Division.

After the completion of its first phase of training under the British, the Division was transferred Southward to the third British army Sector, with headquarters in Deauville. Until August the 20th, it was posted along the secondary lines between Albert and Arras. During this period, batallion units entered the front line trenches of the Artois Sector. The nature of the experiences of the division during this period is evidenced by four hundred casualties in August alone.

On August the 20th the move to the American Sector was begun. The division was transferred by rail through Amiens via Paris to the 14th training area between Chaumont and Chatillon-sur-Seine, where it remained until August 31st. On September the 1st it was again moved by rail to the Stanville and later marched to the Tronville Area. While here it composed the reserve of the First Army during the St. Mihiel operations of September 12-15th.

On the night of September 24-25th the 159th Brigade was assembled in reserve in the Bois-de-Sartelle, several kilometers west of Verdun. On the 25th, the Division Commander, and in turn the unit commanders, were notified that the expected attack was to be made at 5:30 a. m. the following morning. The 80th Division was placed west of the Meuse River opposite the destroyed village of Bethincourt. At 5:30 a. m. the operation began and Bethincourt was reached and taken within a few minutes. That evening the 318th Infantry was hurried westward arriving before midnight at Cuisy. On the evening of the 28th the 318th Infantry moved forward to the Nantil Lois road, west of Septsarges, and on the following day made an attack. On the 30th, a Sector was created for the 80th Division which was relied upon to break through the Bois-de-Ogons. This was a very important place and for this new attack, the 159th Brigade was designated. By this time the 318th Infantry had been relieved from its support position, where it had lain under fire for five days; it was then taken to Namtillion, where it was again prepared for action. The movement took place on ground which had unsuccessfully been attacked many times. It continued until the night of the 11th when the 80th Division was relieved and moved behind the lines to be reorganized and reequipped. The ordeal through which this division passed during those early days of September was the most severe experience of the war and may be classed as one of the most desperate encounters.

After having a brief rest, the Division, on October the 14th, was ordered forward to the vicinity of Les Islettes, where it remained until the 30th concealed in the woods. An attack was then planned to be made on the German Line between Grand Pre and St. Georges. The Division marched twenty-five kilometers through the Argonne forest on October the 30th and 31st. During the next few days it did excellent fighting for which it received thanks and congratulations from the Corps Commander.

On the 3rd of November the 318th Infantry as well as others pressed forward. By night of the 4th, the 5th Infantry entered Beaumont. That afternoon the 318th Infantry attacked the position of Yonco and, before midnight, had occupied hill 275 northwest of town.

On the 6th, the 80th Division was assembled about Sommouthe. After remaining there the following day, it commenced its march to the rear; and on the morning of the 8th, started for the Carnay-Apremont Area. On the 10th of November, official information was received that hostilities were to cease at 11:00 a. m. the following day, and the 80th Division was ordered to march on the 11th to the Les Islettes Area.

In the Meuse-Argonne campaign, the 80th Division advanced nearly twenty-four miles; three times it broke through the enemy's line; it captured 103 officers, 1,710 men, 88 pieces of artillery, and 641 machine guns, as well as other arms and ammunition. All this was accomplished with a total loss of but 210 officers and 5,464 men; of these 37 officers and 592 men were killed.

On the 18th of November, after a rest of one week in the Les Islettes Area, the Division began its march to the fifteenth training camp area, which lay southwest of Chatillon-sur-Seine.

December, January, February, and March comprised a period of dull monotony, more trying in many respects upon the nerves of the men than the period which had preceded it. On March 30th the movement of the Division westward to the Le Mans Area began, preparatory to its embarkation for the United States at Brest early in May.

The signing of the Armistice made very little difference in the condition of things in Madison county. Labor continued scarce; the boys came home in squads, for a period of twelve months or more; as is the case after all wars, those who returned were restless and unsettled. After a short time at home, they began to scatter, to take hold of things and to settle down by degrees. It is hard for a soldier who has been in the army for two or more years to accustom himself to the daily routine of farm life; that must come by degrees through a reconstruction period. Our county is coming through this trying period as well as any other section. It is going to stand its share of loss by the upheaval of all conditions, and will re-adjust itself to normal life and times with that strong fortitude which all patriotic people have shown in every similar period of the world's history.

CHAPTER VII

THE CHURCH HISTORY OF MADISON

Religion has always played a major part in the life of the American people. To begin with, many of the settlements in America were made because of religious persecution. Later government in America was administered through a religious organization. It is, however, not these material changes that religion has made upon the American people, but it is its influence upon the hearts of the people, which makes the religious history so important. The history of the churches in Madison is very interesting, as well as important; for, Madison is a typical example of the influence of religion on American life.

Madison is wholly Protestant and has always been. There have never been any churches established in the county except Protestant ones, and there have been very few people of other religious convictions residing in the county. The Protestant denominations represented in Madison are as follows: Baptists, Methodists, Lutherans, Christians, Dunkards, Presbyterians and Episcopalians. The Baptists and Methodists are by far the strongest denominations.[1]

In 1906 a church census was taken in Madison county from which the following data were obtained: Out of a population of 10,226, there were 4,528 who were members of some church; out of this 4,528, there were 2,448 Baptists; 1,181 Methodists; 150 Christians; 66 Primitive Baptists; 38 Dunkards; 389 Lutherans; 12 Presbyterians; and 17 Episcopalians.[2]

We will now discuss separately the history of each of these denominations.

## Baptists

The origin of the Baptist denomination may be attributed to three sources.

The first mention of Baptists in Virginia was in 1714. In this year some Baptist emigrants came from England and settled in the southeastern part of the state. The second source from which the Baptists originated was a group of settlers of Baptist convictions, who emigrated from Maryland and settled in the northwestern part of the state in 1743.

A third, so far as the Baptists of Madison are concerned, the most important source was a group of people who came into Virginia

---
[1] Answer to Questionnaires from the Churches.
[2] Evans Almanac for 1907.

from New England. This group of people was composed of converts made under the preaching of Mr. Whitefield in the great revival known as the "New Light Stir," in which all who joined were called "New Lights." These became so numerous that they formed new societies and left the Established or Episcopal Church to which they formerly belonged. After leaving the Episcopal Church they became known as Separates. This name was given them about 1744.

In 1754 a group of these Separates was led to Virginia by Shubal Stearnes. They first settled in Berkley county, Virginia, but remained there only a short time before moving on to North Carolina; they did not remain in North Carolina very long, but again pushed northward into Virginia.

The first mention of any Baptist preachers within the limits of Culpeper county (which then included Madison) was in 1765. In January of that year, Elder David Thomas and one of his converts, Allen Wyley, heard that the Separate Baptists were holding a meeting in Pittsylvania, and went there to ask one of the preachers to come to Culpeper to preach. The meeting which they attended was being held by Mr. Samuel Harris. Mr. Harris came to Culpeper and held his first meeting at Wyley's house; in a few days opposition arose in the community and Mr. Harris was forced to leave Culpeper and take refuge in Orange. This seems a very feeble beginning, yet seeds were sown which produced in later years great achievements. From this first meeting there was a gradual increase in the number of converts, and Baptist churches were organized regardless of the opposition and persecution which they received.[1]

There was a great deal of opposition on the part of the Episcopal Church toward the early Baptist, and persecution was often carried on. Only two churches in Madison suffered and one of these very little. Rapid Ann suffered more than any within the limits of the county. This was due chiefly to its being situated only about three miles from an Episcopal "House of Ease." The other congregation which suffered was the Ragged Mountain Church (now F. T.), near the Parish Church of Broomfield Parish.[2]

When these two Baptist churches began there was an established church directly connected with the government. This established church was the Episcopal, just as in England. The colonial government of Virginia was connected with this church, so that every citizen was required to belong, attend and pay taxes for its support. Thus, it is easy to see how opposition would arise against anyone who sought to revolt against this established order of things. The Baptists, unlike the Lutherans, once belonged to the Episcopal Church, but separated themselves from it; consequently, they received more persecution than the Lutherans.

---

[1] Minutes of the Shiloh Association 1893.
[2] Ibid.

Other religious denominations escaped persecution because they were formed after our separation from England and after our statesmen had granted religious freedom to this new nation. Records have preserved the names of some of the Baptists, who were placed in the Culpeper jail on account of their beliefs. Some of them were taken from the pulpits on account of their preaching; others were taken, because they allowed the Baptists to hold meetings at their homes; others, because they tried to make converts. The names of some of those who were placed in jail are as follows: Elijah Craig, Adam Banks, Thomas Maxfield, James Ireland, John Dulaney, Nathaniel Saunders and Anderson Moffatt.[1]

Today the Baptist Churches in Madison county are in what is known as the Shiloh Association, which was formerly called the Culpeper Association, the name having been changed to Shiloh in 1812. The Culpeper Association was once a part of the Orange Association, which in turn was separated from the Dover Association. The Culpeper Association was formed in 1791 and this same year its meeting was held at the Rapid Ann Church on October the 13th.[2]

At present there are two branches of Baptist in Madison; namely, the Primitive and the New School; at the beginning of the Baptist Churches in the county there was but one. The separation did not take place until about 1836. In 1836 several churches withdrew from the Shiloh Association because of differences of belief and formed an Association of their own known as the Rappahannock Association. The churches that formed this were: Robinson River, Battle Run, Thornton's Gap and Gourdvine.[3] Sometime later the Primitive Baptist Churches of the county had a contention, and at present, they do not all belong to the same association.

Each church in the county has an interesting history of its own, a sketch of which will be given.

## Rapid Ann Church

Rapid Ann was organized in 1773 with thirty-seven members. Some of these members originally belonged to the Blue Run Church in Orange county. The first to preach at the Rapid Ann Church were the Rev. Mr. Harrison and the Rev. Mr. Read. These were followed by Mr. Waller and Elijah Craig. When the gospel was first preached to this congregation some persecution occurred. Elijah Craig was taken out of the pulpit and committed to the Culpeper jail; Thomas Maxfield was imprisoned for exhorting; Adam Banks was committed to the jail for praying in the home of John Dulaney; and Dulaney himself, for permitting it. It was in this church that

---

[1] Semple, R. B., A History of the Rise and Progress of the Baptist in Virginia. Pages 114-115.
[2] Minutes of the Shiloh Association 1893.
[3] Semple's History of the Rise and Progress of the Baptists in Virginia (Beale). Centennial Copy of the Baptist Minutes of the Shiloh Association.

88     A HISTORY OF MADISON COUNTY, VIRGINIA

Reverend George Eve, one of the most successful preachers in the early Baptist ministry, and the first to secure license to solemnize marriages in Madison county, was reared, and in 1775 was ordained to the care of the church. During the years of 1776-77-78, as many as one hundred and thirty were added to the church under the ministry of Mr. Eve. He was pastor for twenty-one years, after which he moved to Kentucky and formed North Fork Church in Franklin county.

Joseph Early who became a member of Rapid Ann Church in 1772 should be remembered, because of his great generosity and help in its early history. The pastors prior to 1850 were as follows: George Eve, 1775-96; no pastor from 1796-1804; Joshua Leathers, 1804-1806; Daniel James, 1806-1820; John Garnett, 1820-1836; Barnett Grimsley, 1836-1845; L. L. Fox, 1845-1847; T. W. Lewis, 1847 —.[1]

### Ragged Mountain Church
(Now known as F. T.)

Ragged Mountain is the second oldest Baptist Church in the county. At present the house of worship is in Rappahannock county; when, first built, it was situated in Madison county near the foot of the Old Rag Mountain; hence the name, Ragged Mountain Church. There has been a tradition handed down that the first building stood on the land now owned by W. H. Yowell opposite the rock known as "Sharp Rock." This church was organized in 1778 through the work of Saunders, Eve, Pickett and others. It will be noted that some of these men were persecuted for their religious teaching by the authorities of Culpeper. The house of worship was later moved to Bloomfield; then, to its present site. The records of this church, when it was called Ragged Mountain, have all been lost. The present name, "F. T.," came from the initials of Frank Thornton cut on an oak tree near where the church now stands. George Eve was the first pastor of the Ragged Mountain; he served until 1788, when he was succeeded by Mr. W. Mason. In 1788 a great revival took place and many were received into the church.[2]

### Robinson River Church

Robinson River was organized January 4, 1790. The greater part of the members came from the Ragged Mountain Church, and a few from Rapid Ann. There were 76 charter members; 28 were white males; 39 white females; 3 black males; and 6 black females.

---
[1] Semple's History of the Rise and Progress of Baptists in Virginia (Beale.) Pages 238-39.
[2] Semple, R. B., A History of the Rise and Progress of the Baptists in Virginia. Page 179.

W. Mason was the first pastor and for many years there were no additions to the church. Mrs. Moses Clore, while on her deathbed, obtained a hope of eternal life, and when dying, requested Mr. Mason to preach her funeral, saying at the same time that it would be a great day; at her funeral, a revival began during which many were converted.

The congregation of Robinson River was housed in a wooden structure from 1790 until 1860, when a brick church was erected. The building committee of the brick church was composed of John Fishback, Acrey Berry, Sr., Henry Clore, and Peter Lauck. David Story was the contractor.

Three churches have been formed from this one; namely, Bethcar, Brightwood Baptist, and Swift Ford Colored Church.

The following were the former pastors: William Mason, 1790-1822; Ambrose Booton, 1822-1836; William C. Lauck, 1836-1875; Paul Yates, 1875 —.

At various intervals the roll of the church has been revised and shows the following results: 1790, 76 members; 1823, 52 members; 1863, 110 members; 1878, 74 members; 1924, 10 members.

The first meeting of the Rappahannock Association was held in this church in 1837.[1]

## Mt. Carmel

Mt. Carmel was organized June 10, 1850. In the beginning the church building was to be used as a union church, with Baptist having the preference, but it was not used in this way long. Those who formed it came from Bethcar and F. T. Churches. The lot was given by Mr. Joshua Miller. The names of the first members are as follows: Joshua Miller, Geo. M. Bohannon, Edmund G. Chapman, Edmund P. G. Chapman, Richard Early, Henry Batton, Joel Batton, James L. Mitchell, Richard N. Tanner, Robert N. Tanner, Sarah Miller, Eliza Bohannon, Ann Chapman, Martha L. B. Chapman, Patsy A. Early, Martha L. Batton, Frances M. Henshaw, Elvira Carpenter, Patsy Rouse, Eveline Rouse, Jerima Rouse, Susan Broyles, Margaret Batton, Jane Yowell, Louisa Rossen, Edna N. Tanner, Eliza Tanner, Sarah A. May and Jane, the servant of A. T. Tanner.

The first pastor was Mr. Silas Bruce and the first clerk was Mr. Richard Early.[2]

## Bethcar

Bethcar is a daughter of the Robinson River Church and was constituted in 1823. Because of the great distance which the members who lived near Madison Court House had to go, to attend

---

[1] Church Book of the Robinson River Church.
[2] Church Book of Mt. Carmel Church.

meetings at the Robinson River Church, Michael Yager made a petition in May 1823 asking that letters of dismissal be granted to as many as desired them, to form a new church at the meeting house at Madison Court House. The following members of the Robinson River Church withdrew at this time to form Bethcar Church: Michael Yager, Alfred M. Yager, Moses Clore, Absolom Carpenter, Ephraim Clore, James W. Crow, John Fishback, Edward Graves, Simeon Utz, George Mezingo, George W. Sims, John Weaver, Jr., Abner Deer, Margaret Clore, Anna Fishback, and several colored members.[1] The early pastors of this church were: Oliver Welch, 1823-1833; C. C. Conner, 1834-35; Barnett Grimsley, 1836-52; T. W. Lewis, 1852. ------.[2]

## Shiloh

Shiloh was organized in 1877. Its early pastors were: H. W. Wharton, R. L. Steele, J. A. Chambliss, and T. F. Grimsley. The members who chartered this church belonged originally to Mt. Carmel, F. T., and Bethcar.[3]

## Grave's Chapel

Grave's Chapel was organized in 1885. The people most instrumental in the building of this church were Ed Graves, James Kite and Charlie Kite. Its early pastors were J. M. Farrar, Hugh Goodwin, Roy Temple, A. M. Grimsley, G. Gray, A. J. Harlow.[4]

## New Bethel

B. P. Dublin organized a Baptist Church at Rochelle in 1849, which disappeared in 1858.[5]

## Novum

Novum was organized by members from Mt. Carmel and Slate Mills on October 29, 1911.[6]

## Oldrag Regular Baptist

The Oldrag Church was organized in 1911. The ones most instrumental in building this church were Major Smith, Howard J. Berry, and Elmer Dyer. This church began as a branch of the original regular Baptist Church. Its pastors have been Warren Corbin, D. B. Seal, W. A. Woodard and H. J. Berry.[7]

---

[1] Church Book of Robinson River Church.
[2] Minutes of the Shiloh Association 1924.
[3] Answer to Questionnaire.
[4] Ibid.
[5] Minutes of the Shiloh Association 1893.
[6] Answer to Questionnaire.
[7] Ibid.

## Mt. Zion

Mt. Zion church grew out of the efforts of a union meeting. It was organized in 1833. Some of the people instrumental in building it were: J. S. Twyman, Park Aylor, John Richards and Andrew Carpenter. Its early pastors were Silar Bruce, T. F. Grimsley, Goodwin Frazer, B. F. Robinson and J. W. Morgan.[1]

## Liberty

Liberty Church was organized in 1832. Its pastors have been E. G. Ship, Benjamin Creel, R. N. Herndon, Wm. A. Hill, T. F. Grimsley, T. P. Brown, J. M. Farrar, Hugh Goodwin, Roy Temple and J. N. Doffermeyer.[2]

## Brightwood (Primitive Baptist)

Brightwood Church is a daughter of the Robinson River Church and was organized in 1850.[3]

## Methodists

It is beyond the scope of this book to discuss the rise of Methodism in England. Suffice it to say the Methodist separated from the Episcopal Church as the Baptist did. The separation took place in the eighteenth century, as a result of the teachings of John and Charles Wesley, and of George Whitefield. These three preachers did not desire at first to separate from the Established Church, but wished to reform it. They were very zealous workers and were very methodical in their teachings; hence, they were called "Methodists." These three men sought earnestly to put energy and vitality into their religion; it was this which caused their separation from the Episcopal Church and which remains to this day a distinct characteristic of the Methodist denomination.

There are no records from which we may trace the origin of the Methodist in the county of Madison; it seems that no Methodist church was started there until after 1800. There is, however, a tradition that Trinity Church at Wolftown was begun in 1775; this must be a mistake as there were no Methodist Churches in the adjoining counties, which are older than Madison. Most records seem to point to the fact that the Methodist denomination began in the county between 1800 and 1850.[4]

The origin of the Methodist Church was something like that of the Baptist. Small groups of workers and evangelists came and

---

[1] Answer to Questionnaire.
[2] Ibid.
[3] Ibid.
[4] Statements of Older People.

preached in school houses and arbors, and by this means organized congregations, which later sent out branch churches.

The first circuit to which the churches of Madison belonged was called "Rapid Ann Circuit;" then it included the counties of Orange, Madison, Greene, and a part of Albemarle. The first Quarterly Conference of the Orange Circuit was held at the Providence meeting-house.[1]

The first mention of Madison Circuit was made in the Quarterly Conference at Madison Court House, June 2, 1838, at which Joseph Carson was the presiding elder, and Robert O. Blakey, secretary. In 1840, Madison Circuit which embraced the counties of Madison, Greene, and a part of Albemarle and Rockingham Counties, including the city of Harrisonburg, had twenty-two appointments. At a meeting of the Annual Conference in 1848, Madison and Greene counties were formed into one Circuit and called "Madison Circuit," with S. T. Moorman, presiding elder; Thomas Diggs, preacher in charge; Jesse K. Powers, assistant elder; and J. McCullen, secretary. According to the records this circuit owned a parsonage at Madison Court House, and Madison and Greene remained in the same Circuit until 1863.[2]

At the Virginia Conference of 1863, these two counties were divided and made into separate circuits. The Madison Circuit included the following churches in Madison county: Oak Grove, Trinity, New Bethel, Providence, afterwards Walker's Chapel, Mt. Zion, Huffman's Chapel, since destroyed, and Ford's Schoolhouse, no longer a preaching place. Joseph H. Davis was presiding elder, and E. H. Prickett, preacher in charge.[3]

At the fourth Quarterly Meeting November 7, 1865, seven months after the surrender of R. E. Lee, Reverend J. O. Moss reported that there was but one Sunday School within the bounds of the circuit; this was at New Bethel or Jack's Shop, now known as Rochelle; it had forty-two scholars, eleven teachers, and one hundred fifty books.[4]

At the Annual Conference 1913, over which Bishop Collins Denny was presiding, Madison Circuit was made a four appointment circuit under the name of "Madison Circuit and Mountain Mission," with R. L. Waterfield, presiding elder, and L. L. Banks, preacher in charge. Four churches were included in this circuit, Madison Court House, Oak Grove, Rose Park, and Mt. Olivet. The other churches, Mt. Zion, Walkers and New Bethel were taken from Madison Circuit and, in connection with Westover from Greene Circuit, were formed into what is now known as "Rapidan Circuit."[5]

---

[1] Richmond Christian Advocate August 3, 1922.
[2] Ibid.
[3] Ibid.
[4] Ibid.
[5] Ibid.

At the first Quarterly meeting held by each of the Circuits Dr. E. W. Twyman from Rapidan and Mr. D. M. Pattie from Madison were appointed to make a fair division of the parsonage property. They decided that the property was worth three thousand dollars. The Madison Circuit agreed to take the parsonage and pay the Rapidan Circuit one thousand five hundred dollars for their interest.[1]

Three churches in the county belong to the Brightwood Circuit; namely, Bethsaida, Etlan and Bethlehem. At a church conference held in January 1894, a committee from Bethsaida was appointed to make plans for building a new church; the members of the committee were B. B. Suddith, J. W. Sprinkle, E. M. Blankenbaker, J. W. Palmer, G. W. Huffman, H. S. Thomas, J. K. Botts, Mrs. J. W. Sprinkle and Miss Sarah Carpenter; the following year a building was started. Reverend R. G. James was the first man to preach in the new edifice, though it was not completed and dedicated until Rev. T. W. Ogden became pastor. This Circuit was at first known as the "Blue Ridge Mission" and was supported by the Board of Missions; it has made much progress since then and now pays a salary of $900. This with the appropriation of the Board makes the income of the pastor $1050.[2]

There is very little recorded concerning the history of the individual churches. There are, however, a few of which something is known. Mt. Olivet was organized in 1848. Rev. McMullen was the first Methodist preacher to preach in this vicinity. He held his meetings in an arbor near where the church now stands. As this arbor was in a grove of beech trees, the meeting place was called "Beech Grove." Later, as the congregation grew, a church was built, which came to be called "Mt. Olivet."

About the same time and under the preaching of Rev. Mr. McMullen, meetings were held in an old schoolhouse known as "Gibbs Schoolhouse," on the spot where Oak Grove now stands. Oak Grove Church grew out of these meetings, and a building was erected about 1852. The land for the church was given by Mr. Abe Blankenbaker. The leading people who were active in the work of building this church were George Tanner, Gabriel Aylor, Abe Blankenbaker, John Clore and Nellie Crisler. A new church, one of the most modern in the county, was erected at Oak Grove in 1924.[3]

## Christians

There are two Christian Churches in Madison county, Fairview and Rochelle. It is not known how this denomination started in Madison county. The Christian Church at Rochelle was built in 1859. Those who took an active part in its erection were William

---
[1] Richmond Christian Advocate—August 3, 1922.
[2] Ibid.
[3] Oak Grove Church Book.

Flowers, Nelus Wayland, and Lonza Wayland. The first pastor was Benjamin Creel. More than five hundred have professed Christ in this church since its foundation. In 1880, a part of its membership was organized into a separate congregation, and a new church, known as Fairview, was built.[1]

## Lutherans

The Lutheran faith is the second oldest in Madison county, if not the first. It was brought in directly by German colonists. These colonists lived for awhile at Germanna, but later settled on the waters of the Robinson River. They have played a very important part in the history of the county. It seems best to take up the history of each Lutheran Church in detailed form, as from this we can gather a more definite picture of the community in which the Lutherans settled. From this, also we can see the richness of the past to which the descendants of these people may ever look back.

## Hebron Church

The Hebron Church was organized by a colony of Germans who had emigrated from Germanna and a few years before from Holland. This old church for a long time was known as the "Old Dutch Church." It has stood at its present site successively in three counties Orange, Culpeper and Madison, and its congregation lived there while the land was still in Spotsylvania county.

The church is the oldest of the Lutheran faith in Virginia, and also, the South. The original part of the building is the oldest Lutheran church in use in the United States. The Germans who started it moved to Madison (then Spotsylvania) about 1725. Rev. Casper Stoever in his account of this German colony, claims to have been the first pastor and says that for sixteen years before his arrival, these Lutherans were without a pastor. There is no evidence that these people had a church before they moved to Madison. Their first services after arriving on the waters of the Robinson River, were held by laymen in a stockade that was built as a protection against the Indians.[2]

In 1725 they sent two of their number to Germany to seek a pastor but they returned unsuccessful. About this time a church was built known as "The German Chapel." There are several good proofs that such a building existed and that it stood where the present church stands. It is supposed that this church was built about 1726; it was of unhewn logs; there were openings for windows, but no glass; the floor and benches were made of puncheons.[3]

---

[1] Answer to Questionnaire.
[2] Huddle, W. P., History of the Hebron Lutheran Church. Pages 1-2.
[3] Huddle, W. P., History of the Hebron Lutheran Church. Page 13.

It is not positively known when a congregation was organized, but it is certain that one existed as early as 1733 as Rev. Casper Stoever became pastor there in that year; also the treasurer's report for the same year has been found.[1]

Rev. Casper Stoever, their first pastor, was born at Frankenberg in Hesse, in 1685, and came to America in 1728, landing in Pennsylvania. Where he labored before coming to Virginia is not known. He informs us, through a pamphlet, he has written on the history of his congregation, that the number of souls at the beginning of his duties there, or soon afterwards, was three hundred. He also tells us that his salary was 3,000 pounds of tobacco—about forty dollars—which his congregation paid, in addition to taxes for the support of the English or Episcopal Church.[2]

In 1733 a farm of 193 acres was bought from William Carpenter, and a parsonage known as "Glegehans" was built on it in 1734. The consideration named in the deed was five shillings lawful money of Virginia.[3]

A new church was badly needed, as the old chapel was insufficient. Consequently, in the fall of 1734 the pastor, Rev. Mr. Stoever, Michael Smith, and Michael Holt were sent to Europe to solicit funds to aid in building a church, establishing a school, and supporting an assistant pastor. The outcome of this was the selection of an assistant pastor, Mr. George Samuel Klug, and the collection of about 7841 rix dollars (silver coin of Germany, Holland, Denmark, etc., worth from $.60 to $1.08). A number of theological books were collected for Mr. Stoever, and a valuable library of standard books, for the congregation. On their return voyage the above named gentlemen stopped at Plymouth, England, where they bought at a cost of $125 a hundred pieces of cut-glass and three hundred pounds of putty to be used in making windows. Sadness followed their success abroad, for on the return voyage Rev. Mr. Stoever died; this was in 1739.[4]

After the death of Mr. Stoever, his assistant, Rev. Samuel Klug, became pastor and the work was carried on as planned. On July 21, following, another farm of 685 acres of land, was bought from Mr. Thomas Farmer for five shillings sterling. This farm is often spoken of as being bought with money from Germany. It was situated near the Champlane farm at Etlan. In 1740 the new church was completed. It was a frame structure, rectangular in shape, fifty feet long, by twenty feet wide, by thirty feet high. Slaves were bought to work the church lands in order to help pay the pastor. Some time after the church was built a school was established.[5]

---

[1] Huddle, W. P., History of the Hebron Lutheran Church. Pages 30-38.
[2] Ibid. Page 16.
[3] Ibid. Page 20.
[4] Ibid. Page 22.
[5] Ibid. Pages 25-30.

Hebron Lutheran Church

In 1775 a constitution of the church was drawn up and signed by more than 170 members. This constitution is beautifully written in German. The following year on April 6, 1776, the largest number that ever communed iin this church communed; the number was 176.[1]

The German language was used altogether in this church until Rev. William Carpenter became pastor in 1787. He was also the first minister sent from this congregation. He moved to Kentucky and became the first pastor of Hopeful Church in Boone county.[2]

Rev. Michael Meyerhoffer was the first pastor to administer the Lord's Supper in English. He became pastor in 1815, and for the length of his pastorate, had more converts than any pastor during the history of the church.[3]

The old communion set and pipe organ are highly prized by this congregation. The oldest pieces of the communion service were given the church and bear this inscription, "A gift from Thomas Griffin, London, May 13, 1727." The remainder of the service was a gift of Mr. Furgen Stollim of Lubec, Germany, bearing the date of March 28, 1737. The pipe organ was built by Mr. David Tannenburg at Lititz, Pennsylvania, about the year 1800; from this place it was hauled on wagons to the church by Jacob Rouse and Michael Rouse. It cost 200 pounds.[4]

This church belonged to the ministerium of Pennsylvania until 1820; then, to the Synod of Maryland and Virginia until 1829, when the Synod of Virginia was formed.[5]

The first Sunday School in this church was about 1833. The first prayer meeting in 1844. The first burial in the present cemetery was in 1904.[6]

This church has sent out a group of pastors of whom they may be justly proud. Those who have gone out are: William Carpenter, Jacob Crigler, Bellfield Wayland, James Strickler, John F. Crigler, and Ashby Graves.[7]

## Mt. Nebo

A few years before the Civil War began, some families of the Lutheran faith from Rockingham and Shenandoah counties crossed the Blue Ridge and settled in Madison county within a few miles of Rochelle. They were members of congregations connected with the Tennessee Synod.[8]

This congregation had no pastor until 1866 at which time Rev. James E. Seneker of Augusta county visited these Lutherans and

---
[1] Ibid. Page 45.
[2] Huddle's History of the Hebron Lutheran Church. Page 50.
[3] Ibid. Page 54.
[4] Ibid. Pages 33, 49.
[5] Ibid. Page 106.
[6] Ibid. Page 101.
[7] Hebron Church Records.
[8] Huddle's History of the Hebron Lutheran Church. (Appendix).

preached for them in the old Methodist church of Rochelle. He found at least eight members of the church. They were: Colonel Noah I. Henkel, Mary M. Henkel, Samuel Tussing, Philip Lohr, Catharine Lohr, Mary Kipps, Benjamin Lowry and Rebecca C. Sommers. The congregation applied for admission and was received into the Tennessee Synod. The work of collecting funds to build a church was begun as early as 1875 but the church was not built until 1879. The church lot was given by Mary Jackson.[1]

For the last thirty-one years, this church has been served by the pastors of the Madison Charge of the Virginia Synod, though all the time it has retained its connection with the Tennessee Synod.[2]

## Mt. Pisgah

Mt. Pisgah was organized in 1893 being a daughter of the Hebron Church. Those instrumental in building the church were: J. A. Flickenger, Smith Gibbs, O. J. Utz, J. N. Tanner, Miss Lou Utz, and Alice Marshall. Its pastors have been those of the Madison Circuit of the Virginia Synod. J. A. Flickenger was the first pastor and was followed successively, by Charles B. Miller, W. P. Huddle, E. Grover Morgan, and V. Y. Boozer.[3]

## Hoffman Chapel

Little is known of the history of Hoffman Chapel nor of the congregation that once worshipped in it. It was originally a Presbyterian or German Reform meeting-house. It is supposed to have been built between 1750 and 1770. It has been said that the congregation that had it built, received some of the money collected in Europe by Rev. Stoever and his associates for the Hebron Lutheran Church. Early in the forties it was repaired and used as a union church. No regular German Reformed minister preached in it for years and the only Presbyterian minister now known to have done so, was Rev. Daniel B. Ewing, who was there about 1849. The deed to the lot was made February 9, 1843, from Samuel Hoffman to E. D. Fray, Larkin Deal, John H. Hoffman and Richard Early. The chapel was used for many years, but has now been destroyed.[4]

## Episcopalians

The Episcopal Church was the first to be established in Virginia and, probably, in Madison county. This was the Established Church of England; consequently, as long as the colonies belonged to the mother country, it was the Established Church of the Colonies.

---

[1] Ibid.
[2] Ibid.
[3] Answer to a Questionnaire.
[4] Huddle, W. P., History of the Hebron Lutheran Church. Page 100.

## THE CHURCH HISTORY OF MADISON

In the early history of Virginia, all business and government was transacted through parishes or divisions made by the Episcopal Church. These divisions of land usually conformed to the county lines. All of the people who lived within the limits of a parish, regardless of their religious convictions, were compelled to attend the parish church and to pay taxes for its support. This being true, in order for us to understand the government of colonial days, it is essential for us to know something concerning these early parishes.①

Madison, or at least some of its territory, was in four successive parishes. On May 1, 1721, Spotsylvania was constituted one parish, known as "St. George's Parish." This parish conformed exactly to the limits of Spotsylvania county; Madison, therefore, was then a part of St. George's Parish until it was divided in 1731.②

In 1731, St. George's Parish was divided and a part of it was formed into a new parish known as "St. Mark's." Madison was included in this new parish, the bounds of which coincided with the bounds of Orange county.③

Then again on November 1, 1740, St. Mark's Parish was divided and the new division was called "St. Thomas."④ "The boundary of St. Thomas' Parish was as follows: St. Mark was divided by a line from the Wilderness Bridge up the Mountain Road to the head of Russell's Run; thence, down the said run to the River Rapidan; thence, up the Rapidan to the Robinson River; thence, from the said river along the ridge between the Robinson and the Rapidan and to the top of the ridge of this mountain; and all that part of the said parish situated on the south side of the said bounds to be erected into another distinct parish and called by the name of St. Thomas." It will be seen from the above that all of the county of Madison remained in St. Mark's parish except a narrow strip of land between the divide of the Robinson and Rapidan Rivers and the western boundary of the county.

⑤ The parish of St. Mark's was later divided by a line as follows: "By the meandering of Crooked Run falling into the Robinson River: up to Colonel Spottswood's Corner on that run; thence, by this line north twenty-eight degrees and east to Bloodworth Road; thence, from Bloodworth Road by a straight line to Crooked Run, a branch of the north fork of Gourdvine River; where the main road called Duncans crosses the said run; thence, by the said run to the head of White Oak Run; thence, by that run down to North River; and all that part of St. Mark's parish which lies below the said bounds, except so much thereof as lies in the County of Orange, be one distinct parish and retain the name of St. Mark, and all that part of the said parish

---
① Statement of Oldest People in the County.
② Slaughter, Philip, History of St. George's Parish. Pages 7-9.
③ Slaughter, Philip, History of St. Mark's Parish. Page 6.
④ Henning, W. W., Statutes at Large for Virginia. Volume 5, Pages 96-97.
⑤ Henning's Statutes, Volume No. 6, Pages 256-257.

of St. Mark which lies above the said bounds; together with so much of St. Thomas as lies in the County of Culpeper, which is hereby added to and made part of the same, be one other distinct parish and called by the name of Bromfield." Thus, Madison was then included in this new parish of Bromfield, which was the last parish division made of the land of Madison county.

As has already been stated everyone who lived in a parish was required to attend the parish church or else pay a fine. A tax was levied on everyone who lived within the parish, just as county taxes are assessed today. One reason why everybody had to attend the parish church was to pay these taxes; but there were other reasons also. All marriages, deaths, and births were recorded in the parish church as they are recorded in the clerk's office today.[1]

From the bounds given above one may see that some of the parishoners lived a great distance from the church. Where this distance was very great, provision was made to relieve the people from the duty of attending church. This was accomplished by building what was called "A House of Ease." This "House of Ease" was similar to a branch church and was placed where the people could attend easily. Attendance here relieved one of the duty of attending the parish church.[2]

When Madison was a part of St. George's Parish it was necessary that a "House of Ease" be built within the western bounds of the county, and one was built near Wolftown. Some years later St. Mark's Parish was formed, but the parish church was situated in what is now Culpeper county. Again, after the formation of Bromfield Parish, the parish church was built near Slate Mills on what is now called the Parish Road. This church was called "F. T." It was a brick church and took its name from the fact that it was near the starting point of a survey of land, taken up by Mr. Frank Thornton, who carved his initials on an oak tree near a spring where his lines commenced. There was also another Episcopal Church four miles below the present Madison Court House. This church was called "South Church." It was a frame building and stood on the land of Richard Vauters. Both the F. T. and South Church buildings were old at the beginning of the Revolutionary War and soon after went into gradual decay.[3]

Mr. Iodell, or Indell, was the minister of these churches about the time Madison became a separate county. He gave up these churches or rather was forced to leave because of charges of immorality brought against him, and was succeeded by an Irishman named O'Neal. Mr. O'Neal had charge of the parish for many years in connection with the Pine Stake and Orange Churches. He also kept a school near Raccoon Ford and Mr. John Conway was one of his

---

[1] Statement of Mr. W. E. Bohannon.
[2] Ibid.
[3] Meade Bishop Old Churches and Families of Virginia.

pupils. Mr. O'Neal left these churches about 1800, but his name still survives in the county, in O'Neals Crossing. After that time Mr. Woodville occasionally performed services in the parish; when he left, the churches went into decay. The Lutheran ministers, especially Mr. William Carpenter, officiated at the marriages, baptisms and funerals of the Episcopal families.[1]

The Episcopal families around the churches above were: Ruckers, Barbours, Beales, Keartleys, Lewises, Bladfords, Vauters, Strothers, Thorntons, Burtons, Conways, Gibsons, Pannels, and Gaineses.[2]

Since the resuscitation of the church in Virginia although a long time after the commencement of the same, efforts were made to revive the churches in the old Bromfield parish. A new brick church was built at Madison Court House and for sometime the prospect was very encouraging, but immigration and coming in of other denominations caused this church to lose ground.[3]

Since the first efforts of the churches in behalf of Madison, the following clergymen from Orange, Culpeper, and Rappahannock, have given a part of their time to the Madison church: Rev. Mr. Lamon, Rev. Mr. Doughen, Rev. Mr. Cole, Rev. Mr. Brown and Rev. Mr. Leavell.[4]

The following account of the history of the Piedmont Church was published in the *Madison County Eagle* of July 24, 1925, and was signed by K. J. H.[5]

"The history of this church is interesting from its beginning. Dr. Phillip Slaughter in 'St. Mark's Parish' finds that the beginning was very early when the county of Madison was included in St. Mark's parish.

"In 1752, Bromfield parish (the Anglo-Saxon word is Broomfield) was set off, and its western boundary made to include Madison and Rappahannock counties. In 1754, a dividing line was run for its eastern boundary separating it from St. Mark's parish. It then included Tennants' Church, a church in the fork of Devil's Run, and another at Hazel River. Later, there was a church at F. T. called from the initials of Frank Thornton, the surveyor, marked on an oak tree near a spring. There was also a church near the present site of Washington, Rappahannock county.

"Rev. Andrew Menzies was the first minister of Bromfield Parish, mentioned in Fulham Mss., England, as licensed for Virginia 1754-5. Another minister was Rev. Mr. Harrison, to whom Samuel Slaughter who died in 1859, aged 90 years, went to school. (p. 81) In 1790 Rev. Mr. Iredale officiated at South Church four miles below Madison Court House. If Dr. Slaughter means the southwest

---
[1] Ibid.
[2] Ibid.
[3] Ibid.
[4] Meades'—Old Churches and Families of Virginia.
[5] Madison County Eagle, July 24, 1925.

Mountain Church, (page 14) it was one of the first churches erected and 'in the neighborhood of Messrs. James Barbour and Benjamin Cave, vestrymen.' Rev. James Woodville occasionally preached here; and Rev. Mr. Carpenter, Lutheran minister, baptised and buried Episcopalians, when without a minister.

"The Journals of the Diocesan Councils now become our authority for further items:

"Bishop Meade in his annual report describes a visit to Madison. (1832) August 1, 1832, 'when Episcopal services have been recently introduced. I preached only once for lack of time, and was gratified to see a genuine work of grace going on in the hearts of many there, and a goodly number attaching themselves to the communion of our church.'

"Rev. A. Lamon, deacon, reports to the council, 'I give (1833) half my time to Madison Court House. I found six members there. I baptized seven adults and eight children; fourteen men and ten women have been confirmed. Fourteen hundred dollars has been subscribed for a new church, and a contract let for one costing $1,800 or $2,000. The Lord has done great things for us.'

"In September, Bishop Meade visited Trinity church between Stanardsville and Madison, preached twice and confirmed three persons, and administered the holy communion. One person confirmed was a Revolutionary War soldier, 83 years old, a comrade of the Bishop's father under Washington. When the Bishop told him he was the son of his old comrade, the man was moved to tears. The next three days (September 13-15) the bishop spent in Madison Court House, holding four services a day, Rev. Archibald Lamon, of Culpeper being in charge. The Bishop writes, "Fifteen months ago, when this place was vacant, I scarcely knew a place less promising to our labors. This time I confirmed twenty-three, and saw a neat brick edifice rising out of the ground to be a place of worship of God. He has visited this place with abundant grace. He has blessed the faithful preaching of his word by ministers of different denominations. He has sent to those inclined to us a faithful man, instant in season, who has gathered a little band with whom I spent some of the happiest days of my ministry." Rev. W. G. Jackson of Staunton and W. H. G. Jones, of Orange, assisted in these services; and Rev. Mr. Lamon of whom Bishop Meade writes, 'I also admitted their minister to priest's orders.

"In the council report this year Mr. Lamon has ten baptisms, (1834) two marriages, twenty-three confirmations, twenty-nine communicants, of whom one was colored, twenty Sunday-School pupils; contributions to missionary and educational needs; increased interest in missions; and a monthly service for colored folk. Bishop Meade consecrated the new church Oct. 27, Rev. Dr. P. Slaughter and Messrs. A. Lamon and H. G. Jones assisting. The next day he consecrated St. Thomas, Orange.

"Mr. Lamon's next report is a combined one for the counties of Madison and Culpeper. In November, 1835, he resigned; he later took a parish in Louisiana, serving with the same devotion until overcome by yellow fever. He died after an illness of four days, aged forty-six years. His first wife was a Miss Rapley of Alexandria, who had four children, John H., Archibald Jr., Sarah, and Charles. His second wife was a Miss Toron, who had a daughter, Elizabeth; Rev. Charles Kenneth Thompson, of Coldwater, Mich. is his grandson; John G. Lamon, of Culpeper, was his nephew. Rev. James Doughan succeeded Mr. Lamon in his field of Madison and Culpeper.

"Bishop Meade came to Piedmont Church this year; he preached, 1837, baptized three and confirmed four persons. Dr. P. S. Slaughter, also came to Culpeper to solemnize some marriages. He introduced to the people Rev. John Cole, who was called and who accepted the work of both counties. He found twenty-four communicants in Madison, twelve at Piedmont and twelve at Trinity. The latter was strictly a 'free church,' open winter and summer, in snow and storm, free to everybody and anything.' He included Stanardsville in his unwearied labors, giving 'twelve sermons a month, besides a Bible class, a lecture and prayer meetings weekly, not wholly without encouragement.' He resigned this western half of his field in 1840, taking St. James church, near Remington, with St. Stephens, Culpeper.

"During these twenty years,1840-60 three clergymen officiated in Madison. Rev. R. T. Brown came in 1841; Rev. Joseph Earnest in 1849; and Rev. William T. Leavell in 1854. Each man included neighboring territory in his care. Mr. Brown had Rappahannock, and Mr. Leavell came over from Flint Hill, and later from Peola Mills, where he lived, and also served. In Mr. Brown's day the ladies held a fair, bought stoves for the church and plastered it, spending in Mr. Leavell's time two hundred dollars for repairs. Rev. Mr. Shields, afterwards of Louisville, Ky., held some service here. Bishop Johns made his first visit in 1845, Mr. Cole accompanying him. He came again in 1848, preaching and confirming three. He drove twelve miles in a pelting rain over rough roads for one of these confirmations, where afterwards, he administered the holy communion. 'Weariness and exposure were soon forgotten in the spiritual refreshment of this visit.'

"The Civil War brought a period of loss. A pastorless field 1860-80 could but lie idle, and it did this for three years, except for occasional services by Rev. Dr. Minnegerode, of Culpeper; and Bishop Johns visited it in 1870, and Bishop Tuttle in 1871, 1875, and 1880.

"Help came now from Rapidan, Rev. William Byrd Lee giving a 1880-90 monthly service. A Sunday School was organized; a dozen members found; Mrs. William Cave became treasurer, and contributions were made to various objects. Rev. R. R. Claiborne from Rapidan ministered to them from 1882-1886. Bishop Peterkin held a confirmation in 1883, and seven hundred dollars was spent in repairs on the church. Rev. Frank G. Scott served here awhile and Rev. John Hansbrough of Orange came in 1890. Bishop Newton came for a confirmation in 1894. Rev. Mr. Wroth afterwards of Baltimore also preached here. In 1895 Piedmont church had its resident rector, Rev. Mr. Cowling, who served till 1901, though he lived the last two years in Standardsville, taking charge of the new church there, where his brother, and Rev. H. K. Pendleton, Rev. J. R. Ellis and Alexander Griffith also served.

"In this decade, Bishop Gibson made his first visit in 1901; 1900-10: Messrs. Frank Meade, in 1902; Robb White (August, 1902), William M. Cleveland, coming from Standardsville, and Rev. Mr. Carter, of Orange, also served Piedmont church.

"From 1911-16 Rev. Byrd Turner lived in Madison, and ministered 1910-11 here and to outlying points, of which Madison Mills was one. The church was repaired and a Sunday School and guild organized.

"Rev. William C. Marshall from Rapidan held monthly service in 1918-20; then he went to Maryland. Misses Frances Hay and Norma Cave acted as treasurers, Miss Cave being still a most efficient officer. In 1923, Rev. Dr. Hammond and Frank Cox arranged for a monthly service for eight months of the year. Mr. Cox being called to New York, Dr. Hammond maintained this service during 1924 and 1925 with earnest co-operation from the members. The building was put in thorough order at a cost of more than two hundred dollars; it is a pleasure to use it with the encouraging attendance of the members and community. May the Master's blessing rest upon this venerable parish and all its members always. K. J. H."

## CHAPTER VIII

### THE SCHOOL SYSTEM OF MADISON COUNTY

A school was established by the early German settlers in the Robinson River Valley at the old Hebron Church. It was built, maintained and supervised by this church; yet, it was not strictly a denominational school, for all who chose were permitted to attend, regardless of the religious convictions. Instruction was given in religious matters and in the fundamental subjects; reading, writing and arithmetic. It is not known definitely when the school was started; but it must have been about 1730 or 1740, for at this time money was collected for the church and school. This school, however, was of short duration and many years elapsed before the county public schools were begun.[1]

Before the Civil War all the schools in the county were private "old field schools." That is, each community built its own school house, and financed and supervised its own school system without the intervention of the county government. The patrons who lived near the "old field" school houses employed the best teacher they could secure. The parents of each pupil who attended the school, were required to pay a small sum for its maintenance; however, if there were children in the community whose parents were unable to pay this sum, the county paid it for them. This was the only way in which the county played a part in the school system before the Civil War.[2]

The instruction in these "old field schools" was confined to the fundamental subjects. Spelling and arithmetic were the main ones in the average school. Pike's Arithmetic seems to have been a favorite with the teachers up to the time of the Civil War. The elementary spelling book, Walker's Dictionary, Murray's Grammar and Morse's Geography were the leading textbooks of that day. In fact, textbooks were so scarce that almost any that could be obtained were used.[3]

The methods of teaching differed greatly from those of today, as did also school discipline. The dull and backward child was urged along by means of the hickory rod; this the teacher believed to be the only way of giving him his share of book knowledge. This idea applied not only to small children, but to larger ones also. The goose quill and the teacher's copy were considered an especially important part of school equipment; even today we are impressed

---

[1] Huddle, W. P., History of the Hebron Lutheran Church. Pages 23-24.
[2] Statement of Oldest People.
[3] Virginia School Report 1885. Page 219.

with the beautiful penmanship which was developed in those days. In geography some facts were taught as to location, climate, etc., however, the child was not made certain but that the "sun do move." Technical forms of grammar were but little taught; these forms were not well understood by teacher or pupils, and, therefore, grammar was passed over. Blackboards were entirely unknown and in place of writing tablets, slates were used. The old pedagogue, however, was a little advanced in one thing that is not taught in the public schools today; this was practical surveying. The teacher took the boys out and surveyed plots of land near the school house; thus, practice was given along with theory.[1]

A teacher of the old field school was not required to have a certificate; there was no county school board, no state board, no administrative school officials to whom he was subject. The old field school teacher was his own master, and the only requirement made of him was that he satisfy the patrons to whom he was directly responsible, and under whose sole jurisdiction he was placed. They expected him to maintain good discipline and to teach the fundamental subjects, but not by any improved method but by forcing the pupils to study the subject matter. Some of the old field school teachers whose names have been handed down in sacred memory were graduates of the best institutions of the country. Every neighborhood prided itself in securing the best teacher. Parents who could afford to educate their sons at college, would almost invariably start them to teaching as a stepping stone to some other employment. Besides this class of teachers, there was also another class known at that day as "professional teachers." They knew something of grammar, could read and write, make the boys mind and the girls "behave." This latter class were never known to spare the rod, but would sometimes spoil the child.[2]

The old field schools were located far apart, sometimes as much as five miles. This distance, together with other causes, made the percentage of attendance very low, while the percentage of illiteracy was very high. Although the percentage of attendance according to the school population was exceedingly low, the number of pupils per teacher was very high. One teacher would perhaps have as many as forty or fifty pupils ranging in grades from one to eight. Such conditions made it impossible for the teacher to give the best type of instruction; consequently, it is not surprising to learn that after keeping good order the teacher had little time left in which to give the individual a proper amount of attention.

There was no graded system in these schools; the only classification made was in each subject. Pupils studying the same books were in the same classes. A pupil who liked arithmetic, would be in

---

[1] Virginia School Report 1885. Page 220.
[2] Virginia School Report 1885. Page 220.

a higher grade in arithmetic than he was in any other subject; a pupil would finish one book and be promoted to another in that subject instead of completing an entire grade. There was very little, if any, of what is now called high school work; in those days, the colleges took care of that.

Before the Civil War, public education was looked upon as a Yankee notion or invention, and could not be tolerated in the Old Dominion. The idea seemed to prevail with some, that the rich man had a right to educate his sons, while the poor must remain "hewers of wood and drawers of water."[1]

This idea was abandoned after the Civil War. The State Constitution of 1870 provided for a system of public schools. The public school system was established in Madison county in 1871, under the supervision of Dr. William A. Hill. Dr. Hill continued in office for eleven years, and under his supervision the schools were a success from the beginning; it seems he was especially fitted for the important task of starting the machinery. Some opposition was raised against the public school system because it educated the negro, but by 1885 nearly all of this had passed away.[2]

When the public school system came into effect, practically all of the old field school buildings were converted into public schools, supported by the county. These old field schools had had but one room and so the first public school had but one room; it was not until 1884 that a two-roomed school was built. This was situated at Madison Court House with Mr. R. E. L. Holmes as its first principal.[3]

In 1871 there were twenty schools for white children and five for colored children, all of which were one roomed; by 1920 there were sixty-three schools for white children, and eighteen for colored children; most of these had two, three or four rooms.[4]

In 1871 the county school officials assumed the responsibility of appointing teachers; consequently, the teacher's task became a harder one; he must please both the people of the community, and the county school officials, while under the old system he had only to please the community. Likewise, as it was the school officials' duty to appoint teachers, it was their duty to see that these teachers were well qualified. This duty fell to the superintendent of schools. The first method of selection used was a very interesting one. A prospective teacher would present himself to the superintendent and ask to be examined as teacher for some specific school in the county. There were no regular public examinations; only a few oral questions would be asked the candidate by the superintendent. The candidate and the superintendent would perhaps spend a very sociable afternoon together, after which the superintendent would inform the candidate

---

[1] Virginia School Report 1885. Page 219.
[2] Ibid. 1885. Page 219.
[3] Ibid. 1884. Page 19.
[4] Ibid. 1871. Page 165.

of his appointment or of his failure. Tradition has preserved some interesting questions asked by the superintendent of those days.

In 1871 twenty-four white teachers and one colored teacher were employed by the county, each teacher having an average of forty pupils of all ages and grades. In contrast to this, in 1920, the county employed sixty-three white teachers and sixteen colored ones; the average number of pupils to each teacher was twenty-five; most of these were classified into grades.[1]

In 1871 the teacher's position was quite different from what it is today. At that time the teacher was looked upon as being the most intellectual person in the community. He, or she, was supposed to have all knowledge and was supposed to be able to answer all questions pertaining to books. Teaching as a profession, too, was looked upon as being confined to the female sex or to males, who were physically handicapped or who taught only as a minor profession. Many preachers, lawyers or farmers taught for five months of the year, and devoted the remainder of the year to their regular profession.

Since the beginning of the school system there has not been a very marked increase in the white school population. The census returns for 1900 show the largest number of white school children in the county; at that date there were 2,398 children of school age, as compared with 1,725 in 1871, and 2,010 in 1920. The colored school population has undergone a more marked change. The colored school population was highest in 1890, there being 1,982 colored children of school age in this year, as compared with 1,424 in 1871 and 942 in 1920.

The next thing that we would naturally like to know is how many of these children were enrolled in school and what was the average attendance. Of the white children in 1871, out of a population of 1,725 only 619 were actually enrolled in school and out of this the average attendance was only 403. Thus in 1871, the county had only 403 children in school for ninety-five days out of a population of 1,725; but in contrast to this, there were in 1920, 1,119 children in school for 134 days in the year, out of a population of 2,010. From the above statistics we are able to see what a marked change has taken place in getting the pupils in school.

The next interesting thing is to trace the change that has taken place in improving the equipment of the school and the methods of instruction. In 1872 the county spent only $3,359.00 on schools. This was a little more than one and one-half cents per pupil; in 1920 the expenditures for school was $46,274.00, which was $23.03 per pupil. Until 1900 most of the school buildings in the county were of a very inferior kind. It was the time when the "little log cabin in the woods" was the institution for training future Madisonians.

---

[1] Virginia School Reports. Volume 1871. Page 165; Volume 1920, Pages 100-148.

Practically all school buildings in the county were made of pine logs hewn to about six inches thickness. These buildings were usually built with one door on the front, one window on each side, and a long window in the back. The equipment inside corresponded very fittingly with the building. All of the desks were made of pine boards; the desks for the girls were on one side of the room; the desks for the boys, on the other; the boys' side could always be distinguished from the girls, because the desks were covered with names chiseled out with pocket knives. In one corner of the room was a shelf for lunch boxes; on one side, a blackboard made of smooth boards painted black; and on the other side, a map of Virginia; these practically completed the school equipment. After 1910 a change began to take place; new and more modern buildings were erected and better equipment was installed. Today the pride of most communities is their school buildings.

Many other changes have taken place. When the log buildings were in use, they were often crowded with pupils, there being as many as thirty or forty in one room. The number of these pupils was not such a problem as the nature of the group. All sizes, ages and grades were represented; consequently, the teacher had classes ranging from those learning to "read and spell" to those who were ready to enter what is now high school.

In the beginning of the public school system, the securing of text books was almost as great a problem as it was when the "old field schools" were in use. In 1871 the state made a list of text books from which the various counties might select the ones they chose to use. From this list Madison adopted Holmes' Spellers and Readers, Venerable's Arithmetic, Murry's Geography and Bullion's Grammar.①

Since the beginning of the public school system there have been some marked changes in the method of administration. In 1871 the county was divided into school districts, three in number which as it happened conformed to the magisterial districts of the county and were called by their names, Robinson, Rapidan, and Locust Dale. Each of these districts formed a unit in itself and was under the jurisdiction of three school trustees appointed by the Trustee Electoral Board. One county superintendent had jurisdiction over these three districts; he was the link which bound them together. Each district managed its own affairs, appointed its own teachers, and made its own school levy. These district boards appointed teachers for the schools in their own districts, subject to the approval of the superintendent. The superintendent usually did not question the school board's power in this but confirmed their appointments. All cases and petitions in which the people were concerned were brought before the school board.

---

① Virginia School Report 1871. Page 195.

In 1922 the District Trustee Board was done away with and the county became a unit with three trustees for the entire county, one from each district. This is the system used at the present time.

The School Trustee Electoral Board was composed of the commonwealth attorney for the county, the school superintendent and one man appointed from the county at large. The duty of this board, then as well as now, was to appoint trustees for the various districts. This board also heard cases of appeal from the District Trustee Board and served as a Board of Review for the entire county.

The system of oral examination of teachers used in the beginning of the public school system has been discussed above. This system was later changed from private oral examinations to public written ones. For a few years these examinations were made out by the superintendent, and given and corrected by him; he issued a certificate to teachers without the state's intervention. After a time the system was changed again. Public examinations were still given by the superintendent but the examinations were sent by him to the State Department; the grades were passed upon by the state; and the state issued all certificates for teachers; thus the superintendent became merely an official of the state. At the present time practically all certificates are obtained through normal schools and colleges. County examinations are still held, but very few teachers take them.

The general supervision of county public schools since 1871 has been under the county superintendent. Until 1909 Madison had its own superintendent whose only territory was Madison county; since 1909 Madison and Greene counties have been combined into one district under one superintendent. The superintendents for Madison have been as follows: Dr. W. A. Hill, N. W. Fry, J. W. Banks, T. N. Berry, E. H. Lovell, J. N. Miller and A. W. Yowell.

At present the schools in the county are much better than they were in the past. More pupils are availing themselves of an opportunity to attend school. There are more pupils in advanced classes and more girls and boys from the county attending the leading colleges and universities.

There have been very fine private schools in the county for both boys and girls. For many years the Warwick High School was one of the finest preparatory schools in this part of the state. Mr. J. D. Fray founded it, owned and conducted it for many years, preparing many Madisonians for college and for life. Due to the rise of high schools and the ill health of Mr. Fray the school was discontinued.

Locust Dale Academy located near Locust Dale was a boys' preparatory school and during its existence prepared many boys from many states for the leading colleges and universities. This school started just after the Civil War and continued into the beginning of the twentieth century. Mr. Larkin Willis, now one of the oldest men in the county, taught there for thirty years.

Oak Park Institute was a private school for girls. It gave preparatory work for college and trained girls for teaching.

Woodbury Forest is the only private school in existence in the county at present. It was founded by Captain Robert S. Walker and is at present one of the best preparatory schools for boys in the Old Dominion.

| Date | 1871 | 1875 | 1880 | 1885 | 1890 | 1895 | 1900 | 1905 | 1910 | 1915 | 1920 |
|---|---|---|---|---|---|---|---|---|---|---|---|
| Total Cost of Schools | $3 397 | $4 451 | $3 750 | $7 751 | $8 327 | $8 761 | $8 621 | $3 194 | $17 407 | | $46 274 |
| White Sc. Population | 1 725 | 1 865 | 2 106 | 2 200 | 2 276 | 2 275 | 2 398 | 2 398 | 2 079 | 2 079 | 2 010 |
| Colored Sc. Population | 1 424 | 1 483 | 1 671 | 1 700 | 1 982 | 1 837 | 1 473 | 1 473 | 1 110 | 1 110 | 942 |
| No. White Schools | 20 | 31 | 10 | 41 | 47 | 49 | 50 | 49 | 52 | 52 | 63 |
| No. Colored Schools | 5 | 12 | 6 | 18 | 23 | 20 | 20 | 19 | 22 | 17 | 18 |
| No. Months Taught | 4 3/4 | 5 | 5 | 5 | 5 | 5 | 5 | 5 | | | 6 7/10 |
| No. White Teachers | 24 | 31 | 10 | 40 | 47 | 49 | 51 | 49 | 53 | 52 | 70 |
| No. Colored Teachers | 1 | 12 | 6 | 19 | 23 | 20 | 20 | 19 | 22 | 17 | 16 |
| Average Salary for Teachers | $25 23 | $19 86 | $18 80 | $23 97 | $21 71 | $20 75 | $18 50 | $44 58 | | | |
| Enrollment, White | 619 | 972 | 1 041 | 1 382 | 1 521 | 1 300 | 1 409 | 1 490 | 1 622 | 1 372 | 1 432 |
| Enrollment, Colored | 395 | 753 | 527 | 938 | 978 | 700 | 813 | 730 | 974 | 637 | 639 |
| No. Pupils per Teacher | 40 | 27 | 28 | 32 | 25 | 23 | 25 | 24 | | | |
| Average Attendance, White | 403 | 541 | 792 | 887 | 820 | 749 | 696 | 1 068 | 926 | 1 000 | 1 110 |
| Attendance, Colored | 178 | 333 | 295 | 553 | 490 | 426 | 501 | 448 | | 393 | 482 |

Some of these figures must be wrong, but they are those given by the Virginia School Reports.

## CHAPTER IX

### Economic History

The wealth of Madison county was estimated in 1920 at $3,512,100.00, divided among a population of 10,125 people. This would make the per capita wealth over $346. This is a very fair wealth, for a rural community with not a single town of more than five hundred people. Madison can neither boast of its rich citizens, nor complain of its paupers.[1]

The reasons for this equality of wealth are many. In the first place all the population is in some way connected with the farm. The farms are usually productive and produce a wide variation of crops, which give the laborer a just reward for his labors.

In the second place, all the farms are relatively small, when we consider the method of farming used; consequently, there are few tenants or renters.

In the third place, the nature of the people produces an equality of wealth. The people are industrious and thrifty, and there is a great deal of friendship among all classes. The citizens mingle together and are personally acquainted; thus, they have a community interest.

In the fourth place the climate makes the people healthy and the soil productive. The climate of Madison is mild and equable; while the variation in temperature is greater than in the tide-water section of the state. Its winters are not severe, nor is the heat of its summers oppressive. Being situated on the eastern side of the Blue Ridge, it is somewhat protected from the chilling north winds of winter; and its altitude, of an average of over a thousand feet above sea level, makes the summers mild.

The first census taken after the formation of the county, was in 1800. The returns for this year showed a population of 8,322, of which 3,436 were negro slaves. From 1800 until 1830 the population of the county steadily increased, but from 1830 until 1880 it varied, sometimes being higher, and sometimes lower. Since 1880 the population has varied very little, remaining near 10,000 as follows: 1880, 10,545; 1890, 10,225; 1900, 10,216; 1910, 10,055; 1920, 10,125. From 1800 until 1830 the negro population increased; since that time it has been on a gradual decrease. When the Civil War began, there were 4,397 negro slaves in the county.[2]

Before the Civil War the economic conditions of Madison were very different from what they are today. This change has been

---

[1] Annual Report of the Commonwealth of Virginia. Volume 1920.
[2] Annual Report of the Commonwealth of Virginia. Volumes 1800-1920.

brought about chiefly by the changes of market conditions. In the early half of the nineteenth century it was almost impossible to market Madison produce; consequently, as few things could be exported, there was little money with which to buy imports. Before the Civil War, Madison was its own producer and consumer. Railroads were unknown and all the farm produce that was marketed had to be taken to some water-way. Fredericksburg was the nearest market and the only means of reaching this place was with horses and wagons. There are still a few old men in Madison who remember taking these long trips to market, and they delight in telling the farmers of today about those trips which required a week. These trips were made only a few times each year to exchange home produce for manufactured necessities.

A few years before the Civil War, railroads began to take the place of the old waterways. The Chesapeake and Ohio Railroad Company laid a track by way of Gordonsville, and, thus, this town became the market for Madison produce instead of Fredericksburg. Gordonsville remained the market for Madison people until the Southern Railroad was built connecting Charlottesville with Washington, and on this road there were three places that took the place of Gordonsville and have continued to do so until the present; namely, Somerset, Orange and Culpeper.

After Gordonsville had become the chief market for the county, a pike was built in 1849 and 1850 connecting this place with New Market. This pike passed almost directly through the center of Madison and has to this day been very beneficial to the entire county.

Madison has not only been handicapped by not having a railroad but the system of roads until very recent years has been very deficient. The only road the county could boast of as being at all fit for reasonable service, was the so-called Blue Ridge Turnpike, which as stated above, connected Gordonsville with New Market. This road was not built by the county but by a stock company known as the Blue Ridge Turnpike Company. The cost of this road was $176,000, issued in bonds, a part of which were bought by the citizens and a part by the state.[1] At the time the road was built, it was considered very fine. It resembled a macadam in all respects except the surface was not as smooth, but it was a great improvement over the dirt road. The company that built this road expected to receive large dividends by collecting tolls. The toll was rather high in comparison with the prices of other things of that day, being twenty-five cents for a team every seven miles. These tolls were collected and paid into the company until the Civil War. During the war the road was taken over by the state and when peace was declared it was never returned. The amount of toll collected until 1861 was $22,659.00.[2]

---

[1] Annual Report of the Board of Public Works of Virginia, 1853. Page 10.
[2] Annual Report of the Board of Public Works in Virginia, 1861. Page 16.

All the other roads in the county were at that time dirt roads and have remained so until recent years. Since 1910 there has been a movement for good roads, and at present market conditions are much improved and the prospect very bright for greater improvement. Improved market conditions have greatly increased the amount of exports, that is of farm produce, and increased the amount of imports in the way of manufactured articles.

Madison is, and always has been a rural county; therefore farming has always been its chief occupation. As the years have passed there has been a gradual yet outstanding change in the farms of Madison as well as in the methods of farming. Let us think of the great task that confronted the early settler in clearing this land and rendering it fit for cultivation.

In 1716 when Governor Spotswood crossed the Blue Ridge all of Madison was in forests and swamps. Today in 1925, two-thirds of the land is under cultivation. The immense amount of work required to produce this change cannot be conceived, and it seems that only now the people of Madison are prepared to farm.

During the days of the early settlers all the land in Madison was owned by Lord Fairfax who had patented it from the English Crown. This man never saw the land, but his agents did, and divided it into small tracts and sold these to men who came to settle in this region. It seems that these early settlers would not have wanted large farms, because the land was wooded and hard to clear and prepare for cultivation. This, however, was not true. The farms of the county were at first very large and have gradually decreased in size. The deeds to the lands patented by the German settlers show that their farms contained upon an average, four hundred acres; English settlers usually bought still more. Unfortunately there are no records from which we may calculate the average size of farms until 1851. In 1851 there were five hundred and fifty-one farms in the county; eighty-five of these contained over five hundred acres; seventeen, over a thousand acres; five, over two thousand acres; three, over five thousand acres; and one, owned by Thomas Shirley, contained forty-eight thousand nine hundred and thirty-three acres. The average farm in 1851 contained three hundred and five acres, but in contrast to this, in 1906 there were one thousand two-hundred farms in the county with an average of one hundred and forty acres in each.[1]

The value of farm land has increased many hundred per cent. Many small farms now sell for what the larger ones, of which this farm was a part, brought one hundred years ago. Many of the old deeds in the early part of the nineteenth century show that land sold upon an average for less than one dollar per acre. Now there is land in the county that will sell for a hundred dollars per acre.

---

[1] Tax Bill receipts for Madison County 1851.

Let us now turn to the comparative value of the crops in the county, making our comparison between 1850 and the present. Before the Civil War the farmers bought little and sold little; their produce could not be marketed; and even if it could, prices were low and there was no sale for many things that can be disposed of today. Everything that was needed on the farm was raised there and manufactured there for home consumption; most of the things that the farmer could not produce he did without. At present the condition is very different; few things are manufactured; more raw material is produced and there are more exports and imports.

Corn is the staple produce, not so much because it is exported, for there is very little corn sold out of the county; but it is the staple product because it is the chief food for cattle which are the chief article of export. Since 1850 there has been no material gain in the amount of corn raised per acre, although there are possibilities for this. Farmers consider fifty bushels per acre an average yield; should it be necessary, they could double this. Strange to say there has been little change in the yield per acre during the entire history of the county. The average yield still remains fifty bushels per acre. However, in 1916 one boy in the county, who was in the Boys' Corn Club, raised one hundred and twenty-one and two-thirds bushels per acre. Although there has been no material gain in the amount raised per acre there has been a great change in the number of acres cultivated. There has been about a hundred per cent gain in the amount of corn produced. Corn has been such a standard that should you ask the average farmer in Madison in any period of the county's history how farm prices were he would more than likely give you the price of corn, leaving you to judge other things for yourself. In 1850 corn sold for forty cents per bushel; at present it sells for a dollar per bushel.

Wheat, as a farm product, holds second place. The total value of wheat in the county has decreased since 1850, although the price and the number of acres under cultivation has increased. This decrease in value is due to the amount produced. In the first half of the nineteenth century wheat, or rather flour, was the chief article of export. Wheat was taken to the local mills and made into flour; this flour was hauled to Fredericksburg or Gordonsville, and there sold. Flour brought a much better price than live stock; consequently, in accordance with the law of supply and demand, the farmer devoted more of his time to the production of wheat. Since 1850 the price of live stock has increased to such an extent that the farmer devotes more time to live stock than to the production of wheat. In 1850 wheat sold for a dollar per bushel; at present, it sells for a dollar and a half. If we consider what a farmer could purchase for a dollar in 1850, together with the difference in the cost of production and the smaller yield per acre, the total value of wheat per year is now about a hundred per cent less than it was in 1850.

The value of oats has remained somewhat the same. The yield per acre is the same, but the number of acres under cultivation has decreased. The reason for this change is that in 1850 oats were used more as food for horses than they are today. Hay and other grains have taken their place. In 1850 oats sold for twenty-five cents per bushel; now, they sell for seventy-five cents. The change in price more than balances the decrease in yield, so that the total value of the oats crop in the county remains about the same.

Rye has undergone little change. The total yield per acre and the total number of acres under cultivation have remained somewhat static. The price of rye is usually considered to be the same as wheat.

Hay has undergone a greater change than any crop raised in the county. In 1850 more clover hay was raised per acre than at present, and the total yield was much greater. However, the total yield of all hay is much greater than it was in 1850. In 1850 clover was the only hay known; but, now it is only one of the several grasses and plants made into hay. In 1850 all of the hay was cut with a scythe and raked with a pitchfork or hand rake. Because of this very slow process, there was less acreage devoted to the cultivation of hay. The first mowers and horse rakes came into the county just after the Civil War, and this machinery brought a marked change in the status of hay. Until recent years hay was fed only to horses; at present it is also fed to cattle. This is especially true of pea-hay. In 1850 there was no market for peas, and pea-hay was unknown. It came into use in Madison county in 1900. The price of hay in 1850 was about seventy-five cents per hundred; now it sells for a dollar and twenty-five cents. The total yield of hay, with the exception of clover, has increased.

In 1850 there was little sale for live stock other than for home use. The price was low; consequently, little was raised. There has been an increase in the production of cattle, especially in the last few years. Few beef cattle were raised in 1850 and calves for food were unknown. The chief reason for this was the distance to market. Prior to the Civil War a cow could be bought for twenty dollars; at present the same cow would be worth fifty dollars. Calves sold for five dollars that would bring twenty dollars at present. The value of cattle in the county in 1875 was estimated at $60,816.00; in 1920 at $276,250.00. There has not been any great change in the number or value of horses. Oxen were used in the place of horses in 1850. At present oxen are no longer used, as trucks and tractors have taken their place.[1]

Sheep were raised only for home use in 1850, and the wool was made into cloth. Therefore, every farmer kept a few sheep; but like cattle, there was not much sale for sheep. Lambs were not sold until

---

[1] Annual Report of the Commonwealth of Virginia. Volumes 1875-1920.

after the Civil War, and the number of sheep did not increase until it became possible to market lambs.

Practically no hogs were sold on foot in 1850; all of them were converted into bacon and sold. At present most hogs are sold on foot. The value of hogs in 1875 was estimated at $17,844; in 1920, at $29,035.00. This is an increase of sixty-three per cent.[1]

Very little poultry was raised to sell before the Civil War. It was not until about 1880 that the local stores began to buy chickens, and even then the price was only twenty or twenty-five cents each. Eggs sold in 1850 for eight cents per dozen; now, they sell for thirty cents per dozen. Turkeys were driven in large droves to Washington in 1850 and there sold for a dollar each. Today turkeys sell for five dollars apiece. It is then plainly evident that the production of poultry has greatly increased in the last fifty years, and has become one of the main means of revenue of the county.

Before the Civil War there was no sale for fruit of any kind, and improved fruit trees were unknown. A few apple trees were grafted by the farmers themselves, such as the Milum Apple. Most of the apples grown were for home use, and were used for eating, or for vinegar and apple brandy. Today there are more than two hundred thousand improved trees in Madison. These improved trees were introduced into the county just after the Civil War and apples began to be exported about 1900. Today thousands of barrels are exported. The leading varieties are, Milums, Winesaps, Bonams, Yorks, Ben Davis, Pippins, and Black Twigs. There are many varieties of smaller fruit in the county, but very little is sold. Madison has many possibilities as a fruit growing region.

In 1850, potatoes were not raised to be exported; at present many are shipped.

Tobacco was raised in great quantities before the Civil War. Since that time its culture has gradually decreased until today there is very little raised.

In recent years many other articles have been exported which bring in large dividends, such as dairy products and vegetables.

The things named above about cover the main products of farmers in Madison. It may be said in conclusion that most of the crops have increased, and that market conditions have improved since the Civil War. Still there are many phases of agriculture in Madison that are undeveloped. Among these are the fruit industry, the yield of crops per acre, and better market conditions, etc.

With the great change in the size of farms, in the amount of produce raised and in the increase in price and better market conditions, there has also been a change in the problem of producing these products and in the living condition of the farmer.

---

[1] Annual Report of the Commonwealth of Virginia. Volumes 1875-1920.

One great problem that confronts the farmer in Madison county is that of labor. Before 1850, slaves did the work, but after the Civil War, the negro slaves remained in the county and were hired by their former masters. Today laborers enough cannot be secured to develop the farms to their maximum capacity. The question is not always the price of the labor, but the impossibility of securing it. The laborers, both white and colored, have left the county to secure positions in the city, where working hours are shorter and wages better; the farmer cannot compete with these wages and working hours.

Another problem is in regard to farm equipment. In the first seventy years of the nineteenth century farm equipment did not cost as much as it does at present by many hundred per cent. Labor-saving farm machinery adds to the output of products and decreases the cost of labor, but greatly increases the cost of equipment. Before the Civil War there was a very small sum spent on farm equipment. In the first place, there were very few labor-saving devices; and in the second place, practically all farm implements were made in the shops by the slaves. Labor was cheap and plentiful; consequently, there was no great need for labor saving devices; today conditions are changed. Labor is scarce and farm machinery is a necessity.

The modern farmer spends more not only on his farm equipment but more also on the improvement of the soil. He does this of necessity, for soil that has been under cultivation for a long time requires more care than virgin soil. In the nineteenth century there was little guano or fertilizer sown. Plaster was sown but this was not as costly as modern guano.

We have now compared the price and value of farm produce and have found that the value of produce in Madison far exceeds in value any former period. Let us now compare what the farmer has to buy. This is the only way to secure a balanced sheet on the economic order of the county.

In the early history of the county the court set standard prices for town keepers and they were not allowed to exceed this price. Records show that Madison made several such provisions before 1800, but after that time the custom was discontinued. This was an old custom passed on to Madison by other counties, for there is such a record in Orange county, dated 1735.[1] Let us compare this with two from Madison dated 1793 and 1796. These records were originally made with reference to English money, but translated into our currency they would be as follows:[2]

---

[1] Scott, W. W., History of Orange County, Virginia. Page 150.
[2] Court Order Books of Madison County.

|  | 1735 | 1793 | 1796 |
|---|---|---|---|
| Rum, per gallon | $1.33 | $1.50 | $2.50 |
| Whiskey, per gallon |  | 1.25 | 1.25 |
| Hot meal of victuals | .16 2/3 | .21 | .33 1/3 |
| Cold meal of victuals | .08 1/3 | .12½ | .21 |
| Lodging with clean sheets | .08 1/3 | .08 1/3 | .12½ |
| Brandy, per gallon | 1.00 | 1.25 |  |
| Cider, per gallon |  | .16 2/3 | .21 |
| Stabling of hay 24 hrs. |  | .16 2/3 | .33 1/3 |
| Stabling of hay 12 hrs. |  | .12½ | .16 2/3 |
| Gallon of corn |  | .10½ | .12½ |
| Gallon of oats |  | .10½ | .12½ |
| Common wine, per gallon |  | .33 1/3 | .41½ |

It is easy to see the changes that have taken place. Things were much cheaper then than now, and the purchasing power of a dollar was much greater.

We will go still further and trace the price of other things prior to the Civil War. Farm wagons were not used as much then as they are now. Most farmers possessed one, but for plantation use slides were used and the wagons were kept to make trips to market. All of the wagons were made in local shops and were very inferior to the grade of wagons used today. The bodies were the old-fashioned crooked style and were very heavy. Strange to say, inferior as these wagons were in comparison to the modern ones, they cost about the same. In 1850 a good wagon and body cost $150.00. The change that has taken place is, that the wagon has taken the place of the slide for plantation use, and the truck has taken the place of the wagon for marketing.

The plows used about the time Madison county was formed were chiefly wooden, or perhaps wooden with a very crude iron point. These plows were replaced by the McCormick, which was very little better than the old fashioned wooden plow. Just before the Civil War, the Livingston plow, which cost about six dollars, was used. Then after the war came the Oliver Chilled plow, which now costs about $20.00. The next step in the history of plows is just beginning.

Before the Civil War all of the corn cultivators were made at home. The Rube Milton cultivators seem to have been the most famous in the northern part of the county. These cultivators were made by Mr. Rube Milton who had his shop at Criglersville. Today the cultivators are made in northern factories and cost only about one-third as much, but are considered very inferior by the farmers.

All pitchforks and hoes were made in local shops until about 1870. The forks at that time only had two prongs and were very inferior to those of today. The two-pronged fork cost about fifty cents, while now a four-pronged fork costs about a dollar and a half.

Hoes, like the forks, were all shop made and were very heavy. Most hoes are bought now and are factory made, at about the same cost of the old shop-made hoe.

Until about 1870 all the horseshoes and nails were made in the local shops. These shoes did not look as nice as the modern horse shoe, yet they usually lasted longer. When the shoes were made in the local shops, one dollar was the usual price for shoeing a horse. Today one-fifty is the usual price.

There were no binders used in the county until the extreme latter part of the nineteenth century. All the wheat was cut with a cradle and bound by hand. The cradle came into use about 1800; before this time all of the wheat had been cut with a reaping hook.

Until about 1800 wheat was either flailed out, or was placed on a large floor or a clean place on the ground, and horses were driven over it to tread it out. This latter place was known as a "tread floor." There is a tradition that on the exact spot where Mr. R. E. Weaver's house stands was situated one of these old "treading floors." The next step in threshing grain was the use of the old "pepper box machine," which came into use about the same time as the wheat cradle. These machines consisted of only a cylinder for flailing the grain from the straw. After this the grain had to be separated from the chaff and fanned by hand. These "pepper box" machines were run by horse power. A little later a fanning and sifting apparatus was added which made them almost equal to a modern threshing machine, though for a while they were still run by horse power. A few years later came the steam engine which took the place of the horse, but horses were still used to take the equipment from one yard to another, as all of the engines were stationary. Next came the traction engine and later the tractor.

The farmers cut all of their hay with a scythe and raked it with a fork or hand rake until about 1870. At this time mowers came into use, but of course they were not as good as they are today. When hay was cut with the scythe the farmers could not have as many acres under cultivation, but with the advent of the mower came a far greater acreage of hay.

All the early houses built in Madison county in colonial days, were made of hewn logs, usually forest pine, and were covered with shingles. This style was necessary because there were no saw mills at that time. Saw mills came at a much later date, but the first ones used in the county were very different from those used today. In the first place there were no steam engines; water power was used for everything and, consequently, the first saw mills were run by water power. The first saws were "up and down" saws, and therefore, the work done with them was very slow and expensive. The circular saw and engine was not used much before 1875. These conditions have always made the cost of houses very high. At first there was plenty of timber but no means of getting this timber prepared for houses. Today there is less timber, but better facilities for building purposes.

Modern houses are better furnished than those of olden times. Until about 1860 there were very few cook stoves, all the cooking being done by the open fireplace. Cast iron stoves then came into use, but no one owned a range until about 1900. Today most houses are equipped with steel ranges.

Prior to 1875 all furniture was made in local shops and was not usually sold in sets as it is today. Furniture in those days was usually made of walnut in a very unique style. The beds were all corded, and mattresses were unknown, but most every one owned several feather beds. The carpets were practically all made of rags woven on looms. There were no lamps; candles made at home were used altogether. The candle-sticks were imported. In some homes the means of lighting was lightwood torches and the well known "betty lamps." Homes contained very few books, except the Bible, hymn books, and, perhaps, a few other religious books. There were very few pictures of any kind in any of the homes. The houses were heated entirely by fire-places.

Very little food was imported, for nearly everything was prepared at home. Sugar was bought in loaf form very sparingly. Very little preserves were made, but cake or some sweet desserts were made. No canned goods was bought, nor were there any glass jars in which to can food at home. Most things which are canned today were dried in olden times. The only food products bought were sugar, coffee, tea, spices, soda, salt, and things of similar nature. Thus, things purchased for the table cost very much less than they do today.

Very little was spent for pleasure until recent times. At present, there are many predictions as to the future because of the great desire for pleasure. In this chapter we are not concerned with the moral side of the problem, but with the financial side. It is safe to say, when everything is taken into consideration, that Madison county has been benefited by this desire. The prediction of some that the automobile will bring the county to financial ruin is right in one respect. When a man's home is placed in jeopardy to secure an automobile, for pleasure, or when the natural resources of the county are taken away and not replaced for a similar purpose, evil will result. Those who argue in favor of the automobile are right in this respect, that when people buy automobiles, or anything, that may be called the luxuries of life there must be some way to pay for these. Thus, it makes people more industrious and they strive harder to earn money with which to buy what they want. Thus a condition is created which makes a community more progressive, and makes people strive to accomplish something rather than be content to loaf. One must be dissatisfied with his present state in order to be progressive;

the automobile appeals to more people than does education, culture or other things of similar nature.

This is really an age of luxury, but it is also an age of advancement. All the financial figures of the county show progress except in one thing; that is in timber. Madison is not rich in ore or other natural resources, but it has been rich in lumber. Every year thousands of feet of lumber are being exported and there is no effort made to replace this deficit. No one knows how the money obtained from this lumber is being spent. An economist would tell us that if it is being spent in things that produce a lasting benefit, such as roads and schools, the financial status of the county is not hurt, but benefited; however, on the other hand, if the money received from the lumber is being spent in frivolous pleasure or in something of only a moment's duration, then the county is being harmed greatly. This economic law is more applicable to lumber in Madison county than anything else, though it is true of all things.

In studying the financial status of a county definite conclusions are hard to make and only comparative ones can be made. It takes no great philosopher to find this to be true. Talk with a few men and you will find it so. Some will be optimistic; some, pessimistic; and some will take a middle view. One of the chief complaints heard in Madison today is against high taxes. This complaint is justifiable. From year to year the county has increased in wealth, but taxes have increased much faster than the wealth.

| Year | Value of Real Estate | Value of Horses | Value of Cattle | Value of Sheep | Value of Hogs |
|---|---|---|---|---|---|
| 1875① | $1,893,049.00 | $112,625.00 | $ 60,816.00 | $ 9,159.00 | $17,844.00 |
| 1911 | $1,778,002.00 | $146,421.00 | $116,314.00 | $ 9,657.00 | $10,495.00 |
| 1912 | $1,786,442.00 | $152,629.00 | $111,573.00 | $ 9,525.00 | $10,940.00 |
| 1913 | $1,804,574.00 | $167,912.00 | $131,662.00 | $ 9,145.00 | $12,752.00 |
| 1914 | $1,827,194.00 | $174,097.00 | $154,755.00 | $ 9,079.00 | $13,562.00 |
| 1915 | $1,924,475.00 | $161,515.00 | $168,845.00 | $ 8,117.00 | $11,077.00 |
| 1916 | $1,927,514.00 | $163,172.00 | $169,777.00 | $ 7,128.00 | $14,772.00 |
| 1917 | $1,922,026.00 | $163,580.00 | $188,700.00 | $ 8,455.00 | $19,330.00 |
| 1918 | $1,943,819.00 | $168,140.00 | $216,020.00 | $13,101.00 | $24,105.00 |
| 1919 | $1,966,621.00 | $163,090.00 | $252,550.00 | $14,285.00 | $30,380.00 |
| 1920 | $1,990,993.00 | $166,580.00 | $276,250.00 | $13,455.00 | $29,035.00 |

① The above figures are taken from the Annual Report of the Commonwealth of Virginia, the years named.

# CHAPTER X

## SOCIAL CUSTOMS OF YESTERDAY

Like all other things, social customs and living conditions change as time moves on. Progress creates a new environment, and, consequently, new customs. We so often hear older people speak of what they call, "those good old days when they were children;" and it is to be supposed that the present generation will do the same, when they grow old and a new generation takes their place; for, in every generation, changes come in every field of activity, and cause the older generations to become skeptical of the new. Considering the changes that occur from an ethical and social standpoint, it is to be supposed that some conditions and customs are made better and some made worse. The question then arises: Why consider past customs? The answer is: Because they furnish food for thought, by teaching us what past conditions were, which will enable us to summarize our own conclusion, as to which are the "good old days."[1]

Madison may be said to have had three distinct, yet overlapping epochs in social customs and living conditions. First, the Colonial Period, when men wore knee trousers and powdered wigs; ettiquette then was very stiff and modeled after that of the mother countries of Europe. This period was very brief in Madison county, for the Piedmont sections of Virginia were not settled until this epoch was almost past. The second period was more distinctly American and was better adapted to American ideals and environment. This was the period of the early nineteenth century and the one in which we are interested. In the beginning of it, we find Madison, in its infancy as a county, and, also, in its material development. Its people still possessed some of the qualities and characteristics of former pioneer days spent in the new forest. The pioneers, who came to Madison were not descended from nobility; they were, however, sturdy, brave, and noble-hearted people. Their wealth was not estimated by the currency they possessed, but by the noble lives they lived; consequently, in the early nineteenth century there was much less social distinction along the lines of wealth than there is at present. Although some possessed more wealth than others, all lived alike; they led a simple life, yet it appears to have been a happy one.

First let us consider the means of transportation in the early part of the nineteenth century, or from 1800 to 1860. In this period very few, if any, families in Madison owned a carriage or a buggy.

---

[1] All information in this chapter was obtained from old people who drew from their memory.

All travel was on horseback or on foot. It was customary for the boys to take their sweethearts on horse back behind them to parties or dances or other social functions in which the young people participated. This was also the custom when going to church, the men taking the women behind them. However, if there were horses enough, the ladies rode alone; but, they always rode on side-saddles and wore long riding skirts; one who rode astride was not considered a lady. Horses were valued very highly and all who could afford it, kept very fine ones. Horses seemed to have been the standard of wealth; for a man's wealth was judged by his team or the quality of the horse he rode. Everyone took notice of their neighbors' horses, and everyone could recognize the rider's horse at a distance before they could recognize the rider. Strange as it may seem, distance by this mode of travel was insignificant; people would go for miles to various social functions, covering distances which seem impossible to us today.

Many people did not even possess horses; much walking was done by these and also by those who did own horses. It is reported that in the year during which General Washington and his army camped at Valley Forge, the people near Criglersville and Syria walked to preaching at the Ragged Mountain Church, a distance of ten or twelve miles. They would often carry their shoes in their hands and put them on when they came near the church. They did this to save leather, for shoes were very high and all the leather that could be obtained was needed for the army.

Madisonians would go for miles to visit. The visit was usually made on Sunday; the visitors would spend the day and take both dinner and supper. The housewives competed with each other as to which could prepare the most elaborate meal, or as they would say "put on the greatest spread," for their visitors. Their dinner (the meal at noon) was the most elaborate. This meal was not judged so much by its rare, fine delicacies, for very few imported articles could be obtained; it was judged by the quantity of the so called "spread." Meals were not prepared on ranges but by open fires, for at that time very few owned cook stoves. Even the famous pound cake, so well known to Madisonians, was baked in an open fire; likewise, the corn bread or the old "ash cake" was cooked in the ashes on the hearth. Every kitchen was equipped with a large open fireplace with hooks built in the chimneys and kettles placed over the fire. Some of the oldest houses in Madison still have these old fireplaces, which are relics of by-gone days. The principal part of the cooking was done by slave women.

Not all visiting was done in the day, for there was a very common custom of going to a neighbor's house to "sit until bedtime." All the family, from the youngest to the oldest would go, usually on foot to a near neighbor's house and here spend the evening hours. They would all gather around the open fire and chatter about the happenings in the community, the prospects of the growing crops, and other things of local interest. During the conversations, Milum apples, chestnuts, and other things were served as refreshments. This visit usually lasted from about twilight until the visitors became sleepy.

Clothing and styles were different from those of the present day. The principal part of clothing was home-made. Unlike today, almost every farmer in Madison raised a little cotton for home use. This cotton was spun upon the old familiar spinning wheel by the housewives and made into cloth. Woolen goods were also made at home. Each farmer kept a few sheep to be used for food and to produce wool for clothing. Wool, as soon as it was sheared from the sheep, was carried to a mill where it was carded and combed out; then like cotton, it was spun into cloth at home. Linen goods were made at home. Flax was raised for this purpose and woven into bed linen, table linen and sometimes into men's shirts. Of course, this linen was very coarse and was not bleached as white as the linen bought today. Hemp was raised and made into rope and very coarse clothing. Sewing was done chiefly by hand, and strange to say, there were more tailors than at present. At one time, there were seven tailor-shops in the little village of Madison. Silk was the chief cloth imported into the county, and almost every woman had one silk dress in her possession; this she kept in store for special occasions. Most women wore calico dresses to church and to the usual social functions.

Until near the time of the Civil War, all dresses were made with hoop skirts, but after the war this style disappeared entirely. Ladies over forty years of age wore sun bonnets to church. Some of these bonnets were made of silk; some of straw, and some of calico; but all of them were made at home; there were no millinery shops, nor were there any hats imported. The name "shaker" was usually applied to the bonnets made of straw. Poke bonnets came into vogue a little later and both girls and older women wore these. Sometimes the older ladies wore very elaborate lace caps under these bonnets, but usually they were only worn by married ladies. Jewelry was very much used and a lady's costume was considered incomplete without a large breast pin; the most usual one was a cameo. Rings and bracelets were worn, but they were plainly designed and not very expensive. Almost every girl had her ears pierced when a small child, so that she might wear ear rings when she grew older.

The styles for men have not changed quite so much. The men wore long pigeon-tailed coats, usually black. Their trousers were very much as they are today. The material, out of which these suits were made, was called broadcloth and was an all-wool material. Shirts were made very much as they are today, white being the predominant color. The so called "stock-collars" were worn with these shirts. They were called "stock collars" because they were braced very substantially and stood up very high under the chin.

DAYS OF YESTERDAY

Tradition has left us several instances in which wooden collars made of hickory were worn. There was no standard material out of which the "stock collars" were made, nor was there any standard color used; however, most of them were made of satin, and were usually black.

The shoes of both men and women were made at home. The farmer took his cow-hides to the tannery, where they were tanned on shares. He then took his part of the leather to the shoe-maker, who made shoes for the entire family.

We will now turn to some of the social functions proper. Weddings were very elaborate home affairs, and lasted for about two days' time. The marriage ceremony was usually performed in the home of the bride; it was also very elaborate, but the ring ceremony had not yet come into vogue. The prospective bride and groom usually selected six boys and six girls from among their friends to act as "waiters" in the ceremony. These waiters were in attendance upon the bride and groom while the preacher performed the matrimonial tie. The bride's trousseau usually consisted of two dresses; one, made of white material, was to be worn on the wedding day; the other was to be worn on the second day. All the friends and relatives of the bride and groom were invited to the wedding. The first day was spent in the home of the bride, where a great many things had been prepared to eat and a great feast was held. The next day all the wedding guests were taken to the home of the groom where another feast was held, which was called an "infare." These two days completed the wedding, as a bridal tour was seldom made.

The principal social functions for the younger people were dances and parties. Practically all the dances were held in private homes, for public dances were very little attended. All of the dancing was the old fashioned square dance, and should there be any round dancing, boys danced with boys and girls with girls. Large crowds attended these dances, going for many miles on horseback or on foot. The crowd would begin to gather in the latter part of the afternoon and continue to grow until after dark. Supper was always served by the host or hostess and the dancing would not begin until everyone had eaten and the tables had been cleared. The fiddlers would then tune up and the dance would begin. The music was usually made by colored slaves and some strong-voiced man would call the figures. Many of the pieces they played are still remembered in Madison, such as "Arkansas Traveller," "Mississippi Sawyer," "Whistling Rufus," "Susanna," and others. Thus the dance would continue until after the toll of midnight and would be closed by the dancing of the "Old Virginia Reel."

The parties were more common than dances, as almost every family of young people gave parties. At that time church discipline was strict in regard to dancing and those young people, who were members of some church, did not usually participate in dancing; however, both church members and non-church members attended parties. The supper and other preparations were about the same for parties as for dances. At the parties, the evening was spent in playing games; usually games that required singing, such as "The Farmer's in the Dell," "Go Round and Round the Valley," "Good Night," "Wink," and "Stealing Partners."

Girls were more strictly chaperoned than they are today. Likewise, more attention was given to the boys than is given them today; they were made to choose their companions with more care and to use more discretion in sowing their "wild oats."

The young people also attended singing schools. Some person in the community, who could read music, would establish a class, and most of the girls and boys of that neighborhood would attend. The singing school was considered by the younger generation a great institution, as it furnished a means of recreation which produced both fun and profit. Every one enjoyed these gatherings, which were usually held on Saturday afternoon, and in most cases good vocal training was given.

There were many games which were enjoyed by young and old. Baseball was unknown, but its fore-runner, town-ball, which was played by young and old alike, held its place. Large crowds gathered to see a game of town-ball very much as we go to see a baseball game now. The men and boys would all play horseshoes. Each community had its champion, and it was considered a great honor to be skilled in pitching. Girls and boys enjoyed croquet and nearly every family possessed a croquet set. This may really be called the fore-runner of tennis, for at present, tennis has taken its place. In summer the young people would gather in the afternoon and play croquet until night-fall.

For the girls and boys of school age, the day that school closed in the spring was the greatest day of the year. Most of the people in the community, both male and female, came to the little log school house on that day. The girls and older women would be entertained by recitations prepared by the pupils for the occasion; the girls would usually recite poetry or give a one-act play, while the boys delivered orations in the old fashioned manner of "stump speaking." The larger boys and men would amuse themselves by a game of town-ball; one school would compete against another, or perhaps the older men in the community would play against the school boys. When the ball game and speech-making were done, the teacher served the crowd with lemonade, and the day was over. The girls went home happy, but many of the boys were heavy-hearted, thinking that corn-thinning time was drawing nigh.

There were some events much enjoyed by the men, in which the women participated in the work, but not in the pleasure, such as corn shucking, shooting matches, and threshing wheat.

Corn-huskings, better known as corn-shuckings, were looked forward to with great eagerness by men, both white and colored.

Each farmer broke his corn off the stalk in the husk and piled it up in a large pile; then he would invite his neighbors to help him one day to husk it. The crowd would begin to gather early in the morning; some coming five or six miles. It was a great day of festivity for them all. The owner of the corn would furnish plenty of apple-brandy and the housewife would cook a very elaborate meal. All the huskers would gather around the pile of corn and the colored men would sing their familiar "corn-shucking songs," such as "I Had An Old Hen," and "Ain't You Gwine." Then once in a while, these colored men would take the owner of the corn on their shoulders and march around the corn, singing as they went. Every one was eager to husk a red ear, for this was a token that it was again time to pass around the bottle. Strange to say, few drank enough to become drunk. Every one would stay until all the corn was shucked, even if it were late at night.

Wheat-threshing time was very similar to corn-husking time. The process of threshing was very slow in those days, as machines were very inferior; therefore, farmers helped each other and made it a time of great festivity. Like the corn-husking, all the neighbors would gather and go from house to house, until this task was finished. Very much the same customs were practiced at butchering time.

Shooting matches and tournaments became customary just after the Civil War. We have tournaments at the present time, and they need no discussion, but shooting matches have entirely disappeared. Shooting matches were usually held on Saturday afternoon and prizes were offered to the best marksman. The prize was a turkey or something of that nature. The participants in these matches would pay a small sum for the privilege of trying for the prize.

In the entire history of the county, men have enjoyed attending the county court each month. It was the court in March which was considered the main one of the year. At each court the leading citizens of the county would meet together and discuss topics of interest; thus, court days furnished a time for all the citizens to mingle together and get acquainted. The largest crowd assembled the fourth Thursday in March; this custom is still observed although the crowds are smaller now than they were in the past.

In the past, the ladies had some social events in which the men did not participate, such as quilting and rug-making contests. One lady in the community would have a quilting contest or a rug-making contest, into which all of her friends entered. By this means the housewife secured many beautiful quilts and rugs.

Madison has always been famous for its hospitality, as, in fact, all the South has been. Madison has always prided herself on the friendliness of its people. Madisonians have always shown great kindness to those who visit their homes. They really practice the proverb which says the "latch string is on the outside."

We may draw from the above many conclusions as to the changes which have taken place in the last few generations. The third period in the development of social customs and the mode of life, is the modern, which needs no discussion. As time produces changes, it is to be hoped that the changes will ever be for the better and for the advancement of the county and its citizens.

## CHAPTER XI

### THE PRESENT (1900-1925)

Madison county now has a population of 10,055 contented and prosperous people in contrast to the 8,322 who were there in 1800, one hundred and twenty-five years ago. The population is not increasing at any appreciable rate, but progress is being made in other ways.

Since 1900 the county has made more progress than it ever has done before in its history for the same length of time. This progress has been along the lines of better agricultural methods, better educational opportunities, better religious and charitable work, better roads, and many other things besides.

There are few farms now that are not equipped with the best agricultural implements. Binders were very scarce in the county in 1900, and now wheat cradles are as scarce as binders were then. Mowers and horse rakes have been in use for some time; in the last few years their use has greatly increased. Wagons are being replaced by trucks; buggies by automobiles; steam engines by tractors; and various other changes are being made, all of which lighten the labor of the farmer and bring him more profit. Tractors, trucks, automobiles, self-feeding threshing machines, electric light plants, radios, cream separators, victrolas, telephones, hay forks and many small devices for saving labor and causing pleasure have come into use in Madison county in the past twenty-five years. These labor-saving devices have served two purposes. They have lightened the burdens of labor and at the same time have produced greater profit to the citizen.

The farmers have also made rapid strides in the methods of agriculture in the last twenty-five years. They have, in general, improved the soil by a more extensive use of fertilizers, legumes and proper crop rotation. Farm demonstration has been introduced and the farmers are beginning to see the necessity of this work. The farm demonstration agent is slowly introducing things that will prove valuable to the farmers. So far, his work has been mainly confined to stock breeding, to creating interest in better agricultural methods, and to securing co-operation in their use among the farmers. Corn clubs, pig clubs, canning clubs, and other organizations of this nature have been started and have proven a success. They have taught the farmers that farming is a real science and that greater possibilities are open to them in the future. The first farm demonstration agent was Mr. A. W. Yowell. He succeeded in organizing various clubs which for several years proved successful. He was also successful in beginning a county agricultural fair and in having a Madison county booth at the State Fair. Then for several years the county did not have a farm demonstration agent. However, the movement had begun and only time was required to prove that this work was beneficial and necessary. The farm demonstration work was begun again in 1924 and is now being conducted by Mr. Browning, who is doing excellent work in introducing better bred stock, as well as in creating interest in agricultural methods.

Along with farm demonstration came home demonstration work. This work was begun by Miss Chappel, who rendered excellent service to the housewives, and trained the girls to become better home-makers. Various clubs were organized among the girls and demonstrations were given to the older women, all of which proved successful. Some opposition arose to home demonstration work in 1924, but the issue seems not to have been directed against the work itself; it was used as a means of expressing public opinion against higher taxes. The work, however, continued and is now being conducted by Miss Mary Lippard, who is making excellent progress.

Improvement in methods of agriculture has given more leisure time to the farmers, and the new inventions are making his life more pleasant. Victrolas are now found in most homes in the county. Most of the people are not able to make trips to large cities to hear great musicians and singers, but they are becoming acquainted with a great deal of the best music through the Victrola. Many homes are brought still closer to metropolitan life by the use of the radio. This new device appeared in the county in 1923. Magazine and newspaper reading has greatly increased in the last few years, until at present most of the best magazines are found in the homes of Madison county. Mr. T. T. Mitchell has been conducting a theatre at Madison Court House for several years and this has been fairly well patronized by the people of the county. All of these things show that the life of the people is being revolutionized. We are coming into closer contact with the outside world. Our pleasures are being expanded and our knowledge is being broadened.

One of the outstanding changes that has been made in Madison county during the last few years has been in education. The citizens have taken new interest in this work. At present a large per cent of the boys and girls attend college, universities and schools above the high school. Madison is well represented in the colleges and universities of the state, as well as in many out of the state. Boys and girls are entering all vocations and professions. Not only are the people of Madison sending their sons and daughters to institutions of higher learning, but they are taking more interest in local schools. Schools have been consolidated, and high schools established. There is one accredited high school in the county, the Madison High School, and one other, the Criglersville High School is expecting to be accredited in 1926. There are other schools which give high school work and excellent grade work. All who desire a public school education now have the opportunity of obtaining it. Several schools are being conducted for the people in the Blue Ridge. The Ferrum School under the direction of the Methodist Church is the most prominent one. The most outstanding feature in educational development is the interest of the patrons of the various schools. Each community is boasting of its school; patrons' leagues are being formed; rally days are being held; all of this furnishes a standard by which to judge the prosperity of the future. Education fosters citizenship and prosperity, and it is to be hoped that the educational movement in Madison will continue to grow, for educated people are an advantage to any community.

Religious work is improving in Madison in many ways. Most of the churches have good Sunday Schools and good church attendance. The first county Sunday School Convention was held in 1913. All the churches in the county enter into this convention, regardless of denomination. This proves that there is a tendency in the county toward united work in the fields of religion. Most of the churches have been giving liberally to missions, both home and foreign, and charitable work of all kinds has been well cared for. The religious life of any community is in the hearts of the people, and Madison may well be proud of so many strong and noble-hearted Christian people. It has been rightly said that one of the things by which any nation may be judged is its religious life. History bears out this on all of its pages. Although progress is being made in most of the churches, it would be unfair to be partial and not to look on the other side. The forces of sin are making great progress. Citizens! Let us think. The forces of sin destroy our souls, our bodies, our minds and our nation. Did we fight Germany for might or for right? If we fought for right and then, by our lives, show that we do not believe in right, what are we? When we disregard the laws of our land as we sometimes do the prohibition laws, when we disregard the laws of God, when we disregard the laws of nature, when we disregard duty and follow the ways of selfishness, greed, frivolity and foolishness, whither are we headed? We are making progress in many fields of activity, but there is a question as to our moral welfare and to our power to think. We are better educated and have more churches, but are we better and do we think straighter?

The people of Madison are only beginning to realize the natural beauty of their county and its adaptibility to summer resorts. The altitude ranges from five hundred to three thousand five hundred feet and the climate is cool and healthful. The hillsides abound with thousands of springs which bubble with clear, cool, freestone water. The scenery in the Blue Ridge is wonderful, with its peaks, crags, gorges and other wonders of nature. There are possibilities of many delightful summer resorts, but at present only two have been built. *Skyland*, which was begun a few years ago, is a very modern resort

Madison At Present

with all conveniences and is situated on the summit of the Blue Ridge. *Honeymoon Hut* near Franklin's Cliff was built by Mr. Irvine Graves a few years ago, but has never developed into a real summer resort. At present the National government is contemplating establishing a national park which will include the principal part of the Blue Ridge in Madison county.

Industrial development has been gradual in the last twenty-five years. Madison is a rural community, and practically all of its development has been in agriculture, but there are a few industries that are being developed. Several furniture and chicken coop factories are doing thriving business, and at present a large power plant is being installed on the Robinson River. The capital of this company will be $100,000 subscribed by the citizens of the county. This will be the first large stock company in Madison.

There are two banks in the county, one at Wolftown and one at Madison. The one at Wolftown started only a few years ago; consequently, it has not had time to develop fully. The one at Madison is strong and is now doing excellent business.

The chief problem in the county since the World War has been the problem of labor. Labor cannot be secured regardless of the price paid. The young people, both white and colored, are leaving the farm for the city where they can secure better wages and shorter hours, while at the same time they can satisfy their longing to see various parts of the country. This problem is being met to some extent by better farm machinery and more scientific farming. This only partially solves it and the farmers are raising only a small percentage of what they could raise if they had plenty of labor. This condition carries with it many other problems. Farms cannot be cared for as well as when plenty of labor is available, but taxes and interest on the investments in farms are as high as if they were being run to their maximum capacity. All of this creates, to a certain extent, a farm depression.

During the World War food stuff was high, and this was a period of great prosperity for the farmers. Real estate went to heights unknown in the history of the county. Many farmers bought land while this period of prosperity was at its height, thinking that prices would remain where they were; when the war ended and prices went down, naturally, there followed a period of depression. This period of depression began to be felt in the county in 1920-21 and is still being felt very keenly. Wheat, cattle and other farm products dropped in price in one year. Many cattle dealers were forced into bankruptcy by buying cattle a year before they were to be delivered. The fall in prices of farm produce did not greatly affect the expenses of the farmers as their mortgages, taxes, labor and living expenses remained somewhat the same. Some went into bankruptcy while others were saved from this by a loan from the Federal Government.

This is the present condition: real estate is low, the cattle market is dull, and the farmers are really passing through a period of very great depression.

The parcel post system begun in 1912 has been of great benefit to the farmers of Madison. Much light weight farm produce is now shipped directly to the consumer in this way. Not only is the farmer able to ship his produce direct to the consumer, but he is able to buy directly from the manufacturer. Thus the parcel post system has served two purposes in relieving the burdens of the farmer.

Periods of depression are never absolute; that is, everything does not pass through a period of depression at the same time. While cattle have been very low since 1920, dairy products have been high, and the farmers are slowly relieving the depression by changing from beef production to the production of dairy products. Likewise sheep and poultry have remained high; thus the farmers are gradually lifting the depression by changing their products.

A great change in market conditions has been taking place since 1915. With the introduction of the automobile and truck, there has arisen a need for better roads, and people are beginning to realize this. In 1920 a vote was taken on a $263,000 bond issue, and was carried by the citizens of the county. This was the real starting point of a good road movement. The people, each day, realize more and more the importance of better roads. The improved roads and the use of the truck have greatly increased the amount of products placed on the market. Produce is now being shipped, that before could not be, because of the cost and trouble of getting it to the railroad. The people have almost given up the expectation of having a railroad; in fact, public opinion seems to be opposed to it. The citizens of the county contend that good roads and trucks are better for them than a railroad. Much enthusiasm has been displayed concerning the state road now under construction, which will span the county and form a main line for all other county roads.

Improved fruit began to appear in the county about 1900. Before this time practically all of the fruit trees were seedlings or had been grafted by the farmers themselves. After 1900 nursery trees began to take the place of home grafting. Many varieties of apples were introduced and many orchards were started. The long distance to market made the problem of shipping the apples a great task, and only a few of the very best were shipped. The others were hauled to the still-houses and made into apple brandy. When prohibition came into effect many people predicted that orchards would not be profitable. This prediction proved false, however, as about this time, roads were improved and trucks came into use. This made it possible to market apples that before this time it was impossible to market. Thus a necessity produced a remedy and orchards became more profitable than ever. At present more fruit of all kinds is being grown, but as yet only apples and peaches are being exported. There is a possibility, nevertheless, that in a few years the canning industry will take care of the other varieties of fruit.

There has been comparatively little crime in the county within the last few years, except in regard to liquor. Few murders have been committed and crimes of other nature have been few in number. Being a rural community, the county is free from a class of criminals who inhabit metropolitan districts. Then, too, the people are becoming educated to better order and less crime. At one time in the past, there was a good deal of fighting; now that is seldom seen; in fact, it is less than in most of our larger cities. The people of Madison are to be complimented on the peaceful conditions in which they live.

Our county is, so to speak, now standing on the eve of new endeavors, looking to greater achievements. That bright future must come, for we have the resources and the people.

## CHAPTER XII

### Miscellaneous Data

In gathering material for a history there are always some things that do not exactly fit into the main thread of the story. Many of these things are interesting and valuable in rendering a clear cut mental picture of the people studied. A good deal of such data has been collected in Madison county, some of which will be included in this chapter. Many of the earliest deeds to land in Madison county are recorded in the deed books of Culpeper county. The following is a partial list of such deeds and the date the patents were made.[1]

| | | | |
|---|---|---|---|
| George Anderson | 1732 | Robert Cave | 1749 |
| William Booton | 1749 | Michael Holt | 1726 |
| Michael Wilhite | 1728 | Jacob Barler | 1726 |
| Michael Clore | 1728 | John Clore | 1728 |
| Michael Cook | 1726 | Christopher Yowell | 1733 |
| Daniel Campbell | 1749 | Alexander Campbell | 1749 |
| Adam Garr | 1762 | Peter Flishman | 1728 |
| Zacharias Flishman | 1728 | John Weaver | 1762 |
| George Utz | 1762 | Nicholas Crigler | 1762 |
| John Powell | 1749 | John Frogg | 1749 |
| Michael Wallace | 1749 | Michael Kafer | 1726 |
| Nicholas Yager | 1726 | | |

Just before the Civil War large plantations were numerous in the South. Madison county did not have many plantations, but in 1851 there were seventeen farms that contained more than a thousand acres. These farms were as follows:

| | | | |
|---|---|---|---|
| Thomas Shirley | 48,933 acres | Thomas W. Chapman | 1,270 acres |
| William Twyman | 8,787 acres | George W. Clark | 1,309 acres |
| Milton Kirtley | 5,913 acres | German Glebe Lands | 1,200 acres |
| Alfred Utz | 2,497 acres | Richard Early | 1,780 acres |
| Michael Wallace | 2,392 acres | William Early | 1,780 acres |
| Robert A. Banks | 2,652 acres | James Walker | 1,624 acres |
| Lynn Banks | 2,239 acres | John Harrison | 1,591 acres |
| Merry Aylor | 1,258 acres | Anthony Twyman | 1,235 acres |
| Richard C. Booton | 1,630 acres | | |

One of the most famous men that Madison county has ever produced was James L. Kemper. His ancestry and achievements were somewhat as follows:

---

[1] Deed Books of Culpeper County.

Johann Kemper of Oldenburg came to America in the colony of Germans who settled at Germana in 1714. In 1717 he married Alice Utterback and later moved into what is now Madison county. Their son, John Peter Kemper, married a daughter of Dr. Haeger in 1730. One of their descendants, James L. Kemper, commanded one brigade of Pickett's celebrated division in the battle of Gettysburg and was wounded in the heroic attack of the so called "Round Top," but recovered, and from 1873-1878 was governor of Virginia.[1]

The first records of the Hebron Lutheran Church were written in German. These records have been translated into English by students of German. The following list comprises the names of men spoken of in the treasurer's report of this church in 1733.[2]

| | | |
|---|---|---|
| Andrew Kerker | Christopher Uld | Michael Cook |
| Hans George Utz | Michael Smith | William Carpenter |
| Hans Zeuche | John Willers | Zarachus Flishman |
| Frederick Coppeller | John Hoffman | Michael Clore |
| George Shebley | Urban Tunner | Michael Wilhite |
| John Raussen | Richard Bordine | Richard Blanchenbucher |

From 1748 until 1792 Madison was a part of Culpeper; consequently, those who represented Culpeper in the Virginia Assembly also represented Madison. The list of representatives for this period of time was as follows:

1752-1754. John Spotswood and William Green.
1768. James Barbour, John Field and Thomas Slaughter.
1769-1775. Henry Pendleton and Henry Field.
1781. Henry Field and French Strother.

At various times the voters registration books have been gone over and changed. The correction for 1903 gave the precincts and the number of voters as follows:

| Precinct | White Voters | Colored Voters |
|---|---|---|
| Criglersville | 270 | 26 |
| Dulinsville | 165 | 14 |
| Graves Mill | 83 | 0 |
| Madison C. H. | 166 | 12 |
| Nethers | 109 | 1 |
| Oak Park | 246 | 53 |
| Rochelle | 179 | 24 |
| Wolftown | 118 | 3 |
| Total | 1336 | 133 |

Many years elapsed after the formation of the county before the number of justices was reduced. The following is a list of justices in 1826.

---

[1] Virginia Magazine of History and Biography.
[2] Ibid.

| | | |
|---|---|---|
| Thomas Graves | Michael Wallace | William Walker |
| John Walker | John Hume | Charles R. Gibbs |
| Robert Thomas | James Somerville, Jr. | John Fray |
| Daniel Field | Thomas Shirley | Henry Hill |
| William Booton | Richard C. Booton | James W. Walker |
| Robert Beale | Anthony Twyman | William Early, Jr. |
| William Mallory | William Finks | |

The population of Madison has undergone little change, considering the length of time the county has been formed. The population at various intervals was as follows:[1]

| | | | |
|---|---|---|---|
| 1790 | 22,105 | 1860 | 8,854 |
| (for Culpeper and Madison) | | 1870 | 8,670 |
| 1800 | 8,332 | 1880 | 10,545 |
| (Madison alone) | | 1840 | 8,107 |
| 1810 | 8,381 | 1850 | 9,331 |
| 1820 | 8,490 | 1890 | 10,225 |
| 1830 | 9,236 | 1910 | 10,055 |

Before the text books for the public schools were selected by a state committee, each county had its own committee. The committee for 1904 was as follows:

T. W. Nicol  G. W. Wayland
Dr. C. O. Simms  A. N. Finks
(Several others whose names cannot be deciphered.)

Until recent years each district in the county has had three school trustees. The list of trustees for 1884 was:

*Rapidan District*
J. E. Jackson, J. B. Willis and William Early

*Robinson District*
John J. Clore, Anthony Twyman and J. M. Graves

*Locust Dale District*
J. F. Collins, D. F. Crigler and Dr. G. A. Sommers

There have been in years past many more flour mills than at present. The mills running in 1870 were as follows:

| | | |
|---|---|---|
| Rapidan River | Robinson River | Conway River |
| Conway's Mill | Crigler's Mill | Anderson's Mill |
| Bank's Mill | Weaver's Mill | Booton's Mill |
| Simm's Mill | Reynold's Mill | |

It is interesting to note the changes which have taken place in family names since the formation of the county and how many are

---

[1] Hand Books of Virginia.

still the same. A fairly accurate list of the families represented in the county before 1800 were as follows:

Alcocke
Amburger
Aldridge
Anderson
Archer
Aylor
Back
Baker
Banks
Barbour
Barler
Barnes
Barnett
Beal
Bell
Berry
Bunger
Crisler
Davis
Debord
Deer
Delaney
Delph
Dickens
Duff
Duncan
Earley
Blankenbaker
Bledsoe
Bloodworth
Bohannon
Bomgardner
Booton
Breman
Birk
Bordine
Bradford
Bradley
Breedlove
Brooking
Brown
Broyles
Bullinger
Campbell
Crow
Christopher
Gays
Gibbs
Glassell
Graves
Grayson
Guger
Hans
Hansborough

Cave
Chapman
Christle
Clatterbuck
Clark
Clause
Canady
Carpenter
Clore
Cobler
Cock
Collins
Cooke
Coppeller
Corbin
Cowherd
Craig
Crigler
Justise
Kaiger
Kemper
Kerker
Kirtley
Klug
Lewis
Lillard
Lindsay
Eastham
Eddin
Emmons
Eve
Farmer
Fewell
Finnell
Fisher
Finks
Fleshman
Floyd
Fowles
Fox
Frogg
Fray
Fry
Graines
Garr
Garnett
Newman
Paulitz
Peacock
Petty
Porter
Powell
Pratt
Prentis

Harvey
Harrison
Haynes
Henderson
Henry
Hensley
Herrenberger
Hill
Hoffman
Holt
Holtzclaw
Hughes
Hume
Humfreys
Hunt
Ireland
Jarrell
Jenifer
Jessa
Johnson
Sheible
Shrine
Simms
Slaughter
Smith
Smoot
Snyder
Long
Loyd
Madison
Mayor
Mallory
Manspoil
Marshall
Marry
Maxfield
May
Mayer
Medley
Milum
Miller
Mitchell
Moffait
Morgan
Morris
Motz
Muter
Walker
Walle
Ward
Watson
Watt
Waugh
Wayland

| | | |
|---|---|---|
| Price | Stevens | Weedon |
| Quinn | Stoever | Welch |
| Ramsbottom | Stolts | Wetherall |
| Razor | Swindle | White |
| Rennolds | Taliaferro | Wilhite |
| Redman | Tanner | Willis |
| Richard | Taylor | Willers |
| Riddle | Thomas | Winston |
| Roebuck | Tinsley | Wirt |
| Rosson | Towles | Wood |
| Rouse | Twyman | Woodroof |
| Rush | Utz | Wright |
| Sampson | Underwood | Yager |
| Saunders | Vallick | Yancey |
| Shepherd | Vernon | Young |
| Shebley | Voss | Yowell |
| Shakelford | Wallace | Zachary |
| Ship | Wallis | Zeche |
| Sparks | Weaver | Zimmerman |
| Spauldin | Webb | |

The census returns of 1790 showed that the people of Culpeper county were of the following nationality:

English 20 per cent.
French 20 per cent.
Irish and Scotch-Irish 20 per cent.
German 20 per cent.
All other nationalities 20 per cent.

This was also true of that part of Culpeper now known as Madison, except that the percentage of Germans was a little higher.

The United States records give the names of fourteen men killed in the world war from Madison. Some have died since, due to injuries they received while in the army, but their names have not been recorded in the national reports. The fourteen given are as follows:

| | | |
|---|---|---|
| Acty, George W. | Jackson, Joe | Smith, Jesse |
| Allen, Johnny | Yowell, George | Tusing, Fred |
| Fray, Fernander | Jenkins, James | Utz, Robert |
| Funds, Andrew | Lightfoot, John | Tanner, Jesse |
| Hill, Somerfield | Slaughter, Joe | |

In colonial days all nationalities, other than English Protestants, were required to take out naturalization papers. The following is an example of German naturalization papers in Madison.

"Andrew Garr, John Adam Garr, Lawrence Garr, Lawrence Gays, Duvold Christle, Martin Vallick, John Zimmerman, Peter Flishman, Zachariah Blankenbeker, John Carpenter, John Thomas, Christopher Uhld, and Frederick Bomgardner, German Protestants, having procured a certificate under the hand of George Samuel Klug, minister of the German congregation in Orange county, that they within two months last past had received the sacrament of ye Lord's supper, prayed that they might partake of the benefits of an act of parliament made in the thirteenth year of the reign of our Sovereign Lord, George the Second, by the Grace of God of Great Britain, France and Ireland, King, defender of ye faith, etc., and instituted an act for the naturalizing of such foreign protestants and others therein mentioned as are settled or shall settle in any of his maties (sic) colonies in America. Upon their motion, ordered that they take the oath appointed by act of parliament to be taken instead of the oaths of allegiance and supremacy, and the abjuration oath and subscribe the test, which they all severally did, accordingly between the hours of nine and twelve in the forenoon, and it is thereupon further ordered, that ye clerk give them a certificate of their having taken the afd. oaths and subscribed the test."[1]

The same year another naturalization paper was taken out as the one above. It was as follows:[2]

"Courtney Broyle, Tobias Willite, Jacob Manspile, John Wilhite, and Jacob Miller, German protestants," etc., etc. (same as above).

The colony of Germans employed by Governor Spotswood sued him for wages and the outcome was their removal to Madison. This is an exact copy of the proceedings of their petition before the Colonial Council 1722-1734.[3]

"On reading at the Board of Petition of Zacharias Flishman (Fleshman) and George Ouds (Utz) on behalf of themselves and fourteen other high-Germans, now residing in Spotsylvania county near Germanna, complaining that Col. Spotswood hath unjustly sued them in the Court for the non-performance of a certain Agreement pretended to be made by them in consideration of money advanced them upon the transportation into this colony, although they have heretofore performed, and are always ready to perform any Agreement they made with the said Col. Spotswood; but though they have often applied to him for a Copy of the said Agreement they made with him, he hath refused to give them any such Copy and therefore praying this Board to commiserate their Condition as being Strangers and to make such order as they shall think proper to have the Agreement produced; the Governor with the advice of the Council is pleased to Order as it is hereby Ordered; That in regard to the petition, poor condition and ignorance of the Laws of this Colony, the person acting as Deputy Attorney for the King in the said County of Spotsylvania do appear for the Petitioners in the said suits brought against them in that court, that so the Petitioners may have the benefit of a fair tryal."

---

[1] Court Order Records of Orange County.
[2] Court Order Records of Orange County.
[3] Virginia Magazine of History and Biography.

The Masonic lodge is the oldest secret order in the county. The following is an exact copy of the report of this order in 1801, 1802, 1803, 1804.

Report to Grand Lodge of Virginia A. F. and A. M.
December 14th, 1801.
Madison Lodge Meets at Madison Court House, Virginia.
John Booker. M.
Leonard Barnes, Jr. S. W.
Churchill Gibbs. J. W.
Report December 15th, 1802.
Madison Lodge No. 64 A. F. and A. M.
Meets at Madison Court House the second Friday in every month.

Dr. John Booker. W. M.
Leonard Barnes. S. W.
Churchill Gibbs. J. W.
Benjamin Jennings. Secty.
John Walker. Treasurer.

George H. Allen. S. D.
William Strother. J. D.
John Wright. S.
Richard Booz. T.

M. M.'s. Henry Barnes, Reubin Fry, William Bledsoe, John Walker, David Jones, David Michie, George Eve, Richard Tutt, Isham B. Mason, John Field. E. A.'s Thomas Miller, James Meghan, John Powell, Robert G. Lane, Samuel Smith.

Report December 15th, 1803—Same officers. M. M's. William L. Mickie, Eliakim Colvert, John Gilpin, Joel Bennett, E. A. Thomas.

1804—Richard Tutt died after that Lodge reported "Domant."[6]

It is interesting to know how the various post offices in the county received their names. They received their names in the following way:

Achash—Named by the United States Post Office Department.
Aroda—Named by the United States Post Office Department.
Aylor—Named for the Aylor family.
Banco—Named by the United States Post Office Department.
Brightwood—Named by the United States Post Office Department.

This was formerly called Dulinsville for the Dulin Family, and before that it was called Fleshman's Shop, because of a shop owned by one named Fleshman.

Criglersville—Named for an early settler named Crigler who owned one of the first tanneries in the county. This tannery was situated just below the "Old Brick Church."

Duet—Named by the Post Office Department.
Elly—Named by the Post Office Department.
Etlan—Named by the Post Office Department.
Graves Mill—Named for a mill owned by the Graves family.

---

6. Original Record.

Haywood—Named by the Post Office Department.
Hood—Named for the Hood family.
Leon—Named by the Post Office Department. This was formerly called James City in honor of the James Family.
Locust Dale—Took its name from being situated in a grove of locust trees.
Madison—Named for the county.
Madison Mills—Named for the flour mill built there by the Madison family.
Nethers—Named in honor of the Nethers family.
Novum—Name taken from the Latin word (novum) meaning new.
Oak Park—Took its name from being situated in a grove of oak trees.
Oldrag—Took its name from the Old Rag Mountain.
Peola Mills—Name was derived from the flour mill situated there.
Radiant—Named by the Post Office Department.
Rochelle—Named from French name La Rochelle. This place was formerly called Jack's Shop because of a shopkeeper who lived there named Jack.
Ruth—Named for the daughter of the first postmaster, Mr. Wade Tanner.
Shelby—Named by the Post Office Department. This office was formerly called Glory.
Syria—Named by the Post Office Department.
Twyman's Mill—Named for the Twyman family.
Uno—Named by the Post Office Department.
Wolftown—It is not known how it received its name. This place was formerly called Rapid Ann, taking this name from the Baptist Church situated there.
Woodbury Forest—Took its name from the school of the same name.
Zeus—Name was given by a young lady.

The Robinson River Church is the third oldest Baptist church in Madison. The records of the other two have been destroyed, but fortunately the records of this church are still preserved. The family names that have been connected with this church since its beginning are as follows:

| | | |
|---|---|---|
| Rush | Thomas | Yager |
| Simms | Tucker | Yowell |
| Shultice | Utz | Apperson |
| Shotwell | Wayman | Aylor |
| Shirley | Walden | Bates |
| Smith | Wallace | Batten |
| Story | Weaver | Berry |
| Tanner | Wilhoit | Brown |

| | | |
|---|---|---|
| Broyles | Henshaw | Proctor |
| Britain | Henderson | Fletcher |
| Burke | Hutcherson | Fleshman |
| Covington | Hume | Fray |
| Crigler | Hurt | Garr |
| Crow | Carder | Hill |
| Deal | Carpenter | Jarrell |
| Dickens | Clore | Jenkins |
| Dulin | Colvin | Lauck |
| Dulaney | Leathers | Priest |
| Finks | Lillard | Pratt |
| Fishback | May | Racer |
| Garnett | Mason | Renolds |
| Good | Milton | Ritemour |
| Grimsley | McAlister | Rosson |
| Grayson | Miller | |

For the first few years after Madison was formed into a county most of the land deeds were transferred to the deed books of that county. A list of the deeds recorded in the county between 1792 and 1795 is as follows:

| Grantor | Grantee |
|---|---|
| Robert Alcocke | Nathaniel Goger |
| Robert Alcocke | Henry Bell |
| Edmond Archer | James Barbour |
| Adam Banks | Charles Humes |
| Adam Banks | Francis Harvey |
| Adam Banks | John Graves |
| Adam Banks | Merry Walker |
| John Baker | John Weaver |
| Ambrose Barbour | Watts Barnett |
| James Barbour | Thomas Barbour |
| John Berry | Henry Price |
| Moses Broyles | Stephens Fisher |
| Moses Broyles | Henry Price |
| Michael Broyles | Benjamin Smith |
| Reubin Brooking | John Bunger |
| Fether Bunger | John Bunger |
| Ann Campbell | Augustine Lillard |
| Benjamin Cave | Belfield Cave |
| Benjamin Cave | Benjamin Johnson |
| Adam Clore | Joshua Leathers |
| Adam Clore | Moses Clore |
| Adam Clore | Leonard Crisler |
| Adam Clore | Reubin Medley |
| Michael Clore | Adam Clore |
| Jeremiah Kirtley | Charles Humer |
| Reubin Clark | John Young |
| Charles Cock | John Harrison |
| William Collins | Henry Harvey |
| Adam Cook | John Jessa |
| Jonothan Cowherd | George Eve |
| William Corbin | Thomas Corbin |
| James Crain | Joshua Leathers |
| Nicholas Crigler | Mattias Rouse |
| Reubin Crigler | William Smith |

| Grantor | Grantee |
|---|---|
| Martin Deer | Andrew Deer |
| Benjamin Delaney | Peter Fox |
| Michael Delph | Michael Clore |
| Samuel Delph | Lodwick Major |
| Benjamin Dickens | William Carpenter |
| Jane Early | George Wilhoit |
| Paschal Early | George Wilhoit |
| James Emmons | William Emmons |
| William Eve | James Walker, Jr. |
| Benjamin Tweel | Adam Snyder |
| Benjamin Finnell | John Wayland |
| Peter Fleshman | Andrew Garr |
| Francis Gibbs | Michael Berry |
| Edward Graves | Solomon Carpenter |
| Edward Graves | Philip Snyder |
| John Graves | Absolom Graves |
| John Graves | George Gaines |
| Joseph Haynes | John White |
| Stephen Haynes | James Haynes |
| Elizabeth Hensley | Benjamin Lillard |
| William Hill | James Newman |
| Julius Hunt | Philip Slaughter |
| Ralph Hughes | Thomas Bohannon |
| George Huffman | Michael Snyder |
| Daniel Jarrell | William Jarrell |
| Jeremiah Kirtley | Charles Humes |
| John Leathers | William Blakey |
| Austin Lillard | Ann Campbell |
| Joshua Lindsay | Anthony Vernon |
| Thomas Loyd | Robert Shelton |
| John McAlister | Jacob Rouse |
| Matthias McDaniel | George Harrison |
| Samuel Major | Franky Razer |
| Daniel Mock | Adam Clore |
| Daniel Mock | Acrey Berry |
| Nannonmaker Lewis | William Carpenter |
| Lewis Powell | William Powell |
| Lewis Powell | George Eve |
| Sarah Powell | Thomas Brown |
| Robert Powell | Ambrose Clark |
| Thomas Pratt | Philip Slaughter |
| Thomas Pratt | Elizah Beckham |
| Richard Quinn | Anthony Vernon |
| James Ramsbottom | John Lillard |
| Robert Renolds | John T. Renolds |
| Robert Renolds | James Watts |
| Robert Render | Thomas Bohannon |
| Ann Rice | George Harrison |
| Alexander Rider | Jeremiah Rider |
| John Rice | Susanna Medley |
| Simon Rice | George Harrison |
| Ann Rogers | Joseph Rogers |
| Robert Roebuck | Cornelius Wayland |
| Thomas Sampson | Jonathan Cowherd |
| Thomas Sampson | Benjamin Lillard |
| John Seale | George Thomas |
| Robert Shelton | Thomas Loyd |

| Grantor | Grantee |
|---|---|
| Alexander Simpson | John Harrison |
| Jeremiah Sims | Benjamin Henry |
| Robert Slaughter | Philip Long |
| Benjamin Smith | Milinder Smith |
| Benjamin Smith | William Smith |
| Benjamin Smith | Isaac Smith |
| Benjamin Smith | Nancy Rucker |
| George Smoot | John Yager |
| John Smith | James Yowell |
| Nicholas Smith | George Crisler |
| Peter Smith | James Smoot |
| William Smith | John Stansifher |
| Adam Snyder | Harmon Redmon |
| Michael Snyder | Philip Snyder |
| Margaret Snyder | Edward Graves |
| Henry Sparks | William Clarke |
| Munford Stevens | Thomas Barbour |
| Thomas Standley | Milinder Smith |
| Thomas Stockdell | Joel Cofer |
| Thomas Stockdell | Mary Burton |
| George Swindle | Joseph Carpenter |
| John Swindle | Yager and Fray |
| John Synor | Adam Snyder |
| Henry Terrell | Lawrence and Adam Garr |
| John Thomas | Thomas Wallace |
| Henry Towles | Joseph Towles |
| Daniel Triplet | Joshua Willis |
| George Utz | John Utz |
| Joel Underwood | Benjamin Powell |
| Russell Vawter | Jacob Bunger |
| Richard Vernon | Anthony Vernon |
| Richard Vernon | Richard Vernon |
| Richard Vernon | John Vawter |
| Richard Vernon | Tinsley Vernon |
| Richard Vernon | Benjamin Quinn |
| Hugh Walker | Charles Holloway |
| Merry Walker | Sampson Huffman |
| Merry Walker | William Walker |
| Merry Walker | John Bradford |
| Merry Walker | Adam Banks |
| Merry Walker | John Walker |
| Zachariah Wall | Robert Wall |
| William Walker | James Twyman |
| William Walker | Thomas Terry |
| John Wayt | Churchill Gibbs |
| John Wayt | Leroy Canady |
| Matthias Weaver | Ephriam Fray |
| Jeremiah White | John Rucker |
| Joshua Willis | Daniel Triplett |
| Lewis Wilhoite | Elias Cristler |
| Tobias Wilhoite | Jesse Wilhoite |
| Tarpley Wilson | George Jackson |
| Benjamin Winslow | Paschal Early |
| Benjamin Wroe | Charles Young |
| Benjamin Wroe | Wharton Canady |
| John Wright | George Rouse |
| John Wright | William Twyman |

| Grantor | Grantee |
|---|---|
| Adam Yager | George Cristler |
| Adam Yager | John Adam Yager |
| Adam Yager | Godfrey Yager |
| Elisha Yager | Nathaniel Yager |
| John Yowell | Ambrose Ship |
| John Yowell | Joshua Leathers |
| James Yowell | Lewis Crigler |
| James Yowell | William Story |
| John Zachary | Benjamin Zachary |
| William Zachary | Adam Rouse |

## CHAPTER XIII

### Interesting Incidents

Many local events have occurred in the county which have not greatly influenced its history. These events are not of major importance, yet they are interesting and linger in the minds of the people. This chapter will be devoted to some of these events.

### Erection of the Confederate Monument

In 1902 a beautiful monument was erected in the public square, facing the court house. This monument was erected by the Kemper-Fry-Strother Camp of Confederate Veterans in honor of those who served in the Civil War. Just as this monument withstands the elements of nature, so the hearts of the people will ever honor the courage and bravery displayed by their forefathers in this great war.

### The Town of Madison Incorporated

By an act of the Legislature, Madison Court House was made an incorporated town March 20, 1875. This act was repealed March 15, 1922. This is the only town in the county that has ever been incorporated.

### Family Names Changed

There have been many family names changed in Madison county since the county began. Some of these names were originally German, and have now become Anglicized, while others that were English have undergone some changes. A partial list of such names is as follows:

| Present Name | Name before it was changed |
|---|---|
| Blankenbaker | Blankenbucker, Plunketpeter |
| Rouse | Rausch, Rouce, Rause |
| Clore | Gloor |
| Carpenter | Zimmerman |
| Wilhoit | Wilhite |
| Utz | Ouds |
| Yowell | Youell, Youel, Ewell, Yule |
| Crigler | Craigler |
| Fleshman | Flishman |
| Tanner or Turner | Tunner |
| Rosson | Raussen |
| Twyman | Twiman |

## Dunkard Congregation Emigrated 1780

A community of Dunkards was organized near the Hebron Lutheran Church about the middle of the eighteenth century. This congregation gave the Lutherans much trouble and uneasiness, but in 1780 they emigrated to Pennsylvania under the leadership of their pastor, Johannes Tanner.[1]

## Madisonians Who Emigrated to Kentucky

Several of the Carpenter family emigrated from Madison further west into Kentucky. They blazed the road, which became known as the "Stage Road" to the Kananha and Ohio Rivers, and traversed the territory of the famous Sulphur Springs. Nathan Carpenter came there in 1774 and Sulphur Spring Valley was patented to him. He was killed by the Indians, but his wife, Kate, and their children took refuge in a mountain which today is called Kate Mountain.[2]

## Settlement of Madisonians in Kentucky

Ludwig Rauch (Rouse) about 1800 had ventured as far westward as Florence County, Kentucky, where he found fertile lands. He returned to Madison and there praised the west and declared it his intention to make his home there. He went west again, but returned to Madison in 1804, for his betrothed wife. His success in the west caused such an excitement in Madison that the next year fourteen men with their families started for Boone county, Kentucky. They were: Solomon Hoffman and his wife, Elizabeth; George Rouse and his wife; Ephraim Tanner and his wife, Susanna; Johannes Hans and his wife, Emilie; Ferdinand Zimmerman and his wife, Rosa; Johannes Rouse and his wife, Nancy; Benjamin Aylor; Simeon Tanner; Josia Zimmerman; and Jeremiah Carpenter. In 1806 they erected a church which they called "Hopeful," and in 1813 they induced William Carpenter of Madison to become their pastor. More Germans arrived later in Northern Kentucky where they founded the cities of Frankfort, Lexington and Louisville.[3]

## Emigration to Indiana

About 1857 a group of people left Madison and traveled in wagons to Indiana to settle. Only a partial list of these settlers are now known. They were: John Smith, Mark Delaney, James Garr, James Rush, John Rush, Kirtley Wayman, and Jerry Aylor. An interesting story is often told about Delaney's dog which started on this journey. The dog became frightened as the settlers were crossing the Ohio River and started back home. He left the settlers about

---

[1] Virginia Magazine of History and Biography.
[2] Virginia Magazine of History and Biography.
[3] Virginia Magazine of History and Biography.

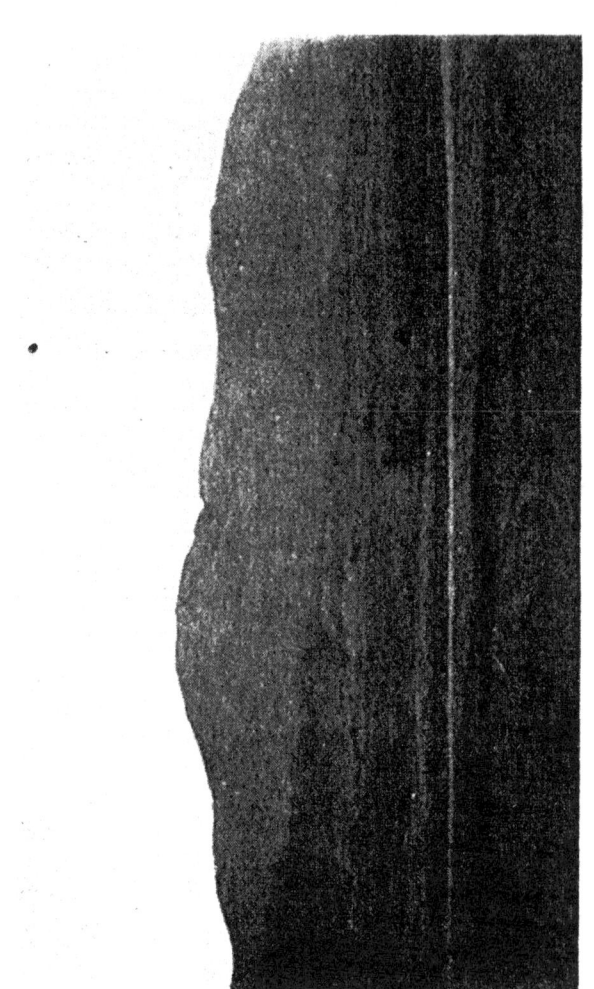

The Old Rag Mountain

sundown one day and reached Madison about sundown the next day. About the same time Joseph Wilhite set his slaves free, and as he had to transplant them to a free state, he employed Albert Weaver to take them. Albert Weaver also finally reached Indiana and there accumulated much wealth.

## Origin of the Scull Bean

Most of the people of Madison are very familiar with the garden bean called the Scull Bean. This bean received its name from one William Scull who settled in Madison, bringing this variety of beans with him from Germany.

## Origin of Milum Apples

The Milum apple, a native of Madison county and very highly prized by the citizens of the county, had its origin near Milum's Gap (sometimes called Fisher's Gap). It originated from a seedling that came up in the yard of one Joseph Milum. The apple proved to be so good that people from far and near came to graft trees from this one. The apples were named for the man who owned the seedlings, Joseph Milum, and afterwards the gap in the Blue Ridge near his home was also named after him.

## Votes Cast in the Election of 1824

One hundred and one years ago there were only one hundred and thirty-nine votes cast in the presidential election in Madison county. In the 1924 election, the number of voters was between one and two thousand.

## Madison Court House Made a Dry Town

Local option was voted upon in the town of Madison as early as 1898. In that year a vote was taken and local option was adopted.

## Madison's Attitude on National Issues

The Federal Convention was held in Philadelphia in 1787. The outcome of this convention was the drafting of the present Constitution of the United States. This constitution was then placed before the states for ratification, and the vote in Virginia, which was one of the pivotal states, was eighty-nine for and seventy-nine against ratification. Madison county voted for it.

Congress passed a tariff bill in 1828, which later became known as the "Tariff Bill of 1828." This bill raised the duty on hemp, flax, and wool. Madison was against this bill.

---

⑤ Huddle, W. P. History of the Hebron Lutheran Church.

# 154  A HISTORY OF MADISON COUNTY, VIRGINIA

Madison voted against the tariff bill of 1832, which placed a high duty upon cotton and woolen goods, as well as upon iron. Thus we see that Madison has always been opposed to high tariff.

Madison voted in favor of holding a State Constitutional Convention in 1828, and after the Convention had been held and a Constitution had been drawn up, Madison voted for it The returns from the vote taken, showed that two hundred and twenty-five votes had been cast in favor of the new constitution, but not a single vote against it.

The people of Madison voted for Crawford in 1824, and Jackson in 1828.

## Land Warrant Issued to Bellfield Cave in 1792

"An act directing the registrar of the land office to issue a land warrant to Bellfield Cave."

### Passed November 17, 1792

"Section 1. Be it enacted by the General Assembly, That the registrar of the land office shall, and is hereby directed to issue a land warrant or warrants to Bellfield Cave, for the amount of certain money paid by him into the treasury of this Commonwealth, under an act for calling in and funding paper money, apportioning the quality of land to the value of the said payment into the treasury, at the time the same was made.

"Section 2. This act shall commence and be in force from and after the passing thereof."[1] This act must have had reference to the funding of National debts after the Revolutionary War.

## First Bank Opened in the County

The first bank to be established in the county was established at Madison Court House in 1900.

## County Newspapers

The first newspaper to be printed in the county was the *American Eagle,* which was begun in 1859. This paper was only published for several years, as the turmoil of the Civil War caused it to be discontinued. Then the county was without a newspaper until 1893, when the *Free Press* was begun. *The Free Press* was discontinued, and the *Madison News* established in 1897. Since that time the *Madison Exponent* has succeeded the *Madison News,* and the *Madison Eagle,* the *Madison Exponent.*

## Clothing Factory—"The Factory"

A clothing factory was built on the Robinson River by a Mr. Larkin about 1870. This factory became known to the citizens of

---

[1] Hennings Statutes at Large for Virginia.

the county as "The Factory." It was operated by different people for about fifty years, but is no longer in operation. The last man to operate this factory was Mr. Hamp Berry.

### Lewis Miller's Tannery

In days gone by, there were many more tanneries in the county than there are at present. It is not known when this tannery was begun, but it must have been some time before the Civil War. Mr. Joseph Fray was the last one to operate it. It ceased to be operated about 1885.

### Booton's Tannery

There was a very old tannery situated below Madison Court House. No one knew when this tannery was begun, as it ceased to operate as early as 1850.

### Tannery Near Banco

There was a tannery near Banco that ceased to be operated about 1875. This tannery was perhaps built by Henry O'Neil. The last man to operate it was Sidney Thomas.

### Wool Carding Mill

At one time all the farmers kept a few sheep, in order to secure wool to make their own clothes. The sheep were sheared and the wool was then washed and carded. The farmers could not card or comb the wool themselves, but took it to a mill where it could be carded. A mill of this kind was situated at Zeus, and at first it was owned and operated by a company. The last man to operate it was Mr. John Hawkins.

### Hemp Mill

In days gone by, many farmers of Madison raised hemp, out of which rope and coarse cloth were made. There were mills situated in various parts of the county that prepared the raw hemp for weaving. One of these mills was situated on the Robinson River, on the land now owned by James Smith. This mill was owned and operated by the Thomas family.

### Pine Blight

About 1890 a blight occurred among the pine trees in the county, and nearly all the pine timber was killed. However, this blight soon passed over and at present no one would know that such a thing ever happened.

ROBINSON RIVER VALLEY

### Chestnut Blight

A disease attacked the chestnut trees in 1918, and at present has killed practically all this variety of timber in the county. The loss has been considerable, but many are hoping that it will soon pass as did the pine blight.

### Locust Blight

Since 1920 there has been an insect attacking the leaves of the locust trees. The insect finds his way between the surfaces of the leaves, and causes the leaves to turn brown and die; however, the trees are not killed. Forestry experts claim that this blight will not prove fatal.

### Grant Reid Murder Case

One of the most famous murder cases in the county occurred in 1898. Grant Reid, a colored man, murdered his wife, Minnie, and his father-in-law, Pete Jackson, in the most dastardly manner. After committing the crime he succeeded in getting away from the scene of the murder. Then, fearing that he would be lynched, he gave Mr. Lester Blankenbaker his gold watch to take him to jail. After a long and hard fought trial, he was convicted and hanged. He made several attempts to end his own life before he was hanged, but all proved in vain and he, after all, had to suffer the penalty of his crime.

### Last Man to be Hanged in the County

The last man to be hanged in the county was William Gillison. He was convicted of murder in the first degree, for killing the wife of William Henry Thomas. After this time, those who received the death sentence were electrocuted instead of hanged.

### Influenza Epidemic

During the World War there was an epidemic of Spanish Influenza in the county. A great many people contracted this disease and many died from it. In fact, more people died of this disease in Madison county during the World War than were killed among the men who went to war from here.

### Smallpox Epidemics

The worst smallpox epidemic known in the history of the county occurred about 1850. It is reported that Mrs. Judie Clore brought the germs in her clothing from Kentucky. During this epidemic many people died of the disease, while others who recovered received scars, which lasted for life. It is reported that people who had been vaccinated sixty years before were unharmed by the disease. Another epidemic occurred in 1903, but this was not as fatal as the one of 1850. A few cases were reported again in 1925.

## Floods

The streams of Madison are swift, for they drain hillsides and mountains. This causes them to become swollen easily and to cause damage to the narrow valleys between the hills. There was a flood in 1870 that did some damage, and many of the citizens remember this date, because this was the same time that Noah Kite and his family were drowned. The next flood was in 1889; this did considerable damage, as did the one that occurred four years later in 1893. The flood of 1893 did considerable damage at Criglersville, for it was then that Mr. Rosson's house was washed away. Cave's dam and bridge were washed away in 1901. In 1924 there was much rain and some damage was done.

## Great Blizzard of 1886

One of the worst known blizzards in the county occurred in January, 1886. Very little is known concerning the damage done by this blizzard.

## Great Windstorm

One of the most destructive windstorms, that ever occurred in the county, was on the night of March 1, 1914. This wind did a great deal of damage to fences, buildings, and timber, especially in the northern part of the county. The vicinity of Criglersville seemed to have suffered most in this storm.

## Killing Frost in June

Many of the older people remember 1859 as a year without a summer. It was an exceptionally cool summer, and a frost that fell June 4, destroyed many crops and vegetables. This was the latest frost we have any record of in the county.

## People Drowned In the County

Many of the streams in the county have not been bridged and oftimes the fords have been dangerous. There have been several instances of people's drowning in these streams, while they were swollen. The following is a partial list of those who have lost their lives in this manner: Lynn Banks was drowned in 1842; John Henshaw was drowned at Criglersville a few years before the Civil War; —— Thompson was drowned at Carpenter's Ford; John Lillard was drowned at Criglersville in 1901.

## Men of Long Service in Madison

There have been some men in the county who have spent their lifetime in public life. It is impossible to make an exhaustive list of these people; however, it should be done. There have been some doctors who were reared in the county, and after studying medicine, practiced in the county practically all their lives. A partial list of these is as follows: Dr. Thrift, Dr. Lindsey, Dr. Simms, Dr. Twyman, and Dr. Taylor. Dr. Taylor practiced for fifty years. We are sure that there have been others who deserve to be mentioned, but their names are not known to us at this time.

Lynn Banks was speaker of the Legislature of Virginia for twenty-two consecutive sessions. This was longer than any other man who has held this position.

Daniel Field was judge of the Circuit Court for thirty-six years.

Angus R. Blakey was commonwealth's attorney for many years.

There have been lawyers, teachers, preachers, and others who have rendered service, who deserve to be mentioned but as no exhaustive list could be made, these will have to be omitted.

## Famous Men of Madison

All through this book men who deserve fame in the county's history have been mentioned, but there are others who have not been mentioned but deserve to be. Some of them are:

Shelton F. Leake, who was elected lieutenant-governor of Virginia in 1852. He was also famed as an orator.

George Muter, who was a member of the Kentucky Convention in 1785 and 1787. He was the elector of Woodford county in 1790 and was appointed first Chief Justice of Kentucky.[1]

Francis Hill, who was for two years the grand master of the Masons. He was the clerk of the County Court from 1859 to 1875. After retiring from this office, he began to practice law in 1875.

William Wirt, who was later United States Attorney-General, was qualified as a justice of the peace in Madison county in 1793.

## First Marriage License Issued in the County

The first marriage license to be issued in the county, was issued to William Smoot and Margaret Jenifer in 1793.

## Overseers of Roads 1793

The following people were named by the court as overseers of various roads in the county in 1793:

Ruben Fry and Ambrose Medley, the road between the Robinson River and Crooked Run up to the Dutch Church;

---

[1] Virginia Magazine of History and Biography.

Henry Hill, William Chapman and John Wetherall, the roads leading from the Dutch Church to Garr's Mountains, and between the north line and the German Ridge;

Jeremiah Kirtley and Thomas Graves, the roads between the German Ridge and Elk Run;

William Walker and Merry Walker, the road between Barnett's road and the South River below Elk Run;

James Barbour and Robert Beale, between Garr's Mills road and Kirtley's road and the Robinson River.

Robert Alcocke and Ambrose Barbour, the road between Barnett's road and Kirtley's road and the Robinson River.

### Last Vote Crier at Criglersville

The custom at one time was to call out aloud the names of those who voted and for whom they voted. That was the method used until the present system of secret balloting came into use. The last man employed at Criglersville to call out votes was Mr. Henry Weaver, known as "Big Henry."

### Voting Precincts in 1852

The present voting precincts have been given elsewhere in this book. The precincts of 1852 were as follows: Madison, Stony Hill, Criglersville, Huffman's Mill, Graves Mill, Rapidan Meeting House, Fleshman's Shop and Locust Dale.

### Dividing Line Between Madison and Culpeper

The dividing line between Madison and Culpeper was surveyed by a surveyor named John Gruman.

### System of Money Changed

Before 1795 all the county records used the English system of money, but after this time they used the present system.

## CHAPTER XIV

### Manufacturing

Madison county is a rural community; consequently, there is very little manufacturing. There are, however, several articles of manufacture that deserve mention. The streams of Madison are especially adapted to corn and wheat mills, and these have not been lacking in the county since its beginning. There was a law in the county that before one could build a mill, he must obtain permission from the court.

The first grant made in the county was to the Madison family, permitting them to build the mill now owned and operated by Mr. T. O. Gillum. This permission was given in 1793 to four of the Madison family, two of whom were James Madison and his son, James Madison, Jr. This is perhaps the oldest mill in the county still in operation.

In the year 1794 six legal grants were made as follows:
Samuel Rouse to build a mill on Stoney Run;
Daniel Mauck to build a mill on the Robinson River;
Benjamin Lillard to build a mill on Hughes River;
Christopher Dickens to build a mill on the Robinson River;
John Henshaw to build a mill on Deep Run;
Ephraim Fray to build a mill on Deep Run;
Crigler's mill on Deep or Muddy Run was built the same year that George Washington died, 1799. The mill at Banco, formerly known as Weaver's mill, now owned by H. C. Tysinger, was built in 1840. Hawkin's mill on Deep or Muddy Run is a very old mill, but it is not known when it was built. The mill at Peola Mills has been destroyed. It is not known when the mill at Wolftown was built, but it is perhaps not so very old. Reynold's mill at Criglersville was built after Weaver's mill. This finishes the list of flour mills in the county.

In times past there were many grist mills on the runs and rivers of the county, but all of these have disappeared. There are more grist mills now in use but they are owned by the farmers and are run by steam or gas engines. The farmers grind much more grain at present than they did in the past, but instead of taking their grain to a mill, they grind it themselves. Of course the mills named above grind meal, but their specialty is flour. In times past these flour mills were equipped with stones for grinding, but today they have modern equipment and steel rollers.

It is not known definitely how much flour is manufactured in the county per year, but it is estimated at over 10,000 barrels. It must

Shop of The Inventor of Rod Coops

also be borne in mind that the farmers of Madison do a great deal of their milling in the adjoining counties, and that large quantities of grain are shipped. Madison produces more flour than is consumed.

As has been stated elsewhere there were in times past more tanneries in the county. There is now only one in existence. This is at Criglersville and is owned and operated by J. W. Wetherall and Son. Not only is leather made there, but harness is also made and repaired.

The most outstanding progress made in manufacturing has been in articles of wood. Madison has an excellent variety of lumber, which makes wooden manufacture profitable.

Before the hickory rod chicken coops came into existence, coops were made of white oak slats covered with wire. These coops were clumsy, hard to handle and could not be packed one upon another. The hickory rod coop was invented by Mr. W. J. Carpenter of Brightwood. Before his invention Mr. Carpenter was engaged in the manufacture of grain cradles in partnership with his father-in-law. They purchased a small machine which turned the ribs of the grain cradles and from this Mr. Carpenter conceived the idea of turning rods for a chicken coop. He began making coops in 1885. At first there was little sale for them, mainly because poultry was not marketed then as it is today. The business, nevertheless, grew until at present his sons, who operate the factory, put on the market between twelve and fifteen thousand coops per year. Mr. Carpenter did not take out a patent on his invention; consequently, other factories have arisen. Still, the output of the original factory is larger than that of its competitors.

There are two coop factories at Brightwood. One owned by Mr. R. C. Aylor, who was the original builder of this factory in 1921. The other is now owned by Mr. M. F. Blankenbeker who bought this factory, it having been in operation for about twenty years with various kinds of work in wood. He, however, converted this into a coop factory in 1922. Before Mr. Blankenbeker came into possession, this factory had been known by several firm names, as follows: Weaver and Johnson, the original ones to establish the shop; Johnson and Somerville; Johnson and Partlow. Mr. E. A. Clore has a coop factory at Madison Court House. Work here is not confined to the manufacture of chicken coops exclusively, but to various kinds of wood work as well. Mr. Ira Utz operates a small factory at Criglersville which furnishes coops for that community, very few being shipped any distance. It cannot be definitely stated how many coops are made per year in Madison county as the number varies from year to year; yet, upon an average more than thirty thousand are made.

The manufacture of chairs was begun in the county by the Clore family. Mr. Moses Clore and his two sons, James and Joel, being the first to build a factory devoted exclusively to the manufacture of oak chairs. The first they made were unlike those at present having straight backs and an acorn top on the posts. The style of chair now made was originally designed by the Clore family. The factory making chairs under the original stamp is operated by Mr. J. C. Clore. Since the beginning of the chair industry several other factories have arisen.

Mr. J. D. Weaver started a factory in 1870 and since has devoted a part of his time to the manufacture of chairs, as well as to the manufacture of furniture and the preparation of lumber for building purposes. The Clore and Hawkins factory devoted to the manufacture of chairs was begun in 1906. Hawkins and Sons started in 1910. E. A. Clore's factory also devotes part of its time to the manufacture of chairs. The total output of chairs in all the factories in the county exceeds twenty thousand per year.

Some, or rather most, of the chair factories also manufacture other furniture. There is one concern which deserves mention, although no longer in operation. This is the factory once operated by Mr. Albert Aylor. Mr. Aylor for years made chairs, furniture and musical instruments. He was an excellent violin maker, one of his violins taking the second prize at the St. Louis Exposition. .

In former days there were many small factories which made farm wagons or did repair work on farm implements. Now that trucks have taken the place of wagons to such a large extent and repairs can be bought much cheaper than they can be made, these shops or factories are fast disappearing.

The growth of the fruit industry has created a demand for barrels in which to export the crop. Several barrel and stave mills have been established in the last few years. The mills at Syria and Banco have the largest outputs.

There are many possibilities for greater development in manufacturing in the county, and it is to be hoped that the citizens will see this and make good their opportunities.

## CHAPTER XV

### THE COLORED PEOPLE OF MADISON COUNTY

The first slaves were brought to America in 1619. These slaves were brought from Africa, and, for the most part, from Liberia. The task here, however, is not to trace the origin of the colored race in America, but only to give a brief history of that race in Madison county.

The exact date of the arrival of the slaves in Madison is not known. It is certain that they came very early; in fact, a good while before the Revolution. There must have been slaves in the county almost at the very beginning, for when the first settlers arrived in what is now Madison, there were slaves in all other parts of Virginia, and, hence, we would expect the settlers in Madison to own them. One of the first records that can be found concerning slaves in the county, states that they were bought by the German congregation of the Hebron Church to cultivate the glebe lands.[1] This, however, does not prove that there were no slaves in the county before this time; but evidently, there were very few. The colored population increased from early colonial times until 1890, and since that time there has been a very slow decrease. At present about one-third of the population of the county are colored people.

Many of the slaves who lived in the county in early colonial days were very ignorant, because they had been recently brought from Africa. Many of the colored people in the county today can trace their ancestry back to slaves brought directly from Africa, and they have also preserved some knowledge of the customs practiced by these early ancestors in their new environment. As they had been reared in Africa, they still retained some of the African customs for several generations. One especially interesting custom, which they preserved, was in regard to death and the ceremony performed at the burial of a friend. At such a time they always knelt at the grave, and by that act signified their farewell to the departed spirit. This custom prevails in many savage tribes today.

We do not have to study histories in order to find accounts of slave days, prior to emancipation, for we can obtain a great deal of information from Confederate veterans and old slaves, who are living witnesses. These sources of information, however, are passing away, for each year these two classes of people are becoming smaller in number.

---

[1] Huddle, W. P., History of the Hebron Church from 1717-1907.

There have been many books written about slave days, yet those books cannot convey the spirit of the time. Slavery had its good and its evil side; there were good and bad masters, and likewise, good and bad slaves. There were masters who were very cruel to their slaves and there were others who were as good to them as if they had been their own children. There were slaves who were not obedient and not respectful and others who were. There was a lack of kindness towards slaves, at times, as there is in the American home today, but it seems evident that the majority of the slave owners in Madison were not cruel.

The people of Madison did not fight in the Civil War in order to keep the colored people in bondage. Most of them realized the evils of slavery, and they saw the good in setting the slaves free. The contention was not over the freedom of slaves but over the manner in which this freedom was to be granted. Madison, like many parts of the South, believed in a gradual emancipation. The people saw the evil effects of absolute emancipation taking place at once. As a proof of this, there were people in the county who set their slaves free before the Civil War. The following extract is taken from the will of Albert Early, dated the 25th day of May, 1839, and admitted to probate the 25th day of November, 1847:

"I give and bequeath unto my above named executors all the negro slaves I now own or may own ——. I do most solemnly and seriously request and exhort them to do with my said negro slaves as I now prescribe, that it is my wish that they—— should be liberated so that they may enjoy all the liberties and blessings of a free and independent people and not approving the custom of liberating slaves to remain in the United States, I would recommend to my said executors to select for their residence some section of the country, which —— may supply them, the above named negro slaves, with all the comforts and necessities that may render their lives as agreeable and easy as possible."

The will further authorizes the executors to sell so much of the land and other property of the testator, as may be necessary to pay his debts and then to apply as much of the proceeds as the above named "executors may think proper for the removal and settlement of my above named negro slaves."

The will concludes:

"That it is owing to no malignity of feelings toward my relations that I have thus disposed of my negro slaves, but because I think they own enough of them without mine and I think that they are a general evil and withal I deprecate the principle."

---

① Munford, B. B., Virginia's Attitude Towards Slavery and Secession. Pages 117-118.

Extract of will of Joseph Early, of Madison county dated the 22nd of December, 1852 and admitted to probate August 24th, 1854:

"My will is that my executors hereinafter named send my negroes that I now have to Liberia—give each of the men—three in number—fifty dollars each and Verindy and all her children, one hundred dollars, to take with them besides getting them out, and bacon enough to last them six months after they get to Liberia."[1]

These wills show the attitude of many people concerning slavery. There was a great deal of friendship between master and slave. There is no greater proof of this than the fact that very few slaves deserted their masters during the Civil War, and that after emancipation the former masters tried to help their slaves get established. We are impressed today with the scene, which takes place when Confederate Veteran and an old slave meet. These two show the closest friendship of the two races.

Lincoln's Emancipation Proclamation was issued on September 22, 1862, but it did not immediately have very much effect upon conditions in the county. Emancipation did not really take place there until after the war in 1865. After obtaining their freedom, many of the former slaves remained on the old farm and worked for their master for wages, or perhaps rented a part of the farm to cultivate. The colored people were a newly emancipated people, and they were new in the art of earning a livelihood. They knew how to work, but had never developed that power which enables one to live alone. They had acquired the habit of toil, but not the regulating of this toil to a definite end, to provide homes for themselves.

Emancipation brought a great change in the life of both white and colored. Each race had to become adjusted to the new situation. Problems always arise in any country when there is an abrupt change in the system of labor, and naturally there were problems for both races during Reconstruction.

The white and colored in Madison were in a much better condition during Reconstruction than the people were in the farther south, where there were large plantations and men owned thousands of acres of land and hundreds of slaves. These large plantations made the problem of Reconstruction greater, for it made more problems for the white and colored. So far as the white people were concerned, there were the problems of debt and labor. Labor could not be secured for running large plantations, and by necessity the land was divided into smaller farms. This meant a change in life, because the people had to adapt themselves to life on a small farm, rather than on a plantation. Their homes had to undergo a complete change, as did also their business; for there had to be a change in the method of the culture of the cotton. There was no variation of crops in the

---

[1] Munford, B. B., Virginia's Attitude Towards Slavery and Secession. Page 120.

far south. Cotton was king; thus, there was more profit in cultivating it in large quantities. From a financial viewpoint cotton was adapted to large plantations, and when emancipation occurred the people of the South had to become accustomed to raising cotton on smaller farms.

Madison county did not have to undergo a very great change. The nature of its soil, the variation of its climate and the topography of the county did not render it fit for large plantations, and very few had ever been established. This meant that when the slaves were set free, there was not as great a change in the condition of labor; thus, the farms in Madison remained somewhat constant. As the farms and crops did not have to undergo a change, life and business remained somewhat static.

As to the slaves, they did not feel such a great change in Madison as those did farther south, for in that place they had only been trained to do one thing; namely, to cultivate cotton; this made them less self-sustaining when they were thrown upon their own resources. They did not know how to cultivate several crops, and they did not have money to raise cotton. Again the slaves in the South had worked in large groups, and knew only the command of the overseer; thus, they were robbed of the personal contact with the white man, who took an interest in them.

The conditions in Madison were different. There was a variation of crops, consequently, the slave had been taught to do many different things. There were few large slave holders in Madison; few men owned more than twelve or fifteen slaves, the average number being five or six. There were a few men who owned a large number; namely, General Banks and Thomas Shirley. It was advantageous to slaves for their master to own but few, for when this was true, they came in closer contact with their master and he took more personal interest in them; thus, they received a lot of useful information through him.

The profit derived from slavery was never as great in Madison as in other sections of the South. This was due to the fertility of the soil, the variation of crops, and the condition of the climate. The profit received from slavery was greater in the cotton states or in places where there was one staple crop. It was these sections that kept the price of slaves high; it was not places similar to Madison. Very few slaves were imported into Madison county just before the Civil War, but many were exported to the cotton fields, and this condition made the price of slaves high.

The greatest evil of slavery was the buying and selling of slaves. They could be sold from their old homes in Madison and carried to the South, where they were more profitable. As a usual thing, only those slaves who were considered bad by their masters, and those left on an estate after the death of their master, were taken to Richmond to be sold. The average price paid for a good slave just before the war was from $500 to $1000, while some brought as much as $1500. Some of those, who were sold by their masters to traders, and were taken farther South, returned after they were given their freedom. These slaves were able to give in detail an account of their life in those sections. A typical example of this is Tumps Berry.

After receiving freedom, the first efforts made by the colored people were to secure homes. Unsettled conditions and lack of capital made this a somewhat difficult task. In many sections of the South, the former slaves wandered from place to place, waiting for the promised "forty acres and a mule." This was not the condition in Madison, for most of the colored people were not deluded by this promise. They realized that if they were to obtain forty acres and a mule, they would have to work for them, so they at once went to work to win their own homes. The first real estate owners recorded in the county were Lena Scott and Catharine Gordon.

After emancipation, the former slaves began to enter into various trades requiring manual labor. Most of them continued to work on the farm; some in the capacity of laborers, and others as renters. However, there were a few who opened shops of various kinds. James Strother was the first colored person to have a harness shop in the county. John Jackson and Edmond Jefferson were the first to run a blacksmith shop. Noah Roebuck and James French were the first to operate a shoemaker's shop. There were only two professions into which the colored people entered after they were freed; these were the ministry and teaching. Benjamin Gray and Beverly Jones were the first to attend College, to prepare for the ministry and Benjamin Gray was the first minister to be ordained in the county. Barnett, an African minister, conducted the ordination with a council from Charlottesville, Virginia.

The colored people soon began to try to secure an education. The first colored school to be founded in the county was in 1868. This school was situated near the public square at Madison Court House. It was a private school, taught by J. A. Manaway and promoted by Edmund Jefferson, Catharine Gordon and Robert Campbell. The first to teach under the Peabody Fund was Roberta Scott of Richmond, while the first to teach under the present school system was a preacher by the name of Hope.

Very soon after emancipation, the colored people began to withdraw from the white churches, to which they had belonged in slave time, and to form churches of their own. All the colored churches are Baptist. There are thirteen New School Baptist and two Primitive Baptist Churches in the county. Their names and locations are as follows:

### New School Baptists

| | |
|---|---|
| Antioch | Madison |
| Elk Run | Shelby |
| Mt. Sinai | Seville |
| Locust Grove | Radiant |
| Oak Grove | Oak Park |
| Mt. Pisgah | Twyman's Mill |
| Maine | Uno |
| Chestnut Grove | Brightwood |
| Mt. Vernon | Ruth |
| Rock Hill | Wolftown |
| Mt. Calvary | Haywood |
| Pleasant Grove | Etlan |
| Mt. Zion | Criglersville |

### Primitive Baptists

| | |
|---|---|
| First Robinson | Criglersville |
| Second Robinson | Banco |

The history of these churches has been somewhat as follows: The Antioch Baptist Church was organized in 1868. It was organized by the Bethcar Church (white). Its first pastor was Reverend Gaskin, and from 1868 until 1924 this church has been served by eight pastors.

Elk Run Church was organized in 1874, with Frank Tibbs as its first pastor. This church was organized under a chestnut tree near the home of the late Deacon Henry Spotswood, Sr.

Mt. Sinai was organized in 1876. It was organized on account of a difference which arose in the Elk Run Church. A part of the members remained in the former church, while a part withdrew and organized Mt. Sinai. The pastor, Frank Tibbs, followed the dissatisfied members and became pastor of the new church. Burl Malone, of he white church, set the new church apart.

Rock Hill Church was organized on Kinsey Creek near Grave's Mill in 1875 by Augusta Lewis. The land on which the present church stands was given by George Garth, a white citizen of Wolftown.

Mt. Pisgah was organized in 1879, James Scott was its first pastor; Ernest Francis was the first clerk; and Andrew Francis, its first treasurer. The first public school taught in this community was taught by the Rev. Willis Robinson, who became one of the most noted pulpit orators in that section.

Locust Grove was organized in 1871 near its present site. Frank Tibbs was the first pastor of this church, and it still retains his name, being called "Tibbs' Church."

Maine Church was organized July 17, 1921. U. B. Johnson of Washington, D. C., was the founder of this church, and the charter members came from different churches of the county.

Mt. Vernon Church was organized in 1915. The founder was B. F. Towles. The congregation grew from prayer meetings held on

Hood's Mountain. Those who attended these prayer meetings were finally organized into a church and H. P. Clay became the first pastor.

The First Primitive Baptist church was organized in 1873, and Noah Taylor was its first pastor. The Second Primitive Baptist Church was organized in 1875, with Jesse Lee as its first pastor. These two churches have not been in union for many years.

Mt. Calvary Church was organized in July, 1893. Benjamin Gray was the first pastor and William Jackson, Wash. Burrell, and Angus Arrington were the first deacons. James Carpenter was the first clerk. This church was organized from Mt. Carmel (white) Church.

Pleasant Grove was organized in September, 1910. The first pastor was Philip Brown. James Smallwood, Charlie Blakey, and William Smith were the first deacons. Charlie Blakey was the first clerk.

Mt. Zion Baptist Church was organized in 1882. This church was organized by Augusta Lewis, but the first pastor was James Woodson. The first deacons were: Wash. Clay, A. B. Smallwood, N. Hill, G. W. Barbour and H. B. Clay.

The colored people in the county have five secret orders. These orders have a large membership and are very active. They are the Odd Fellows, Knights of Pythias, Stars of Gideon, Love and Charity, and Household of Ruth.

The colored race has accumulated a large amount of real estate and personal property in the county. Many have farms and are prosperous in agriculture, while others have gone into various trades and are making a success in mechanics. The colored people of the county as a whole, are as well behaved as the same number of people anywhere. They are obedient to the laws and respectful to authority. They live in peace with their white neighbors and there is a warm personal friendship between the two races. They are trying to make the county a more beautiful place in which to live and are doing much to increase the wealth of the county. Many have nice homes and are making rapid progress in home conditions. The colored people have progressed, and seem satisfied with present conditions. They have given up politics and are putting their strength into other developments, especially industrial ones. It is to be hoped that in the future the colored people may take an interest in the affairs of the county and feel that they have a part to play in its history and development.

## CHAPTER XVI

### Conclusion

Never was there a truer saying than, "What we do for ourselves dies with us, but what we do for others lives on." The past belonged to our ancestors; the present is ours; but the future will belong to others. That future depends upon the present, for we are guardians of the past and moulders of the future. The present is always curious about the future and neglectful of the past. Men have a great desire to know what is going to be, yet they neglect the study of the past which could help them to know the future. Men would like to look ahead and make plans, but that power is only partially theirs, for they cannot know definitely what will be, yet if they avail themselves of the opportunity there is a great deal to be known about the future.

Men so often overlook the great truth of the Bible which is a formula to the future. They think that this formula applies only to the spiritual life of men, and has nothing to do with his temporal life. This theory is untrue for it is plainly true in spiritual and temporal life, that "Whatsoever a man soweth, that shall he also reap." By following this formula the future may be solved, for if we know the present and the past, which are the sowing, the reaping may be foretold.

The sowing is the controlling of tendencies which grow and create events. Did you ever read United States history that dealt with conditions that led up to the Civil War, and, as you read, did you not wonder why it was that people did not realize war was hovering over them? The tendencies of separation had been sown and unless they were checked they would bear fruit. Did it ever seem strange to you that the Allies were not expectant of war when the World War occurred? Germany had sown the seeds of war; militaristic tendencies had been created, and war followed as a natural result.

In fact, before any event, does it not seem strange that men do not realize that something is going to happen? No! It is not strange, for we are often not careful how we sow and therefore we do not know what we shall reap. We carelessly start tendencies without a thought, and these tendencies grow until they are of such magnitude that it is beyond our power to check them; then we call the result fate.

Scientists tell us of conservation of matter and energy in the scientific field; they do not apply it to human action, but it is just as true there as anywhere else. There is nothing lost in the world. We eat that our bodies may live; we work that we may buy the necessities of life and some of its luxuries. We have a purpose in all we do, and that purpose produces a result. Then, if we are to know about the future we must make a diligent study of the present and past.

One of the inborn characteristics of man is dissatisfaction. He is dissatisfied and hopes for an expansion of his activities and resources. We have seen how the Virginia colony gradually expanded westward and formed new counties. That was an external expansion of the colony; it was a broadening of the original territory. This extension did not have any marked effect upon the internal development of the colony as a whole, for each new-formed county was a unit in itself. The powers of decentralization were at work; for it was the tendency of the age.

Since that time all the land has been taken up; there can be no more outward expansion. Therefore, the powers of decentralization have ceased. The only expansion that can be made now is an internal one. The future development must be in the management of resources that we now possess. This is an age of centralization. We are able to see that the present and future is an age of centralization for we see that each day the county assumes more power over the districts; the state over the counties; and the federal government over the state governments.

Not only has this condition produced a change in our government, but it is producing a change in the life of the people. When there was plenty of land that could be secured out in the wilderness there was no great need for co-operation among the people; if they could not get along together, they could separate and live almost a secluded life. Now that the farms have become smaller and smaller there is need of greater co operation; this will come in the future, for with centralization there must be co-operation.

In the early history of our county there was a period of exploration. It was an exploration of the earth, the finding of new land. This period has passed, the surface of the earth has been discovered, so in the future there will be exploration, but it will be an exploration of the earth itself. The farmers will explore the fields of agriculture. They will study the soil to find what it can best produce; they will study the possibilities of making the soil better; they will study the nature of crops and will seek to find new crops, which they may raise with profit; they will try to evolve the plants that they raise to a higher plane; they will study market conditions and how to better market their produce. These and various other things will the farmers do to improve their condition by exploration of the things unknown. The orchardist will explore the possibilities of better fruit culture, and better market facilities; the cattle raiser will seek to find more profitable ways by which to raise cattle; thus, in all activities there will be an exploration of more scientific methods which will mean an improvement in the resources we now possess, but which are yet undeveloped.

After our county had been explored there came an age of settlement. The settlers were seeking better homes, more fertile lands, or, in other words, were endeavoring to make their lives more comfortable. No longer will our people seek new lands, but they will still seek to make their lives more comfortable and happier. One line of endeavor will be to lighten the burden of labor. More and better machinery will be used, not only to lessen the man power needed, but to do work that is considered drudgery. Along with better methods of farming will come better equipment with which to farm. Machines will take the place of human hands, and home life will be improved. Machinery will also enter the home and relieve the housewife of much drudgery; houses will be built more convenient and with better sanitation, and the housewife will no longer attempt to manufacture as many things for the home use as she has done in the past; but she will buy the manufactured product, which will be better and cheaper. Her time will be devoted to the things that make the home happier.

The age of machinery and better living conditions will mean a greater amount of leisure time. This may be a problem or it may be a benefit; in fact, it will be what we make it. Since we have had more leisure more things have come into our lives to occupy this leisure time, such as movies, plays, magazines, books, and so many things, which in the future will be increased.

Men will seek a more comfortable life by training the mind instead of the muscle. Each day brings us to a greater realization that mind is greater than muscle. The future will be an age of specialization; men will no longer have a fair knowledge of many things, but each will be trained in one special work. This will mean greater efficiency, and with that greater efficiency will come problems.

Madison county was formed by necessity, because of the distance that some citizens lived from Culpeper Court House. Necessity is often called the "mother of inventions." New necessities arise each day; they are with us now and will be with us in the future. There are two laws of necessity that we can be sure of in the future. The first is that by necessity we make progress; the second, that we must make progress in everything. The world is moving on and we cannot stop it. Other communities progress and we must keep up with them. Only a few years ago the roads of Madison county were neglected; they were rough and muddy; now the people have at last realized that something must be done about this, and roads are being built. They are not being built without opposition, but sometime this opposition will cease. The county has to have roads, for as other parts of the state build them, we are compelled to build ours in order to show ourselves progressive. Roads cost, but they pay in the end, for they lighten the life of the people. Not many years ago it required two days to make a trip to market with a team. These trips were tiresome and were often made in very bad weather. Such trips now belong to history; that day has passed and the people are glad of it. Trucks now make the trip in a few hours with much greater profit and more ease to the driver. We could not go back to the old days now if we wanted to, for conditions have changed and we have made progress in all activities. Easier marketing conditions, brought about by use of trucks and by better roads, have aroused the people to produce more and their lives are becoming adapted to this change. We then see that the means of transportation affect the amount of produce; and the amount of produce affected the means of transportation. This is only one example of the net work into which all activities are woven. They all have a two-fold relationship, to each other which makes progress in everything a necessity.

We have seen that Madison did her part in our country's wars. I believe that Madison will always do her part in everything. It is the spirit of the people not to be slackers. It is our duty to do our part. There will be duties in the future; they may not be in the nature of war, but in the pursuits of peace, such as the duty of enforcing the laws. It is the duty of every citizen to abide by the laws and to see that the law is enforced. Madison has not been a lawless county, and there is less law breaking now, with the exception of the prohibition laws, than there ever was. We may question the desirability of the prohibition law, but we cannot question our duty towards it. It is a part of our constitution and it is our duty to uphold it. Then we have a duty as a voter. It is our duty to see that our officers are the best citizens, and we should see that politics are kept clean.

We have seen that the public school system had a very feeble beginning in 1870, but since that time it has been making progress. Now there is no reason to believe that this progress will not continue in the future; for each day brings greater necessity for better trained minds and better educational facilities. We are making progress in agriculture, and science; in fact, in everything. Consequently, we cannot fall behind in education. Since the beginning of the public school system the percentage of illiteracy has been slowly decreasing and this will continue in the future. We are beginning to realize more and more that we make progress as a group and not as individuals. Hence it is to the advantage of the entire community for everyone to secure an education. Compulsory education will come; in fact, the seeds for this have been sown. We have made loose and feeble compulsory educational laws, but in the future they will be made more stringent. The public schools will require better trained teachers in the future; therefore, there will be more college graduates; more young men and women will seek higher education. It may be in the distant future, but the time will come when the officers and teachers of the schools will be professional people, and the parents will dictate very little in regard to school affairs. We have become accustomed to depend upon a physician when we are sick; upon a lawyer, when in legal need; and we will learn to depend upon teachers in matters of education. The changes in the methods of teaching have been very marked since 1870, and will be greater in the future. The tendency will be to make the studies more practical and better adapted to individual needs. All of the pupils will not be given academic training, but there will be more vocational guidance and better training in the vocations of the community.

The future will produce great changes in the economic conditions of the county. We have seen that the county has not only made progress in the individual products but that there has been an expansion of products; every few years the people of the county learn to market a new product. There are many changes that could and will occur in the economic order of the county, but there seems to be four industries which will lead in the future.

First is the fruit industry. A large part of Madison is well adapted to the growth of fruit. The quality of this fruit is very fine; in fact, as good, if not better, than that raised in Frederick county. The fruit industry has not been developed in Madison because that part of the county which is best adapted to the culture of fruit is a long distance from a railroad. Now since better roads are being built there is an opportunity to market the fruit at a reasonable cost. By the use of improved methods of orcharding and a saving of by-products, fruit growing can be made a very valuable industry in the county.

The second field of development is in the lumber industry. Lumber is becoming more and more valuable and Madison possesses a vast amount of very valuable timber. If this timber could be properly handled, it would mean an immense revenue for the county; if it is pillaged and carelessly disposed of it will mean very little. Think of the difference it would make if we could manufacture our lumber right here at home, and there is no reason why this could not be done. There is plenty of water power and plenty of lumber to develop excellent business in the manufacturing of furniture and other articles of wood. If it could not be made into finished products of this nature, it could be made into building material ready for use, and this would mean more profit than selling it just from the saw.

The third industry is the development of water power. The streams in Madison are all swift, and the power that could be developed is almost unlimited. Mills of all kinds could be run by this cheap power; not only could mills be run, but electricity could be generated. This electric power could be sent by wires for a long distance, or used at home to lighten the burdens of the farmers. There are almost boundless possibilities in this field in Madison in the future.

The fourth industry is dairy products. Only a few years ago no one in the county sold any dairy products; now people in all parts of the county are selling cream. Madison is well adapted to dairying. Its altitude is high and its hills afford excellent grazing, thus in the future this is one of the great possibilities of Madison.

There are many other possibilities of economic development which it is useless to mention. Our county is just entering upon an era of development, the like of which has never been known in its history, and it will continue if the citizens get behind it and boost it.

Social customs have changed a great deal since the Civil War and there will be great changes in the future. Social customs reflect the life of the people; as the economic order, the educational conditions and all other things change we may expect a change in social customs. Madison in the past has been somewhat excluded from the world, but now due to better transportation, more magazines, newspapers and things of this nature, it is coming more and more into contact with other communities. This will mean a change in the life of the people.

It is hard to say what the future will produce in the moral and religious field. We can only hope for better and greater things, but we cannot get them without the co-operation of the people. We must work together for the good of mankind and the advancement of God's kingdom on earth.

I could go into all the activities in which the people of Madison participate, but this would be useless. My purpose in this chapter was not to foretell the future definitely, but to point out to you some general truths and get you to think along those lines. I want you to see the necessity of progress, and that progress must come. We cannot stand still; we must move in some direction. This fact gives us great responsibility, for the future rests upon us. We can make our county a great community if we—so to speak—put our shoulders to the wheel and push in the right direction. We all owe a duty to our county; we all love it. May we all help to make it a better place in which to live. Others have done their part in the past; let us do ours in the future.

6

# APPENDIX

## CIVIL WAR VETERANS
## COMPANY "C," 4th VIRGINIA CAVALRY

Company Mustered April, 1861

William Thomas, Captain; resigned in 1861.
Theo. Smoot, First Lieutenant; resigned May, 1862; age 38.
B. T. Yager, Second Lieutenant; elected First Lieut. 1862; age 34.
Daniel Slaughter, Third Lieutenant; elected Captain 1861; resigned May, 1862.
H. M. Reid, First Sergeant.
R. T. Hume, Second Sergeant.
M. W. Strother, Third Sergeant; First Sergeant July, '61, Third Lieut. Dec., '61.
A. B. Bradford, Fourth Sergeant; Captain 1862.
W. P. Finks, First Captain.
Edwin Henshaw, Second Captain.
H. C. Reid, Third Captain.
John Henkel, Fourth Captain; 3rd Lieut. 1862; killed May 9, 1864.

### PRIVATES

Aylor, Jefferson, age 38; captured Oct., 1864; died 1865.
Bates, C. B., age 25; wounded.
Brown, D. E., age 22; captured Nov., 1863.
Booton, John, age 38; put in substitute.
Berry, Hamp T., age 22.
Berry, Merton F., age 32; lost an arm in 1862.
Blankenbaker, J. A., age 18; wounded.
Carpenter, M. M., age 17; from Green county; elected corporal 1862.
Carpenter, H. B., age 21; elected Lieut. in 1864; wounded.
Carpenter, A. H., age 39.
Carpenter, R. B., age 19; captured in 1864.
Carpenter, Wm. P., age 19; elected corporal May, 1862.
Clore, John J., age 29; First Sergeant July, 1862.
Clatterbuck, Wm., age 39; discharged in 1862; deaf.
Chapman, J. C., age 23; wounded.
Coppage, J. W., age 18; wounded.
Collins, W. A., age 17; wounded.
Dulaney, A. G., age 33; wounded and discharged.
Fletcher, Robert, age 28; Sergeant in 1861; Second Lieut. in 1862.
Ford, John, age 38.
Garth, Geo. C., age 22; First Sergeant 1862; Third Sergeant 1863.
Hutcherson, Robert, age 37; discharged July, 1862.
Hutcherson, Press, age 33; died.
Herndon, D. B., age 23; wounded.
Harrison, B. L., age 25; wounded; elected Sergeant 1862.
Harrison, John N., age 18; died from wound in 1864.
Hague, John, age 36; discharged July, 1862.
Hawes, John, age 22.
Jackson, W. A., age 20; wounded; elected Corporal 1862.
Jarrell, A. G. F., age 37; discharged.

Jones, Jesse, age 27; wounded; elected Corporal 1862.
Kilby, Hamp, age 22.
Lindsay, I. N., age 31; put in substitute in 1862.
Milton, Reubin, age 29.
Marshall, W. H., age 19; died.
McMullen, T. W., age 26; killed in 1864.
Patrick, Wm., age 21; killed in 1864.
Rittenour, Dr. M., age 30.
Rivercomb, George L., age 40; Corporal 1861; discharged July, 1862.
Smith, B. F., age 40; discharged 1862.
Strickler, James F., age 28; put in substitute in 1863.
Simpson, Emmanuel, age 20; wounded.
Story, E., age 23; killed in 1864.
Simms, J. T. E., age 20; wounded.
Seal, J. J., age 24; wounded.
Sparks, John W., age 22; captured in 1864.
Taliferro, Fitzhugh, age 34; discharged in 1862.
Utz, John, age 25; died.

The above list embraces all of the company that left the county on the 24th day of April, 1861. The following are those that joined after that date.

## COMPANY "C," 4th VIRGINIA CAVALRY

Aylor, F. H., age 18; joined in 1862; wounded.
Aylor, G. D., age 18; joined in 1863; wounded.
Brown, Hill, age 25; joined in 1864; Culpeper.
Beasley, W. L., age 18; joined in 1864; Greene.
Brooking, W. E., age 38; joined in 1861; wounded.
Buckner, A. W., age 26; joined in 1862.
Busick, W. W., age 24; joined in 1861. Wounded.
Berry, W. J., age 28; joined in 1863.
Berry, Howard M., age 30; joined in 1864.
Blankenbaker, Geo., age 18; joined in 1862; died from wound.
Blankenbaker, Jas. H., age 25; joined in 1863.
Blankenbaker, J. N., age 25; joined in 1864.
Blankenbaker, Finks, age 25; joined in 1864.
Broyles, Albert T., age 25; joined in 1863; Corporal in 1864.
Bohannon, W. E., age 18; joined in 1864.
Bates, Wm., age 30; joined in 1863.
Bowler, Richard, age 17; joined in 1861.
Bowldridge, Joseph, age 36; joined in 1863.
Bradford, F., age 22; wounded.
Bardford, Landon, age 24; joined in 1862.
Conway, Wm. B., age 18; joined in 1863; made Corporal in 1864.
Cowherd, P. H., age 25; joined in 1863; wounded.
Collins, Q. J., age 17; joined in 1864.
Cook, John, age 27; joined in 1862.
Clatterbuck, Henry, age 30; joined in 1862; wounded.
Clatterbuck, Thomas, age 19; joined in 1863.
Clatterbuck, David, age 18; joined in 1862; wounded.
Clatterbuck, Daniel, age 18; joined in 1862; died.
Carpenter, A. F., age 25; joined 1863; wounded.
Carpenter, John T., age 18; joined 1863.
Carpenter, John, age 20; joined 1863; killed.
Carpenter, T. P., age 22; joined 1863; made First Sergeant 1864.
Carpenter, Hiram J., age 18; joined 1863; wounded.
Carpenter, J. S., age 22; joined 1864.

APPENDIX 181

Carpenter, O. P., age 18; joined 1863; wounded.
Carpenter, Thomas, age 30; joined 1863.
Carpenter, Howard, age 16; joined 1863; transferred to Infantry 1864.
Carpenter, Henry, age 16; joined 1863.
Carpenter, G. F. (Tip); joined 1863; captured.
Chapman, T. A., age 18; joined 1861.
Chapman, B. T., age 18; joined 1863; wounded.
Clore, Henry, age 30; joined 1864; wounded.
Clore, Alfred, age 30; joined 1863.
Clore, Jason O., age 18; joined 1862.
Dodd, William, age 18; joined 1861; from Loudoun; wounded.
Dowell, James, age 27; joined 1863; from Green.
Eheart, Clark, age 28; joined 1863; wounded.
Estes, James C., age 18; joined 1863; died from wound.
Eddins, Joel, age 27; joined 1863; died from wound.
Eddins, (Tip), age 25; joined 1863.
Early, T. W., age 18; joined 1863; wounded.
Early, Robert E., age 18; joined 1863; wounded.
Emmons, James, age 30; joined 1864.
Gordon, Woodville F., age 17; joined 1861; wounded.
Garth, J. W., age 20; joined 1863; killed.
Graves, T. D. C., age 28; joined 1864.
Graves, Morgan G., age 26; joined 1864.
Graves, Joel, W., age 18; joined 1863; Orange; wounded.
Graves, B. F., age 28; joined 1864; made Sergeant 1865.
Graves, Wm., age 29; joined 1865.
Garr, A. W., age 27; joined 1863.
Gains, Thomas, age 23; joined 1863; died.
Graves, Lynn.
Honsworth, R. H., age 30; joined 1863.
Hill, J. Polk, age 18; joined 1862; lost arm.
Hill, Richard C., age 18; joined 1863; killed.
Hill, Wm. P., age 18; joined 1863; wounded Oct. 9, 1864.
Harrison, J. W., age 22; joined 1863.
Harrison, G. W., age 18; joined 1863.
Herndon, W., age 30; joined 1863.
Herndon, Jas., age 25; joined 1864; Green.
Henshaw, J. O., age 33; joined 1861; wounded.
Henshaw, Fayette, age 34; joined 1861.
Huffman, Charles, age 19; joined 1862; died.
Huffman, R. Angus, age 18; joined 1863; wounded.
Huffman, W. R., age 40; joined 1864.
Harlow, Wm., age 25; joined 1863; died.
Hudson, Bruce, age 25; joined 1863; Culpeper; killed.
Jackson, J. C., age 17; joined 1863; wounded.
Jenkins, H., age 30; joined 1861; transferred.
Johnston, A. S., age 40; joined 1864.
Jarrell, J. Morgan, age 18; joined 1864.
Kipps, Geo. W., age 18; joined 1864.
Lindsay, R. L., age 35; joined 1863; wounded.
Lindsay, Dr. J. L., age 24; joined 1865.
Lohr, Philip, age 38; joined 1863; captured.
Lillard, George, age 22; joined 1862; wounded.
Murray, John.
Miller, Jas. N., age 18; joined 1864; wounded.
McMullan, J. W., age 40; joined 1863; Green county.
McMullan, Ed., age 30; joined 1864; Green county.
McMullan, W. H., age 30; joined 1864; Green county.

McMullan, Alexander, age 38; joined 1864; Green county.
Renolds, Marcellus, age 18; joined 1864; wounded.
McGill, Thomas, age 18; joined 1861; Loudoun county.
Megert, J. W., age 18; joined 1861; Loudoun county.
Malone, J. W., age 22; joined 1863; Green county.
May, Thomas, age 19; joined 1863; wounded.
McAlister, J. B., age 22; joined 1863.
Mitchell, W., age 25; joined 1862.
McAlister, A. S., age 18; joined 1864.
Mitchell, Albert, age 30; joined 1862.
Nicol, George, age 18; joined 1863; captured; died.
Nichols, age 18; joined 1863.
Petty, W. C., joined 1864, March 1st; Culpeper.
Price, J. W., age 24; joined 1864.
Price, Charles, age 19; joined 1863; wounded.
Payne, John M., age 18; joined 1863; died.
Peyton, Charles.
Quaintance, M., age 20; joined 1863; killed.
Quaintance, Taylor, age 18; joined 1864; wounded.
Reynolds, James H., age 40; joined 1864; wounded.
Reynolds, J. Q., age 30; joined 1863; wounded.
Richards, Joseph, age 30; joined 1862.
Ready, George W., age 46; joined 1864.
Rose, B. F., age 24; joined 1862.
Rose, John, age 18; joined 1863; captured; died.
Rowzee, J. W., age 18; joined ———.
Reid, Hiram M.
Skinner, Thomas, age 26; joined 1863.
Skinner, John, age 19; joined 1864.
Shipp, J. H., age 20; joined 1863.
Smith, Fielding, J., age 34; joined 1864; wounded.
Smith, W. N., age 35; joined 1863; wounded.
Smith, A. W., age 35; joined 1863.
Smith, Thomas, age 25; joined 1863; died.
Smith, Downey, age 28; joined 1863; Green county; wounded.
Simms, Mat., age 18; joined 1863; Loudoun.
Simms, A. H., age 18; joined 1863; wounded.
Shackelford, J. W., age 22; joined 1863; wounded.
Shelton, M. L., age 18; joined 1862; Green county; wounded.
Shelton, G. W., age 17; joined 1864; Green county; wounded.
Shepherd, Wm.
Story, Wm., age 40; joined 1863; captured; made Corporal 1864.
Stockdell, B. S. H., age 40; joined 1863.
Sparks, A. T., age 19; joined 1863.
Stout, W. H., age 46; joined 1863; substituted for J. W. Strickler.
Seal, J. W., age 18; joined 1863.
Sprinkel, G. A., age 18; joined 1863; captured.
Shotwell, T., age 35; joined 1863; Green county.
Thornhill, James, age 25; Rappahannock county.
Thornhill, Wm., age 25; Rappahannock county.
Thomas, Wm., age 43; joined 1863; died.
Thomas, A. R., age 18; joined 1864.
Thomas, James, age 18; joined 1864.
Thornhill, George, age 38; joined 1863; Rappahannock.
Thornhill, J. H., age 28; joined 1863; Rappahannock.
Thornhill, Thomas, age 18; joined 1862; Rappahannock.
Taylor, Evans T., age 40; joined 1864; Green county.
Twyman, J. W., age 17; joined 1862; wounded.

APPENDIX 183

Tate, Joseph, age 19; joined 1864; Fauquier county.
Tinsley, A. W., age 24; joined 1863; Culpeper county.
Thompson, J. W., age 18; joined 1863; killed.
Thompson, G. W., age 19; joined 1863.
Tucker, Gratton, age 18; joined 1863.
Tennerson, T. A., age 48; joined 1863; substituted for J. C. Utz.
Tysinger, D. C., age 18; joined 1862; wounded.
Utz, J. H., age 18; joined 1863; killed.
Utz, George, age 44; joined 1864; wounded.
Utz, G. W., age 26; joined 1864; killed.
Utz, J. C., age 20; joined 1863; put in substitute.
Utz, W. H., age 18; joined 1862; wounded.
Utz, R. E., age 18; joined 1865.
Vernon, William, age 19; joined 1864; wounded.
Verbel, Charles, joined 1863; substituted for J. W. Strickler.
Weatherall, W. H., age 45; joined 1863.
Weatherall, J. W., age 18; joined 1864.
Wilhoit, Walker, age 18; joined 1863; killed.
Wilhoit, D. S., age 20; joined 1864.
Wright, W. H., age 27; joined 1863; Green county.
Weaver, John M., age 30; joined 1864.
Weaver, J. Henry, age 31; joined 1863.
Weaver, George, age 30; joined 1862; wounded.
Weaver, W. H., Jr., age 18; joined 1864.
Wayland, B. F., age 18; joined 1863; wounded.
Walker, William, age 26; joined 1864; wounded.
Williams, M. A., age 47; joined 1863; substituted for J. Booton.
White, Richard; killed, Yellow Tavern, 1864.
Welch, W. M., age 18; joined 1864.
Yowell, W. L., age 18; joined 1863.
Yowell, Champ, age 19; joined 1862.
Yowell, Walker, age 18; joined 1864.
Yowell, A. E., age 18; joined 1862; wounded.
Yowell, Johannas, age 18; joined 1864.
Yowell, M. W., age 34; joined 1862.
Yager, Moyette, age 18; joined 1863; wounded.

## BROOK'S BATTERY, POAGNER BATTALION

Anderson, Robert A.
Anderson, Herod
Aylor, Henry
Back, Bombry
Brown, David
Butler, James
Cary, James
Calvin, James
Fry, Hugh N.
Fincham, James
Fincham, ———
Gallehugh, Andrew

Hoffman, John
Jenkins, Absolom
Lloyd, Columbus
Lloyd, Gratton
Lillard Sinclair
May, John
May, W. Robert
Mitchell, Love
Rosson, Henry
Rush, John
Rush, James
Shotwell, George
Shotwell, Harvis

Shotwell, Ally
Teasley, William
Thomas, Joseph
Utz, Gus
Utz, A. G.
Utz, T. S.
Weakley, Carnett
Weakley, Churchill
Wayland, F. H.
White, John W.
Yowell, C. Story
Yowell, Frank

## CARTER'S BATTERY, CUTSHAW'S BATTALION

John Harrison                                         George E. Gibbs
                        W. T. Brown

## COMPANY "G," 12th VIRGINIA CAVALRY

Dodson, Lloyd
Dodson, W. R.
Jenkins, Joseph R.
Norman, Henry
Nicholson, John W.
Nicholson, Vancouver
Nethers, Arnold
Weakley, James K.

## CHARLOTTESVILLE ARTILLERY, CUTSHAW'S BATTALION

D. M. Pattie, Jr.

## COMPANY "I," 1st VIRGINIA CAVALRY

Willis, James B.

## SECOND ROCKBRIDGE BATTERY, McINTOSH BATTALION

Cave, John I.
Jenkins, Churchill

## CAPTAIN RICE'S BATTERY, McINTOSH BATTALION

Jenkins, Henry
Jenkins, Banks

## COMPANY "K," 7th VIRGINIA INFANTRY

William Lovell, Captain
Abram W. Garr, First Lieutenant
A. N. Jones, Second Lieutenant
Benjamin F. Garr, Third Lieutenant
B. C. Wayman, First Sergeant
J. O. B. Racer, Second Sergeant
Geo. H. Racer, Third Sergeant
William J. Blankenbaker, Fourth Sergeant
Geo. W. Utz, Corporal
Joel H. Eddins, Corporal
Robert B. Wayland, Corporal
Robert H. Weaver, Corporal

### Privates

Austin, James W.
Amos, John W.
Aylor, Benjamin J.
Adams, Robert
Brown, Crismond A.
Berry, Chadwell, Jr.
Bledsoe, Wm. H.
Coats, Fountain
Coats, William
Coppage, Robert
Cave, Lorenzo F.
Cubbage, Reuben
Clore, Charles
Clayton, John W.
Dodson, John
Dawson, James F.
Darnold, Zachariah
Fincham, William T.
Fincham, Wesley
Gaines, Reuben W.
Taylor, Thomas J.
Weaver, John M.
Wayland, Thomas M.
Weaver, Lord M.

Those registering later were as follows:

Amos, Jefferson
Amos, Jackson
Breeden, Joseph
Carpenter, Robert
Carpenter, Horace
Carpenter, Jerry
Carpenter, A. J.
Carpenter, H. T.
Dixon, William
Davis, William
Delph, William
Darnold, John
Estes, C. W.
Groom, B. F.
Grayson, Robert
Gooding, William W.
Hoffman, J. W.
Harlow, J. W.
Herndon, George
Hill, William
Hunton, Horace
Herring, Nimrod
Jenkins, Wesley
Jenkins, Carnett
Kirtly, W. B.
Kinsey, Richard
Gooding, Robert
Hicks, Herndon F.
Hill, Joseph W.
Hunton, George W.
Huffman, Moses A.
Harlow, John W.
Huffman, Robert N.
Hundley, Robert
Harlow, Lewis B.
Jackson George W.
Jackson, William
Jenkins, Austin
Jenkins, John W.
Jenkins, James H.
Jenkins, Powell S.
Kennedy, James F.
Kirtley, John A.
Layton, Henry S.
Long, Edward J.

Leavell, Joseph W.
Lucas, William D.
Moore, John W.
McIntyre, Eldridge W.
McGhee, Garrotte C.
Nicholas, William
Rosser, James M.
Rosson, Barnette
Roberts, Benjamin D.
Smith, William H.

Smith, Joseph B.
Skinner, Robert
Shipp, James H.
Thomas, John
Lindsay, Thomas
Layton, John
Lee, James
Morris, Churchill
Robertson, John J.
Roberts, St. Clair

Rosson, Edwin
Racer, Charles
Rose, James
Shipp, John
Scott, John
Thompson, J. H.
Thompson, George
Weaver, W. F.

## COMPANY "L," 10th VIRGINIA INFANTRY

Elliot F. Blankenbaker, Captain August, 1861.
Alexandria M. Finks, First Lieutenant August, 1861.
Jason C. Crigler, Second Lieutenant August, 1861.
Mellville C. Gordon, Third Lieutenant August, 1861.
Robert F. Carter, First Sergeant August, 1861.
Howard S. Hoffman, Second Sergeant August, 1861.
Albert Aylor, Third Sergeant August, 1861.

Jonas Blankenbaker, Fourth Sergeant August, 1861.
John W. Tatum, Fifth Sergeant August, 1861.
Jacob C. Bowman, First Corporal August, 1861.
William R. Hoffman, Second Corporal August, 1861.
George Wise, Third Corporal August, 1861.
Richard T. Jacobs, Fourth Corporal August, 1861.

*Privates*

Broyles, Benjamin F.
Broyles, Yancy
Burton, Arthur W.
Blankenbaker, Richard U.
Blankenbaker, William
Blankenbaker, Smith F.
Blankenbaker, John M.
Berry, Chadwell
Clatterbuck, John M.
Clatterbuck, Henry F.
Colvin, John F.
Colvin, William G.
Cubbage, Ephriam
Dodson, John
Dodson, Morgan
Dodson, Andrew C.
Fogle, John
Finks, Horace
Finks, S. H.
Finks, M. F.
Gaines, James W.
Gully, James H.
Goode, Joseph M.
Gillerham, Robert
Gooding, Benjamin W.
Graves, James M.
Hurt, Harrison

Hundley, John W.
Hoffman, Robert A.
Hawkins, J. W.
Hutcherson, Fisher
Hutcherson, Harvey
Hutcherson, Thomas
Jenkins, Lillard
Jenkins, Charles
Jenkins, William M.
Jenkins, John L.
Jenkins, Oliver
Jenkins, Benjamin
Jenkins, Isaac C.
Jackson, John
Jenkins, Harvey
Knight, Richard
Knott, Richard
Knott, James W.
Lillard, Wyatt C.
Lillard, Franklin N.
Lowry, Alexander
Lohr, Michael
Lindsay, I. N.
May, Noel
Marks, John
Marks, Elias
McAlister, Henry
McAlister, Albert
Nicholson, Lewis B.

Nicholson, Thomas
Nicholson, Loyd
Prickett, Edmons
Renalds, James
Renalds, William
Rosson, Martin Va.
Richards, William N.
Richards, Franklin
Ryder, Albert T.
Smith, John W.
Smith, Earley
Smith, Asa
Smith, Austin
Smith, Presley
Shipp, John N.
Thomas, William F.
Thomas, Mark M.
Thomas, Sinclair M.
Thomas, John
Taylor, Franklin
Tucker, George
Thomas, James M.
Utz, M. H.
Weakley, Franklin
Weakley, John
Weakley, William H.
Wayland, James O.
Weaver, Jonah
Yowell, Edmond M.

Yowell, Yager C.
Yager, A. B.
Wilhoit, Abraham
Wise, George
Colvin, Henry C.
Colvin, M. F.
Carpenter, A. J.
Crigler, F. J.
Clore, William
Clore, W. B.
Clore, A. F.
Clore, Henry
Carpenter, Marcellus
Carpenter, Howard
Murray, J. Frank
Melton, Henry T.
Marquis, John
Marquis, William
Seal, David C.
Sprinkel, M. M.
Strickler, James F.
Smith, W. O.
Steighl, D. B.
Thomas, William
Tusing, Samuel
Taylor, Arthur H.
Tucker, William

## COMPANY "A," 7th VIRGINIA INFANTRY

John Welch, Captain; retired spring, 1862.
W. J. Cave, First Lieutenant; retired spring, 1862.
W. W. Gordon, Second Lieutenant; retired spring, 1862.
N. W. Crisler, Third Lieutenant; made Captain and Quarter Master, 1861.
W. O. Fry, Captain; wounded at Gettysburg; made Captain in 1862.
Thomas V. Fry; First Lieutenant; wounded at Gettysburg; made First Lieutenant, 1862.
W. F. Harrison, Second Lieutenant; wounded at Milford Station; made Second Lieutenant, 1862.
George N. Thrift, Third Lieutenant; made Third Lieutenant spring, 1862.

Aylor, Robert H.
Aylor, John W.
Blankenbaker, J. C.
Blankenbaker, G. M.
Blankenbaker, E. F.
Blankenbaker, James N.; transferred to Co. "C," 4th Va. Cavalry.
Blankenbaker, Jerome N.; died in hospital in Richmond, Virginia.
Broyles, Yancy, discharged in 1862
Burdette, James; Culpeper county.
Bowler, N. B.
Bowler, Benjamin; died in hospital.
Bradford, Osmond.
Bohannon, Thomas Y.; died.
Bohannon, J. A.
Bledsoe, J. T.; discharged in 1862.
Brown, John J.
Booton, Edwin; discharged in 1862.
Booton, Sinclair; wounded at Gettysburg.
Carpenter, C. G.
Clatterbuck, A. W.; killed at First Manassas.
Carpenter, W. B.; killed at Drury's Bluff.
Carpenter, R. F.
Carpenter, John W.; deserted.
Carpenter, John A.
Carpenter, A. W.
Carpenter, James H.
Carpenter, H. L.; died.
Carpenter, James O.
Conway, Battle; wounded at Gettysburg.
Conway, Charles C.
Clore, James O.; transferred to Q. M. Department.
Clore, Robert W.
Clore, James T.; killed at Williamsburg.
Clore, W. H.; transferred to Quarter Master Department.
Collins, John W.
Darnold, R. T.
Davis, John W.
Estes, C. W.; transferred to Co. "K," 7th Virginia.
Early, W. D.; lost arm at Frazier's Farm.
Evans, T. L.; substitute; killed at Gettysburg.
Fray, William H.
Foulkner, R. B.
Ford, W. N.
Ford, John S.
Finks, S. H.; transferred to Co. "L," 10th Virginia Cavalry.
Finks, M. F.; transferred to Co. "L," 10th Virginia Infantry.
Garr, W. H.
Gooding, W. W.; transferred to Co. "K," 7th Virginia Infantry.

Gully, John W.; wounded at Gettysburg.
Gullyhue, George W.
Hume, W. S.
Hill, J. Booton; transferred to Tr. Department, Richmond, Virginia
Hoffman, Jos. F.; transferred to Medical Department.
Hunton, John
Hawkins, John W.; wounded and captured at Gettysburg.
Hanison, James; substitute; killed at Gettysburg.
Jones, W. A.
Jones, E. O.; substitute; died in hospital.
Jackson, John H.
Jackson, George
Keeseer, John W.; Green county; wounded at Gettysburg.
Layton, John L.
Lillard, John H.
Lillard, H. M.
Lightfoot, John; transferred to A. P. Hill's Corps.
Leetch, John.
Lacey, W. J.
Lacey, D. W.
McLelary, James T.
Newman, T. J.; died of wounds at First Manassas.
Nicol, T. W.

Price, John W.; transferred to Co. "C," 4th Virginia Cavalry.
Rush, J. C.
Rush, Thomas H.
Rowzee, Thomas E.; discharged in 1862.
Renalds, John M.
Seal, R. A.; discharged in 1862.
Story; killed at Frazier's Farm.
Spark, R. W.
Sisk, C.; discharged in 1862.
Snyder, R. T.
Shepperd, Walton
Thomas, R. S.
Thomas, R. A.
Tatum, Edmond; killed at Seven Pines.
Teasly, George R.; wounded at Second Cold Harbor.
Tansill, Robert; killed at Frazier's Farm.
Watson, James; killed at Boonsborough.
Watson, William; Green county; wounded at Gettysburg.
Wallace, G. M.
Wallace, Michael.
Wayland, John W.
Wayland, James E.
Weaver, B. F.
Weaver, E. F.
Yager, C. C.

## "THE RICHARDSON GUARDS"

John Welch, Captain
W. J. Cave, First Lieutenant
N. H. Crisler,
J. Booton Hill
O. B. Jenks
John W. Carpenter
W. A. Jones
John Hunton
Osmond Bradford
Albert Clatterbuck
A. W. Buckner
A. W. Garr
A. J. Eaheart
William Lacey
James C. Blankenbaker
William R. Burnette
W. F. Harrison
James T. Wayman

George H. Allen
David W. Lacy
John J. Brown
Alphonso N. Jones
James W. Eddins
John M. Renalds
E. Frank Blankenbaker
G. M. Wallace
Robert F. Carpenter
Cumberland G. Carpenter
E. Finks Blankenbaker
Edwin Booton
Thomas Utz
William S. Hume
George M. Blankenbaker
Moses W. Yager
James T. Clore

M. C. Gordon
John J. Fray
Francis Harvey
Robert H. Aylor
Robert T. Hume
John Lightfoot
Reuben Bates
William B. Sprinkle
James N. Blankenbaker
William David Early
Thomas E. Rouzee
R. M. Kinsey
Robert A. Thomas
H. W. Gordon
William A. Banks
Reuben S. Thomas
S. N. Banks
William Lovell

The above list was published in the Madison News, July 17, 1903. This company was present at the execution of Cook and Copprice (white), Green and Copeland (negroes), accomplices of John Brown at Charlestown, Virginia, now West Virginia, in February, 1860.

## CAPTAIN GEORGE BOOTON ARTILLERY COMPANY, YORKTOWN, VA.

George Booton, Captain
Smith, F. Blankenbaker, First Lieutenant
John J. Fray, Second Lieutenant

Broyles, Howard
Breeden, Isaac
Burrows, Thomas
Crow, Philander
Crow, Lemuel
Corbin, James
Colvin, Robert
Easton, John
Estes, Lindsay
Gibbs, J. F.
Good, B. F.
Grennan, John
Jasper, Henry F.

Jenkins, Henry
Jenkins, Benjamin
Kirtley, Thomas
Kirtley, Abraham
Leathers, William
Leathers, Ephriam
Lillard, Sinclair
Long, John "Dink"
McAllister, J. Burwell
Mitchell, John
Mitchell, Benjamin
Nicol, Benjamin

Rosser, H. Glendemning
Rosson, Barnett
Southard, Newton
Southard, G.
Southard, Robert F.
Taylor, J. Morgan
Utz, Robert O.
Utz, Mallory
Weaver, B. F.
Weakley, Minor
Yowell, B. F.
(Frog Eye)

## CAPTAIN GEORGE BOOTON COMPANY "RESERVES," RICHMOND, VA.

George Booton, Captain
Thomas E. Rouzee, First Lieutenant
M. H. Gibbs, Second Lieutenant
M. S. Bowman, First Sergeant

A. H. Lacy, First Corporal
W. E. Bohannon, Second Corporal
James Sparks, Third Corporal
Horace Booton, Fourth Corporal

Anderson, Obediah
Anderson, Benjamin
Aylor, A. F.
Aylor, Gabriel
Aylor, John P.
Brown, John
Booton, Hiram
Booton, Ed.
Burton, William
Burnett, Robert A.
Bledsoe, William H.
Berry, William R.
Breeden, William
Conway, B. F. T.
Conway, Gibbon S.
Carpenter, Jeremiah
Carpenter, J. P.
Chapman, Thomas W.
Coats, Fountain
Cole, Battle
Corlin, John
Carpenter, Nelson H.
Clore, Henry
Clore, N. J.
Davis, Robert F.
Everett, John

Ford, B. J. W.
Fry, Henry
Fray, Joseph M.
Fray, Joseph E.
Graves, A. W.
Hague, John B.
Hill, Edwin F.
Higgins, Arthur
Huffman, Henry P.
Hutcherson, R. Fisher
Jones, William
Jacobs, Berkley
Lillard, Henry
Lowrey, Daniel
Marshall, James
Marshall, Wingfield S.
Murray, Dick
McAllister, Albert S.
Marks, Benjamin
Price, John H.
Parker
Richards, Thomas
Rowzee, John
Richards, William A.
Rider, Andrew
Rosson, Constantine

Rutter, Bartholemew
Rose, Andrew L.
Sparks, W. J.
Sparks, Joseph L.
Shotwell, Frank
Scott, John
Smith, Joel M.
Smith, B. F.
Sparks, Henry T.
Tanner, Robert H.
Twyman, Smith F.
Taylor, George
Utz, Robert N.
Utz, R. Edwin
Vernon, Isaac
Weaver, Thomas J.
Weaver, Adams
Weaver, William H., Jr.
Weaver, Moses S.
Wayland, Nathaniel S.
Wayland, Benjamin
Yowell, James
Yager, Albert
Zirkel, Louis

## LETCHER BATTERY, PEGRAM'S BATTALION

Walker, Samuel F. C.
Bazzle, Michael
Clore, John A.
Eddins, Robert
Estes, John
Estes, James
Gordon, Arthur

Grayson, Edward
Jacobs, John
Lohr, Martin
Lohr, John
Lohr, Henry
Lowery, Benjamin
Lowery, Daniel

Layton, Joseph M.
Loyd, Sinclair
Mauck, Robert F.
Nichols, Albert L.
Rosson, G. P.
Rosson

## WORLD WAR VETERANS
### Drafted White Men

Anderson, Oliver
Aylor, Charles Philip
Aylor, Wharton A.
Aylor, Benj. W.
Back, Clyde G.
Banks, T. Newton
Bates, Lester T.
Berry, Frank
Berry, Charlie T.
Berry, Ray
Blankenbaker, J. H.
Blankenbaker, Joseph F.
Blankenbaker, John Edwin
Bowman, John J.
Botts, William B.
Brown, Frank
Brown, J. D.
Campbell, Wilmer A.
Carpenter, Albert Q.
Carpenter, Webster J.
Cash, Jesse D.
Cave, Albert S.
Cave, Marvin
Cave, Frederick
Clark, William L.
Collins, John D.
Colvin, William
Corbin, Benj. H.
Dodson, John D.
Dodson, Willie
Dodson, Henry C.
Davis, Jack
Eddins, Roy
Eaheart, Joe
Eaheart, Frank
Estes, Creel
Fincham, George R.
Fincham, James C.
Fray, Jesse H.
Fry, Harry W.
Garr, John W.
Gallihugh, Weldon
Gallihugh, John

Graves, Fred M.
Goodall, L. S.
Goodall, Asa A.
Gordon, Edwin J.
Gibson, Clarence
Hanes, Roy J.
Hamilton, John W.
Henshaw, Roy E.
Herndon, William H.
Hicks, Willie D.
Hicks, Charles E.
Hill, Henry L.
Hoffman, E. H.
Hudson, Festus
Hurt, Soley F.
Jackson, Joe
Jackson, William C.
James, Corbett H.
Jeffres, John R.
Jeffres, Claude M.
Jenkins, James H.
Kilby, Elwood B.
Knight, Henry
Lohr, D. Preston
Lohr, Arthur S.
Lohr, Emmit
Lohr, Jess
Lohr, George
Leathers, E. K.
Lacy, Burrows W.
Mahann, Sam
Marshall, Hubert
Marsh, Roy B.
Marshall, George R.
McMullen, Evans H.
McDaniel, Hiram J.
Nicholson, John R.
Nicholson, B. L.
Nicholson, George W.
Parker, Robert
Powell, William E.
Price, Harry B.
Peyton, Robert M.
Ready, George C.
Ricks, James B.

Rider, Lewis
Rider, Haywood L.
Rosser, Turner A.
Sprinkle, Clyde G.
Southard, Burgess R.
Sours, Fred
Sours, John
Somerville, Morris A.
Smith, Shirley H.
Smith, Oscar W.
Smith, Jesse F.
Smith, Fred
Slaughter, John E.
Sisk, Bennie
Skinner, George L.
Skinner, Linton
Skinner, James L.
Skinner, Charles W.
Shotwell, Kemper G.
Shiftlett, Ira T., Jr.
Shiftlett, William H.
Seal, James M.
Tanner, Jesse
Tappy, Charles Davis
Tappy, Benjamin F.
Thrift, James H.
Tucker, Waller
Tussing, Jesse L.
Tussing, Wesley A.
Twyman, Willie A.
Twyman, Eddie F.
Tysinger, Joseph J.
Utz, Robert E.
Utz, Raymond
Weakley, Gilbert
Weaver, Otis J.
Weaver, Herbert E.
White, Irvin D.
White, Burnett G.
Wise, Albert L.
Yager, James A.
Yowell, Lester L.
Yowell, George E.
Yowell, Harvey W.
Yowell, Gideon

190        A HISTORY OF MADISON COUNTY, VIRGINIA

Darnold, Charlie
Tussing, Cleadus
Clore, Delma
Fray, John H.
Smith, James J.
Pettie, David
Lillard, Claude

Clarke, D. E.
Addennius, C. H.
Jenkins, Russell W.
Thomas, Hobert W.
Nicholson, Kenneth M.
Clatterbuck, Raymond P.

Tanner, Irvine F.
Back, Claude
Lohr, Rex
Duff, Milton W.
Lohr, Wallace
Hawkins, Eugéne
Thompson, Otis

VOLUNTEERS

Shoemaker, Thomas B.
Long, Cecil E.
Back, George W.
Beohm, C. R.
Clatterbuck, H. A.
Dulaney, Leslie
Goodall, Kenneth

Hoffman, Ashby
Rider, Winston
Yowell, Fred
Nicholson, B. L.
Nicholson, John R.
Back, Robert W.
Breeden, George E.

Burton, Clyde R.
Dodson, Willie
Donald, Charles E.
Skinner, George S.
Thornhill, John R.
Utz, Youie L.

COLORED DRAFTED MEN

Allen, John
Blakey, Haywood
Brown, John
Clay, Willie
Clay, Floy
Carpenter, John Seldon
Carter, Wayman
Carter, James E.
Carter, Atwood
Cave, George
Cooper, John
Collins, Joe
Crow, Melvin C.
Dade, James
Dade, Walter
Furish, Jesse
Fry, Daniel
Fry, Nachman
Fry, Thomas Lee
Gilmore, Ben
Goodall, Jonah
Goodall, Sie
Goodall, Pleas

Hill, Somerfield
Jackson, Sidney F.
Jackson, Don
Jackson, Minn F.
Jefferson, Charlie
Jefferson, Carter Dale
Gibbs, George H.
Morton, Somerfield
Porter, Horace A.
Price, William H.
Right, Jonnie
Robert, Jesse
Roebuck, Thomas
Rucker, James
Rufner, Jesse
Rowzie, Burt H.
Rowsy, Sam
Simms, Scott
Slaughter, Harry
Slaughter, Joe
Smith, Willie E.
Spotswood, Noah
Spotswood, McDowell
Strother, Charlie

Strother, George
Stewart, Sam
Taylor, Stewart
Taylor, Lewis Jerone
Taylor, William
Terrill, George S.
Thornton, Douglas
Tinsley, James P.
Vaughn, George
Walker, Ezra
Walker, Burnett
Walker, Thomas
Washington, Clarence
Weaver, Daniel
William, Virgil
Davis, James
Fry, Fernando
Lewis, Robert
Tibbs, James
Ferrish, Elma
Atty, Stratman
Blakey, Homer
Jackson, John

SHERIFFS OF MADISON COUNTY

Henry Hill
William Chapman
----------------------
----------------------
----------------------
Daniel James
Nathaniel Welch
Pascal Early
William Booton
John Walker
William Mallory
John Hume

Robert Thomas
Daniel Field
Richard C. Booton
Anthony Twyman
Charles R. Gibbs
Henry Hill
James Walker
William Early
John Harrison, Jr.
Alexander H. Simms
George A. Smith
Richard C. Booton
Eliott Blankenbaker

Reubin S. Thomas
Simeon Carpenter
Thornton F. Berry
John P. Aylor
Thornton F. Berry
Monroe Walker
R. A. Seal
W. F. Harrison
D. M. Pattie
Travis Twyman
John T. Hall

## CLERKS OF MADISON COUNTY

John Walker, Jr.
Benjamin Cave
Belfield Cave

Francis Hill
Sidney Thomas
Henry Hill

Nelson Crisler
G. H. Taylor
A. H. Cave

## ATTORNEYS FOR MADISON COUNTY

John Walker
Richard Henry Field
Horace Stringfellow

James T. Hill
Angus R. Blakey
Theophelus Smoot
D. S. Simms

T. J. Humphreys
James Hay
N. G. Payne

# BIBLIOGRAPHY

## PRINTED COLLECTIONS

*Annual Reports of Officers, Boards and Institution of the Commonwealth of Virginia.* Published each year by the Superintendent of Public Printing for Virginia.

*Annual Report of the Board of Public Works for Virginia.* Published each year by the Superintendent of Public Printing for Virginia.

Crozier, W. A., *Virginia Colonial Militia.* 1905. The Genealogical Association. New York City.

Dodge, T. A., *A Birdseye View of Our Civil War.* 1911. Houghton Mifflin Company. New York City.

Early, J. A., *Autobiographical Sketch and Narrative of the War Between the States.* 1912. J. B. Lippincott. Philadelphia, Pa.

Green, T. W., *Notes on Culpeper County and Slaughter's History of St. Mark's Parish.* 1903. Culpeper Exponent. Culpeper, Va.

Garr, J. W., *Genealogy of the Descendents of John Garr.* 1896. John C. Garr, Printer.

Howe, Henry, *Historical Collections of Virginia.* 1845. Babcock and Company. Charleston, S. C.

Huddle, W. P., *History of the Hebron Lutheran Church 1707-1907.* 1908. Henkle and Company, New Market, Virginia.

Henning, W. W., *Statutes at Large for Virginia.*

McDonald, W. N., *A History of the Laurel Brigade.* 1907. Sun Job Printing Office. Baltimore, Md.

Meade, Bishop, *Old Churches and Families of Virginia.*

Munford, B. B., *Virginia's Attitude Towards Slavery and Secession.*

Robinson, M. P., *Virginia Counties: Those Resulting from Virginia Legislation.* 1916. Bulletin of the Virginia State Library. Richmond, Va.

Slaughter, Philip, *A History of St. Mark's Parish.* 1877. Innes and Company. Baltimore, Md.

Slaughter, Philip., *A History of St. George's Parish.* 1847. John R. M'Gown. New York City.

Semple, R. B., *A History of the Rise and Progress of the Baptist in Virginia.* 1810. John O'Lynch.

*School Reports of Virginia.* Published each year by the Superintendent of Public Instruction.

Scott, W. W., *A History of Orange County, Virginia.*

*Virginia Magazine of History and Biography.* Published Quarterly by the Virginia Historical Society.

Whitehead, Thomas., *Virginia: A Handbook.* 1893. Everett Waddey Co., Richmond, Virginia.

Watson, T. L., *Mineral Resources of Virginia.* 1907. J. P. Bell Co. Lynchburg, Va.

*William and Mary Quarterly Review.* Published by William and Mary College.

## PERIODICALS NOT BOUND

Christian Advocate.
Madison County Eagle.
Minutes of the Shiloh Association.
Madison County Almanac. Printed by J. H. Evans.

## ORIGINAL MATERIAL NOT IN PRINT

Assessors Books of Madison County. Madison County Clerk's Office, Madison, Va.

Court Order Books of Madison County. Madison County Clerk's Office, Madison, Va.

Deed Books of Madison County. Madison County Clerk's Office, Madison, Va.

Mt. Carmel Church Records. Now in possession of Mr. C. M. Twyman. Haywood, Va.

Muster Rolls of Madison County. Madison County Clerk's Office, Madison, Va.

Novum Church Records. Now in possession of Mr. Harrison Hitt, Novum, Va.

Oak Grove Church Records. Now in possession of Mr. Wilmer Aylor, Aylor, Va.

Records of the School Superintendent. School Superintendent's Office, Peola Mills, Va.

Records of the Hebron Lutheran Church. Now in possession of Mr. J. H. Fray, Madison, Va.

Records of the Magisterial Boards of Madison County. Madison County Clerk's Office, Madison, Va.

Registration Records of Voters in Madison County. Madison County Clerk's Office, Madison, Va.

Report of Madison County War History Commission. Now in possession of Mrs. W. R. Clore, Criglersville, Va.

Tax Bill Receipts of Madison County. Madison County Treasurer's

Will Books of Madison County. Madison County Clerk's Office, Madison, Va.

Record of the Robinson River Church. Now in possession of Mr. Dave Berry, Criglersville, Va.

## PERSONAL INTERVIEWS AND QUESTIONNAIRES

*Statement of the Oldest People of Madison County.*
    A questionnaire was sent to the post-offices to ascertain the oldest people in the county. These people were then interviewed concerning events that happened during their life.

*Statement of Church Officials.*
    Questionnaires were also sent to the churches, asking for information recorded in the church records.

*Statement of Prominent Families.*
    Questionnaires were sent to many families asking for family records.

*Study of Mr. W. E. Bohannon.*
    Mr. W. E. Bohannon is one of the oldest citizens of the county, and has for many years been interested in the history of the county. He has been very generous to impart his knowledge to me.

# INDEX

Achsah 61, 144
Acty, George 142
Albemarle Co. 23, 33, 93
Alcocke, Robert 56, 160
Allen Mountain 28
Allen, George H. 60, 144
Amburger, Conrad 40, 42
American Eagle 154
Anderson's Mill 140
Anderson, George 47, 138
Andre 66
Anglo-Saxon 62
Appomattox 71, 72
Archer, John 51
Aroda 61, 144
Arras 82
Asher, John 44
Augusta Co. 97
Aylor 61, 144
Aylor, Albert 164
Aylor, Benjamin 151
Aylor, Gabriel 93
Aylor, Jerry 151
Aylor, Merry 138
Aylor, Park 91
Aylor, R. C. 163
Aylor Mountain 28

Babylon 14
Ball, Samuel 44, 46
Ball, William 64
Ball Mountain 28
Ballenger, Edward 42
Banco 33, 61, 144
Banks, Adam 87
Banks, J. W. 110
Banks, L. L. 92
Banks, Lynn 68, 138, 158, 159
Banks, Robert 138
Bank's Mill 140
Bank's Mountain 28
Barbour, James 46, 51, 55, 56
57, 64, 102, 139, 160
Barbour, Ambrose 51, 56, 160
Barler, Jacob 138
Barlow, Christopher 40
Barnett, James 60
Barnes, Leonard 60, 144
Barnes, Martin 60
Barnes, Henry 144
Batton, Henry 89
Batton, Joel 89
Batton, Martha 89
Batton, Margaret 89
Battle Run 87

Beale, Robert 56, 59, 60, 140, 160
Beaumont 83
Beamer's Head 28
Beller, Mathias 41
Bell, James 55
Belle, Island 72
Berry, Acrey 89
Berry, Anthony 51
Berry, Hiram 66
Berry, Roland 68
Berry, T. N. 110
Bennett, Joel 144
Berkeley, William 35, 39, 48
Berkeley Co. 86
Bethcar Church 89, 90
Bethsaida Church 93
Bethlehem Church 93
Bethincourt 82
Bledsoe, Abraham 47, 52
Bledsoe, Isaac 47, 52
Bledsoe, William 144
Blind, Tom 34
Bloodworth, Joseph 42
Blue Ridge Mountain 23-6-7-8, 30-4-5-7, 42, 56, 73, 75, 81, 97, 133
Blue Ridge Mission 93
Blue Run Church 87
Boarman, Robert 44
Bohannon, Ambrose 66
Bohannon, Eliza 89
Bohannon, George 89
Bohannon, W. E. 12, 34, 77
Bohannon, William 47
Bomar, John 47
Bond, John 44
Booker, John 60, 144
Booton, Captain 72
Booton, Richard 138, 140
Booton, William 60, 138, 140
Booton's Mill 140
Booton's Tannery 155
Booz, Richard 144
Bordine, Richard 139
Botts, J. K. 93
Borden, Benjamin 46
Bowman, John 52
Branham, John 48
Brandywine 66
Bradford, William 60
Bransford, John 47
Brest 81, 83
Breedlove, John 67
Brightwood 31, 61, 144, 163
Brightwood Circuit 93
Bridgeforth, James 43

| | |
|---|---|
| Broadus, Edmund 45 | Carpenter, Samuel 67 |
| Broadus, John A. 45 | Carpenter, William 41, 44, 47, 56 |
| Broile, Adam 51 | 67, 95, 97, 101, 139 |
| Broyle, Courtney 143 | Carpenter's Mountain 28 |
| Broyles, Susan 89 | Carter, Charles 39, 44, 48 |
| Broyles, John 40, 41 | Carson, Joseph 92 |
| Brock, Joseph 60 | Caroline Co. 23 |
| Beverley, Henry 37 | Cave, Bellfield 153 |
| Beverley, Robert 43 | Cave, Benjamin 46, 60, 102 |
| Birk, John 67 | Cave, Robert 47, 138 |
| Blakey, Angus R. 159 | Cavenaugh, Philemon 44 |
| Blakey, Robert 92 | Cedar Mountain 72 |
| Blakey's Mountain 28 | Cedar Run 73 |
| Black Walnut Run 47 | Charles River 21 |
| Blankenbeker, Abe 93 | Charleston 71 |
| Blankenbeker, Balthaser - 40, 41 | Charlottesville 72, 113 |
| Blankenbeker, E. M. 93 | Chapman, Ann 89 |
| Blankenbeker, John 52, 67 | Chapman, Edmund 89 |
| Blankenbeker, Jonas 60 | Chapman, Martha 89 |
| Blankenbeker, Knelus 68 | Chapman, T. W. 138 |
| Blankenbeker, M. F. 163 | Chapman, William 56, 60, 160 |
| Blankenbeker, Matthias 40, 41 | Chamblies, J. A. 90 |
| Blankenbeker, Nicholas 40, 41 | Champlain 28, 95 |
| Blankenbeker, Pattas 42 | Chaldea 14 |
| Broomfield Parish 86, 88, 100, 101 | Chew, Larkin 43 |
| Brooks, Thomas 36 | Chestnut Blight 157 |
| Brown, Daniel 54, 64 | Chichahomminy 35 |
| Brown, John 71 | Clayton, Sam 64 |
| Brown, T. P. 91 | Clem, Abraham 68 |
| Brown, William 52, 64 | Clore, E. A. 163 |
| Browning, Francis 47 | Clore, Henry 89 |
| Bruce, Silas 89, 91 | Clore, J. N. 59 |
| Bryant, William 47 | Clore, J. C. 164 |
| Buford, John 75, 76 | Clore, John 93, 138, 140 |
| Buford, Abraham 66 | Clore, Judie 157 |
| Bull Run 71 | Clore, Ephriam 90 |
| Bullinger, Andrew 40 | Clore, Michael 40, 41, 60, 138, 139 |
| Burn, Thomas 44 | Clore, Moses 90, 163 |
| Bush, Thomas 44 | Clore, Mrs. Moses 89 |
| Bush, Philip 47 | Cobler, Frederick 42 |
| Byrd, William 39 | Columbus, Christopher 19, 53 |
| | Collins, J. F. 140 |
| Calais 82 | Conway, John 100 |
| Campbell, Alexander 138 | Conway River 25, 26, 28 |
| Campbell, Daniel 138 | Conway's Mill 140 |
| Camp Lee 81 | Confederate Monument 150 |
| Campe, William 51 | Cook, Michael 40, 41, 44, 138, 139 |
| Canada 67 | Copper, Joseph 44 |
| Captain John Smith 32 | Coppeller, Frederick 139 |
| Captain Tom 32 | Cornwallis, Lord 66, 67 |
| Carpenter, Andrew 52, 91 | Costler, Michael 42 |
| Carpenter, Absolom 90 | Cowherd, James 46 |
| Carpenter, Elvira 89 | Craig, Elijah 87 |
| Carpenter, Jeremiah 151 | Creel, Benjamin 91, 94 |
| Carpenter, John 42, 142 | Crisler, N. W. 71 |
| Carpenter, Joseph 60 | Crisler, Nellie 93 |
| Carpenter, J. W. 193 | Crisler, Absolom 68 |
| Carpenter, Nathan 151 | Criglersville 31-4, 61, 119, 124, 139, |
| Carpenter, Sarah 93 | 144, 158, 160 |

## INDEX

Criglersville H. S. 132
Crigler's Mill 140, 161
Crigler, D. F. 140
Crigler, Jacob 41, 68, 97
Crigler, John F. 97
Crigler, Lewis 60
Crooked Run 26, 99, 159
Crosthwait, William 47
Crow, William 60
Crow, James 90
Culpeper C. H. 73, 77, 113
Culpeper Co. 24-5-6-7-8-9, 33, 43-4, 50-2-3-4-5, 62-4-5, 86, 101
Chicacoan 21
Cimberman, William 41
Clark, George 138
Clatterbuck, James 67
Clawse, Michael 42
Clawse, John 42
Culpeper Minute Men 65, 66
Culpeper Association 87
Cumberland Gap 37
Curtis, Charles 46

Dark Hollow 28, 29, 34
Deal, Larkin 98
Deal's Mountain 28
Debord, David 52
Debord, James 67
Deer, Abner 90
Deep Run 28, 161
Delaney, Daniel 52
Delph, Samuel 67
Delaware 66
Descartes 13
Devil's Run 101
Dickens, Christopher 161
Diggs, Thomas 92
Dixon, Roger 50
Doffermeyer, J. N. 91
Double Top Mountain 28, 45
Dover Association 97
Downs, Henry 47
Duet 61, 144
Duett, John 44
Dulaney, John 87
Dulin, B. P. 90
Dulinsville 139, 144
Dunkard Congregation 151
Dunmore, Lord 64, 65

Early, Jubal A. 77, 78
Early, Joseph 88, 167
Early, Patsy 89
Early, Paschall 60
Early, Richard 89, 98, 138
Early, William 140
Eastham, Robert 44, 46
Eastham, W. 64

Eddins, Adolphus 44
Egypt 14
Elk Run 28, 160
Elly 61, 144
England 28, 35, 39, 62, 67, 87, 91
Essex Co. 22
Etlan 34, 61, 95, 144
Etlan Church 93
Eve 49
Eve, George 55, 88, 144
Ewing, Daniel 98

Fairfax 50, 65, 95
Fairfax, William 39
Fairview 93
Farmville 72
Farmer, Thomas 95
Farrar, J. M. 90, 91
Farnsworth, C. S. 81
Fauquier, Francis 63
Fauquier Co. 24, 33, 64, 65
Fennell, Jonathan 47
Field, Abram 46
Field, Daniel 60, 140, 159
Field, Henry 64, 139
Finalson, John 44, 46
Finks, Andrew 55
Finks, A. N. 140
Finks, John 78
Finks, Major 68
Finks, Mark 47
Finks, William 140
Fishback, John 89, 90
Fisher, Lewis 52
Fisher's Gap 153
Fleshman's Run 28
Fleshman's Shop 160
Fleshman, Cyracus 42
Fleshman, Peter 42, 138, 142
Fleshman, Zacharias 40-1, 138, 139, 143
Flowers, William 94
Foolish, Zach 34
Fork Mountain 28
Ford's Schoolhouse 92
Fowles Hy 67
Fox, L. L. 88
Fray, Ephriam 161
Fray, E. D. 98
Fray, John 110, 140
Frazier, Godwin 91
Franklin's Cliff 135
Franklin, Edward 47
France 81, 82
Free Press 154
Fredericksburg 23, 28, 67, 75, 115
Frogg, John 138
F. T. Church 86, 90, 100, 101

Fry, Joshua _____ 44, 46
Fry, N. W. _____ 110
Fry, Thomas V. _____ 71
Fry, Reubin _____ 56, 144, 159
Fry, W. O. _____ 71
Gaines, Edmund _____ 60
Garr, Andrew _____ 42, 142
Garr, Adam _____ 51, 138, 142
Garr, Benjamin _____ 68
Garr, James _____ 151
Garr, Solomon _____ 68
Garr's Mountain _____ 28, 160
Garr's Mill _____ 160
Garth, John _____ 46
Garnett, John _____ 88
Gassell, Andrew _____ 60
German Glebe Lands _____ 138
German Ridge _____ 28, 160
German Chapel _____ 94
German Ford _____ 36, 41
Germantown _____ 66
Germana _____ 36, 79, 94, 139
Gibbs, Charles _____ 140
Gibbs, Churchill _____ 60, 66, 144
Gibbs, John _____ 55
Gibbs, Smith _____ 98
Gibbs' Schoolhouse _____ 93
Gillum, T. O. _____ 162
Gillison, John _____ 66
Gillison, William _____ 157
Gilpin, John _____ 144
Goodwin, Hugh _____ 90, 91
Gordonsville__ 23, 73, 75, 113, 115
Gourdvine Church _____ 87
Graves, Ashby _____ 97
Graves, Ed. _____ 90
Graves, Edward _____ 90
Graves, John _____ 51, 56, 67
Graves, J. M. _____ 140
Graves, Thomas _____ 56, 140, 160
Graves Mill _____ 31, 61, 139, 144
Grave's Chapel _____ 90
Grant, U. S. _____ 71, 72
Gray, G. _____ 90
Great Bridge _____ 65
Great Run _____ 28
Green, John _____ 66, 77
Green, Robert _____ 46, 64
Green, William _____ 50, 64, 139
Greene Co. 23-6-7-8, 33, 43, 92, 110
Grimsley, Barnett _____ 88, 90
Grimsley, T. F. _____ 90, 91
Gruman, John _____ 160
Guy, Thomas _____ 44

Haddock, John _____ 44
Haddock, Joseph _____ 44
Hanover Junction _____ 71

Hanover Co. _____ 24
Hansford, William _____ 43
Harrison, John _____ 67, 138
Harrison, W. F. _____ 71
Harris, Samuel _____ 86
Harrisonburg _____ 23, 92
Haywood _____ 61, 144
Haywood Mountain _____ 28, 34
Harpers Ferry _____ 71
Harnsburger, Hans _____ 40
Hasinugaes _____ 33
Hawkins, John _____ 155
Hawkins' Mill _____ 161
Hawksbill Mountain _____ 28
Hazel River _____ 27, 101
Head, Anthony _____ 47
Head, George _____ 47
Hebron Church 27, 31, 34, 39, 46,
   94, 105, 139
Henderson, John _____ 67
Henderson, William _____ 46
Henshaw, Frances _____ 89
Henshaw, John _____ 56, 158, 161
Herndon, R. N. _____ 91
Henkel, Mary _____ 98
Henkel, Noah _____ 98
Henry, Patrick _____ 64, 65
Hill, A. P. _____ 73
Hill, Francis _____ 159
Hill, Henry ____ 54, 59, 140, 160
Hill, L. W. _____ 34
Hill, Robert _____ 54, 60
Hill, William _____ 91, 107, 110
Hobson, George _____ 46
Hoboken _____ 81
Holmes, Hugh _____ 60
Holmes, R. E. L. _____ 107
Holt, Michael ____ 40, 41, 95, 138
Holtzclaw, Jacob _____ 42
Hoke, General _____ 71
Hood _____ 61, 144
Honeymoon Hut _____ 135
Hopeful Church _____ 97
Howard, John _____ 46, 47
Huffman, G. W. _____ 93
Huffman, John __ 42, 44, 98, 139
Huffman, Samuel _____ 98
Huffman's Chapel _____ 92, 98
Huffman's Mill _____ 160
Hume, George _____ 55
Hume, John _____ 140
Huddle, W. P. _____ 98
Hughes River _____ 26, 27, 161

Indian Trace _____ 34
Indian Emigration _____ 151
Ireland, James _____ 87
Iodell, Mr. _____ 100

## INDEX

Jackson, J. E. 140
Jackson, Mary 98
Jackson, Stonewall 73, 75
Jack's Shop 75, 77, 92, 145
Jamestown 21, 32, 37
James City 23, 60, 144
James River 73
James, Daniel 88
Jameson, John 50, 64, 66
Jefferson, Thomas 70
Jenifer, Margaret 159
Jennings, Benjamin 144
Jones, Edward 52
Jones, David 144
Jones, Gabriel 66
Jones, Robert 44
Jones, Tavener 67
Jones, Thomas 43
Jones, William 52, 60

Kaifer, Michael 40, 41, 138
Kate Mountain 151
Kelly, William 47
Kemper, James L. 68, 71, 138
Kemper, Johann 139
Kennedy, Leroy 67
Kentucky 37, 103, 151, 157, 169
Kentucky Emigration 151
Kerker, Andrew 40, 139
Kilpatrick 75, 76, 77
Kipp, Mary 98
King William Co. 22
King and Queen Co. 22
Kirtley, Jeremiah 56, 59
Kirtley, Milton 138
Kite, Charlie 90
Kite, James 90
Klug, Samuel 95, 142

Lancaster Co. 22
Lane, Robert 144
Lauck, Peter 89
Lauck, William C. 89
Leake, Shelton F. 159
Leathers, Joshua 88
Lee, Robert E. 71, 72, 73, 77, 78, 92
Lederer, John 35
Leon 60, 145
Leonard, Pat 49
Lewis, Simeon 60
Lewis, T. W. 88, 90
Lewis, Zachary 46
Liberty Church 91
Liberty Mills 73, 75, 76, 77
Lightfoot, Goodrich 46
Lightfoot, John 46, 158
Lillard, Benjamin 161

Lillard, Jack 78
Lillard, John 158
Lincoln, Abraham 167
Lindsey, Dr. 159
Little Zach 34
Locust Dale 28, 34, 60, 61, 109, 110, 144, 160
Lohr, Catharine 98
Lohr, Philip 98
Long, Gabriel 66
Long, George 42
London 35, 39
Lord Hopton 37
Lord Culpeper 37
Lord Fairfax 24, 37, 39, 114
Lost Mountain 28
Louisa Co. 24
Lovell, E. H. 110
Lowery, Benjamin 98
Lynchburg 72

Madison County Eagle 101, 154
Madison H. S. 132
Madison News 154
Madison Exponent 154
Madison Circuit 92, 93
Madison C. H. 26, 30-1, 41, 73-5-7-8, 89, 90, 92, 101, 102, 107, 144
Madison Mills 41, 61
Madison, Ambrose 66
Madison, Francis 55
Madison, John 43
Madison, James 55, 66, 67, 68, 162
Madison, William 55, 67
Medley Mountain 28
Medley, Ambrose 56, 57
Mercer, John 44, 46
Meuse River 82
Meyerhoffer, Rev. 97
Mezingo, George 90
Miller, Adam 68
Miller, Joshua 89
Miller, Jacob 143
Miller, J. N. 110
Miller, Sarah 89
Miller, Thomas 144
Mallory, William 140
Maple Run 28
Magruder, John 77
Mannahoacks 32, 33
Manincassa 34
Manassas 72
Marshall, Alice 98
Marshall, John 65
Marshall, Thomas 65
Mason, Isham 144
Mason, W. 88, 89
Massanutten Mountains 75

| | | | |
|---|---|---|---|
| Mattaponi | 21 | Oak Grove Church | 92, 93 |
| Mauldin, Richard | 46 | Ohio River | 33, 151 |
| Mauck, Daniel | 161 | Oldrag | 61, 145 |
| Maxfield, Thomas | 87 | Old Rag Church | 90 |
| Mayer, George | 40, 41 | Old Rag Mountain | 28, 34, 88 |
| May, Sarah | 89 | Old Dutch Church | 94, 159, 160 |
| Maryland Synod | 97 | Ontponies | 33 |
| McClanahan | 66 | O'Neal, Mr. | 100, 101 |
| McClellan, General | 73 | O'Neal's Crossing | 101 |
| McClellan, J. | 73 | O'Neal, Henry | 155 |
| McIrvine, Major | 76, 77 | Orange County | 23-4-5-6-7, 33-4-6, 40-3-6-8, 50, 64, 65, 73, 75, 86, 92, 101, 118 |
| Meadow Mountain | 28 | | |
| Meade, Bishop | 102 | | |
| Milum Apple | 117, 153 | Orange Association | 87 |
| Milum's Gap | 28, 29, 72, 153 | Orange Circuit | 92 |
| Milum, Joseph | 151 | Oxford, Roger | 44 |
| Mine Run | 78 | | |
| Michie, David | 144 | Page Co. | 27, 33 |
| Mitchell's Mountain | 28 | Palmer, J. W. | 93 |
| Mitchell, James L. | 89 | Pannill, William | 47 |
| Mitchell, T. T. | 132 | Pamunkey River | 24, 35 |
| Morgan, Charles | 44 | Pattie, D. M. | 93 |
| Morgan, J. W. | 91 | Paulitz, Philip | 40 |
| Morgan, Morgan | 46 | Payne, W. L. | 54 |
| Moorman, S. T. | 92 | Peacock, Robert | 55 |
| Morris, Samuel | 60 | Pendleton, Nathaniel | 50, 64 |
| Moss, J. C. | 92 | Pendleton, Henry | 64, 139 |
| Motz, John | 40, 41 | Pennsylvania | 39, 40, 66, 95 |
| Moffait, Anderson | 87 | Peola Mills | 61, 103, 145, 161 |
| Muddy Run | 28 | Pisgah Church | 77 |
| Mulato Run | 28 | Pittsylvania Co. | 86 |
| Muter, George | 159 | Pollard, James | 44, 46 |
| Mt. Carmel Church | 89, 90 | Porter, Benjamin | 47 |
| Mt. Zion Church | 91, 92 | Porter, John | 51 |
| Mt. Olivet Church | 92, 93 | Porteus, James | 47 |
| Mt. Nebo Church | 97 | Powell, Ambrose | 64 |
| Mt. Pisgah Church | 98 | Pope, General | 73 |
| | | Popham's Run | 28 |
| Neal's Mountain | 28 | Potomac River | 29, 37 |
| Nethers | 31, 61, 139, 144 | Powhatan Indians | 32 |
| New Kent Co. | 22 | Pratts | 61 |
| New Market | 75, 113 | Phillips, David | 47 |
| New Light Stir | 86 | Phillips, Leonard | 47 |
| New Bethel Church | 90, 92 | Price, Henry | 60 |
| Nicol, T. W. | 140 | ′ Providence Church | 92 |
| Nicholson Hollow | 27 | | |
| Northumberland Co. | 22 | Quaker Run | 28 |
| Norman, Isaac | 44 | Quarles, John | 43 |
| Norfolk | 65 | Queen Anne | 28, 37 |
| Norton, Major | 71, 72 | | |
| North Anna | 23 | Raccoon Ford | 47, 100 |
| Northern Neck | 37 | Radiant | 61, 145 |
| North Carolina | 86 | Ragged Mountain Church | 86, 87, 88, 124 |
| Nott, Governor | 37 | | |
| Novum | 61, 145 | Rapidan Circuit | 92, 93 |
| Novum Church | 90 | Rapidan River | 24-5-6-7-8, 36- 9 40-1-7-8, 73-9, 99 |
| Oak Park | 31, 61, 110, 139, 145 | Rapidan Church | 86, 88 |

# INDEX

Rappahannock River 21-2-5-8, 32-7 8-9
Rappahannock Co. 22-3-4-6-7, 44, 50, 63
Randolph, John ............ 65
Ramsbottom, Abraham ...... 60
Raussen, John ............. 139
Read, Grant ............... 157
Read, John ................ 44
Reynold's Mill ........ 140, 161
Richards, Ambrose ......... 67
Richards, John ............ 91
Richardson, William ....... 47
Richmond ........ 22, 26, 72, 73
Robinson River 26-9, 30-6, 41-2-3, 50-9, 77-8-9, 94-9, 135
Robinson River Church 87, 88, 89, 90, 91, 145
Robinson, John ............ 39
Robertson, William ........ 47
Roberts, John ............. 44
Rockingham Co. ........ 26, 27, 97
Rochelle 31, 61, 92, 93, 97, 139, 145
Rochelle Church ........... 93
Roebuck, William .......... 67
Rogers, John .............. 43
Rossen, Louisa ............ 89
Rose Park Church .......... 92
Rouse, Eveline ............ 81
Rouse, John ............... 41
Rouse, Jacob .......... 67, 97
Rouse, Lewis .............. 67
Rouse, Matthias ....... 52, 67
Rouse, Michael ............ 97
Rouse, Patsy .............. 89
Rouse Mountain ............ 28
Rucker, John .............. 60
Russell, Peter ............ 48
Russel, William ........... 48
Russell's Ford ............ 59
Rush, Benjamin ........ 44, 67
Ruth ................. 61, 145

Sag Mountain .............. 28
Sales, John ............... 51
Sampson, John ............. 51
Saunders, Jacob ........... 49
Saunders, Nathaniel ....... 87
Scott, W. W. .............. 42
Scott, Thomas ............. 64
Schull Bean ............... 153
Schull, William ........... 153
Seville ................... 28
Shenandoah Co. ... 26, 27, 73, 97
Sheep Mountain ............ 28
Shelby ............... 61, 145
Shebley, George ........... 139
Sheible, George ....... 40, 41

Shelton, John ............. 44
Shirley, Thomas ... 114, 138, 140
Shirley, Zachariah ........ 60
Shiloh Association ........ 87
Shiloh Church ............. 90
Shipp, E. A. .............. 91
Snider, Henry ......... 40, 41
Snow, John ................ 46
Snow Creek ............ 23, 24
Somerville, James ......... 140
Somers, G. A. ............. 140
Somerville's Ford ......... 48
Southwest Mountain ........ 23
South Church ......... 100, 101
Spauldin, John ............ 67
Sperryville ............... 77
Spotswood, Alexander 23, 24, 35-9 40-2-3-8, 79, 114, 143
Spotswood, John ........... 139
Spotsylvania Co. 22, 23-4, 33-7, 41-3, 99, 143
Sprinkle, J. W. ........... 93
Stony Man ................. 28
Stony Hill ................ 160
Stegarkies ................ 33
Stolts, John .............. 42
Stodgill, James ........... 47
Stoney Run ................ 161
Shotwell's Hollow ......... 33
Shotwell, Jimmie .......... 67
Simpson's Mountain ........ 28
Sims, Edward .............. 60
Sims, C. O. .......... 140, 159
Simm's Mill ............... 140
Slaughter, George ......... 66
Slaughter, Francis .... 46, 48
Slaughter, John ........... 64
Slaughter, Philip ..... 50, 101
Slaughter, Mary ........... 44
Slaughter, Robert .... 44, 46, 50
Slaughter, Samuel ......... 101
Slaughter, Thomas ..... 44, 139
Smith, Augustine ... 43, 44, 46
Smith, Benjamin ........... 67
Smith, Fielding ........... 68
Smith, Jesse .............. 142
Smith, John ....... 46, 60, 151
Smith, Michael 40, 41, 44, 95, 139
Smith, Thomas ............. 51
Smith, William ........ 44, 67
Smith's Island ............ 41
Strother, French .......... 139
Strother, John ............ 64
Strother, Anthony ......... 44
Strother, Captain ......... 68
Strother, Lawrence ........ 34
Strother, William ..... 43, 144
St. John's Church ......... 64

St. Mark Parish -- 24, 99, 100, 101
St. George Parish ---- 24, 99, 100
St. Thomas Parish ------ 99, 100
Strickler, James --------------- 97
Stevens, Edward --------------- 65
Stoever, Casper -- 40, 94, 95, 98
Stuart, J. E. B. ----------- 73-5-6
Stearnes, Shubal -------------- 86
Story, David ------------------ 89
Steele, R. L. ----------------- 90
Suddith, B. B. ---------------- 93
Sulphur Spring Valley -------- 151
Swift Run Gap ----------- 23, 35
Swindle, Michael -------------- 51
Syria -------- 33, 61, 75, 124, 145

Taliaferro, Lawrence ---------- 65
Taliaferro, John ----------- 46
Tanner, Abraham --------------- 67
Tanner, George ---------------- 93
Tanner, Jacob ----------------- 67
Tanner, Jesse ---------------- 142
Tanner, J. N. ----------------- 98
Tanner, Robert ---------- 42, 89
Tanner, Urban ---------------- 139
Taylor, Dr. ------------------ 159
Taylor, James ------------- 43, 47
Taylor, Robert ---------------- 55
Taylor, William --------------- 67
Taylor, Zachary --------------- 46
Tarleton, General ------------- 66
Tauxitanians ----------------- 33
Tenant's Church --------- 26, 101
Tennessee Synod -------- 97, 98
Telph, Michael --------------- 51
Temple, Roy -------------- 90, 91
Thornton, Anthony ------------- 43
Thornton, Frank -------- 88, 101
Thornton, Francis ------- 43, 44
Thornton, John --------------- 66
Thomas, David ---------------- 86
Thomas, Christopher ---------- 41
Thomas, John -------- 41, 52, 142
Thomas, H. S. ---------------- 93
Thomas, Robert --------------- 140
Thomas, Sidney --------------- 155
Thornton's Gap ---------- 77, 87
Thourafare Mountain --------- 28
Thrift, George N. ------------- 71
Tom's Mountain --------------- 28
Towles, Joseph --------------- 60
Towles, Hy ------------------- 67
Trinity Church ----------- 91, 92
Tussing, Samuel -------------- 98
Turner, Robert --------------- 46
Twyman, Anthony ------ 138, 140
Tywman, E. W. --------- 93, 159
Twyman, J. S. ---------------- 91

Twyman, William - 52, 60, 67, 138
Twyman's Mill ---------- 61, 145
Tysinger, H. C. -------------- 161

Uld, Christopher ------------ 139
Uno ------------------- 61, 145
Utz, Alfred ------------------ 138
Utz, Ephriam ----------------- 67
Utz, George -- 40, 41, 51, 138, 139
Utz, Thornton ---------------- 42
Utz, Simeon ------------------ 90
Utz, O. J. ------------------- 98
Utz, Lou --------------------- 98

Valley Forge ----------- 66, 124
Vauters, Richard ------------ 142
Vallick, Martin-------------- 142
Verdun ---------------------- 82
Virginia Conference --------- 92
Virginia Synod -------------- 97
Voss, Robert ----------------- 55

Walker, John ---- 54, 60, 140, 144
Walker, James ------ 54, 138, 140
Walker, Merry --------- 56, 160
Walker, Robert -------------- 111
Walker, William --56, 57, 140, 160
Walker's Chapel -------------- 92
Wall, William ---------------- 52
Wallace, Michael ----------- 138
Wallace, William ------------- 54
Warren County --------------- 24
Washington, George 50, 66, 124, 161
Washington, B. C. -------- 76, 77
Waugh, Alexander ---- --44, 52
Waxham --------------------- 66
Wayland, Adam --------- 52, 60
Wayland, Bellfield ----------- 97
Wayland, Knelus ------------- 94
Wayland, John --------------- 51
Wayland, G. W. ------------- 140
Wayland, Henry ----- 55, 56, 59
Wayland, Lonza ------------- 94
Wayland, Thomas ------------- 42
Weaver, Matthias ------- 52, 67
Weaver, John ---------- 90, 138
Wayland, W. H. ------------- 33
Weaver, Henry -------------- 160
Weaver's Mill --------- 140, 161
Wells, Bryant --------------- 81
Welch, Captain -------------- 67
Welch, Oliver --------------- 90
Welch, Reubin --------------- 43
Wetherall, J. W. ----------- 163
Wetherall, George ------ 52, 64
Wetherall, John ------- --56, 160

# INDEX

Westover Church ----------- 92
Wheatley, George ---------- 44
White Oak Run -- 28, 41, 50, 99
White, Stanford ----------- 57
Whonketeis ---------------- 33
Willis, Henry --------- 44, 46
Willis, Larkin ----------- 110
Willis, J. B. ------------ 140
Wilhite, John --------- 52, 143
Wilhoit, David ------------ 68
Wilcox -------------------- 76
Wilderness Run ------------ 24
Williams, William ----- 50, 64
Williams, Francis --------- 47
Williamsburg ---- 39, 50, 64, 65
Wilson, John -------------- 51
Willers, John ------------ 139
Wirt, William ----- 55, 60, 159
Wood, George ------ 42, 44, 47
Woodberry Forest -- 36, 61, 66, 80, 111, 145
Woodville -------------- 77, 102
Wolftown 31, 61, 78, 100, 139, 145, 161
Woodroof, George ---------- 41
Wright, Thomas ------------ 42
Wright, Daniel ------------ 52

Wyley, Allen -------------- 86
Yancey, Davis ------------- 44
Yancey, R. H. ------------- 55
Yager, Lathan ------------- 68
Yager, William ------------ 52
Yager, Alfred M. ---------- 90
Yates, Paul --------------- 89
Yowell, William ----------- 67
Yager, Nicholas 40, 41, 52, 67, 138
Yager, Adam --------------- 40
Yager, John --------------- 54
Yager, Michael -------- 60, 90
Yowell, W. H. ------------- 88
Yowell, Jane -------------- 89
Yowell, A. W. -------- 110, 131
Yowell, Christopher ------ 138
Yowell, George ----------- 142
York --------------- 21, 22, 23
Yorktown ---------- 67, 71, 72
Zachary, General ---------- 67
Zeus -------------- 61, 145, 150
Zeuche, Hans ------------- 139
Zimmerman, Christopher 40, 41, 46
Zimmerman, John ---------- 142

www.ingramcontent.com/pod-product-compliance
Lightning Source LLC
Chambersburg PA
CBHW071420160426
43195CB00013B/1759